PHENOMENOLOGY OF

THE VISUAL ARTS

(even the frame)

PHENOMENOLOGY OF THE VISUAL ARTS

(even the frame)

PAUL CROWTHER

STANFORD UNIVERSITY PRESS

Stanford, California 2009

Stanford University Press
Stanford, California

This book has been published with the assistance of the Visual
Communication and Expertise Initiative at Jacobs University Bremen.

Library of Congress Cataloging-in-Publication Data

Crowther, Paul.
   Phenomenology of the visual arts (even the frame) / Paul Crowther.
      p. cm.
   Includes bibliographical references and index.
   ISBN 978-0-8047-6214-4 (cloth : alk. paper)
      1. Art—Philosophy.   2. Phenomenology and art.   3. Aesthetics.
I. Title.
N66.C76   2009
701—dc22

                                                    2009007529

Printed in the United States of America on acid-free, archival-quality paper

Typeset at Stanford University Press in 10/14 Minion

Contents

Illustrations

Acknowledgements

In terms of its origins, this book has evolved over a number of years. It consists of new material, together with revised and, in some cases, much extended versions of work previously published (sometimes in hard to find sources).

A few very short extracts from Chapter 1 are included in *Art History Versus Aesthetics*, ed. James Elkins (Routledge: London, 2006), 123–128. Chapter 2 is a much extended version of a paper entitled 'Pictorial Space and the Possibility of Art,' published in the *British Journal of Aesthetics* 48 (2008): 175–192. Part of Chapter 4 was published as 'Painting, Abstraction, Metaphysics: Merleau-Ponty and the Invisible', in *Symposium* 8, no. 2 (2004): 1–14. Chapter 5 appeared as 'Transcendence and Sculpture' in *Painting, Sculpture, and the Spiritual Dimension: The Kingston and Winchester Papers*, ed. Stephen J. Newton and Brandon Taylor (Oneiros: London, 2003), 123–132. Chapter 6 is a much extended version of a paper entitled 'The Logic of Abstract Art' published in *The Structurist* (Fall, 2008): 58–63. Chapter 9 is a slightly revised version of a paper of the same title that was published in *The Journal of Aesthetics and Art Criticism* 66, no. 2 (2008): 161–170.

Thanks are due to my assistant Carin Baban for her exemplary work in preparing the manuscript for publication.

PHENOMENOLOGY OF
THE VISUAL ARTS
(even the frame)

Introduction

This book discusses a realm of complex meanings which gives the visual arts a distinctive character. Key questions of method arise at the very outset.

In this respect, it is striking that the influence of poststructuralist thinkers (such as Derrida, Foucault, and Lacan) has led many art historians and theorists to reinterpret their task in terms of histories of representation and visual culture. The idea of art as a unique form of meaning has been subjected to sustained critique.[1]

This critique, however, has its own shortcomings. In Chapter 1 of this book, I will clarify the limitations of reductionist approaches to art (which are especially influenced by poststructuralism). These approaches tend to assimilate meaning in the visual arts to the socio-historical context in which the works were produced or to models derived from literary analysis; and to neglect the distinctively visual dimension. Detailed descriptions of the artwork's aesthetic and phenomenal structure are marginalized—if they are offered at all.

The analytic tradition of aesthetics fares little better. It has the great merit of offering lucid argumentative techniques which do not fall into the error of taking obscurity and elliptical expression for signs of profundity, *per se.*

Unfortunately, it also has significant shortcomings in terms of engaging with the concrete artwork.[2] Characteristically, its descriptive strategies fixate, somewhat, on the general logical character of the work (e.g. the type/token relation, or the referential structure of pictorial representation).

Indeed, the main orientation in this tradition is towards *how aesthetic and artistic terms are used.* Analytic approaches employ notions such as 'aesthetic' and 'expressive' qualities but mainly without explaining what makes those qualities so significant over and above the mere fact of being aesthetic or expressive. Description stops just where the significance of the aesthetic (and cognate terms) becomes a question.

Now whilst I will make some more detailed critical points against reductionism and aspects of analytic aesthetics elsewhere in this work, my main strategy is constructive. I formulate a theory of the visual arts based on what the *creation* of such art achieves cognitively and (as a correlate of this) aesthetically.

For this purpose, I combine two philosophical approaches. The first is analytic philosophy in the sense of an orientation towards conceptual distinctions and carefully connected steps of argument. This allows the terrain of artistic phenomena to be mapped in terms of its most logically fundamental structures. The second approach involves the elaboration of such structures more concretely through descriptive insights derived from a tradition which has not, perhaps, reached its full potential in terms of the aesthetics of visual art, namely phenomenology.

In developing my *analytic phenomenology*, I am, of course, cognizant that there is already a long-standing tradition of general phenomenological aesthetics, encompassing thinkers such as Witasek, Veber, Geiger, Heidegger, Sartre, Merleau-Ponty, Dufrenne, Ingarden, Gadamer, and, more recently, Edward S. Casey. That this tradition has not been more influential in terms of visual art is because visual idioms have not been a central concern for most of the aforementioned thinkers. Indeed, even the two who have assigned special significance to it (namely Heidegger and Merleau-Ponty) have not pursued the subject at monograph length. And whilst Casey's important work has recently taken a strong visual turn, it has yet to develop into a comprehensive theory of the visual arts.[3]

Some art historians, notably Michael Fried, Richard Shiff, and (in her earlier work, at least) Rosalind Krauss, have made use of phenomenology, but this has been in relation to the understanding of specific artists and tendencies (most notably minimalism) rather than as a basis for understanding the visual arts, *per se.*

Perhaps the major reason for phenomenology's somewhat restricted application to visual art is that its recent manifestations have tended to be exegetical. On these terms, the understanding of a specific philosopher's or tendency's thought is made the end-in-itself of investigation. The opportunity for a more wide-ranging engagement with visual aesthetics is, thereby, underplayed.

Now such exegetical work should not, of course, be underestimated. Indeed, the present book has several chapters which closely expound and develop ideas from other thinkers.[4] However, it is important to negotiate exegesis in open terms—with a view to *extending* its insights in new critical directions.

This can overcome a further restriction. Key thinkers such as Heidegger and Merleau-Ponty (in his later work) approach the visual arts very much in terms of broader philosophical agendas. Such approaches have the advantage of illuminating visual art's important embodiments of Being and reality understood in the most general ontological senses (a thematic to which I will devote an entire volume, as a follow-up to the present one). However, this more general interest means that some features that are distinctive to *individual visual art media* are not dealt with in the requisite detail.

To ensure a balance, therefore, the present work will, as it were, begin at the beginning by placing an emphasis on the ontology and perception of the major idioms of visual art in their own particular characters. Its key interpretative concept will be that of *phenomenological depth*—a notion formulated by myself, but arising (loosely) from a convergence of ideas in Merleau-Ponty and Hegel, and, to a lesser extent, Kant.

Phenomenological depth centres on the *ontological reciprocity* of subject and object of experience. The embodied subject is immersed in a physical world which is not dependent on that subject for its existence and which, indeed, determines the character of the subject (in terms of both its physical constitution and the activities in which it must engage, in order to survive).

At the same time, however, the nature of the physical world *as perceived* is itself given a specific character through the range of cognitive and motor capacities which the subject brings to bear upon it. The ontological structure of the subject and its objects of experience are thus reciprocally correlated in key respects. At the experiential level, each is, in effect, part of the full definition of the other.

I will use the term 'phenomenological' in relation to aspects of this reciprocity. Specifically, my usage will centre on *descriptions of how the relation between subject and object of experience changes character on the basis of different modes of perception and action.*

One aspect of this relation is of particular importance for the present study. It is the fact that most of our perception and cognition has a *pre-reflective character*, i.e. we do and think things without always being explicitly aware of the fact that we are so doing and thinking.

These operations are possible because cognition's pre-reflective modes are informed by a massive stock of tacit background knowledge, and cognitive competences and dispositions which give sense to the subject's particular perceptions. How these inform behaviour is a question of the utmost complexity, but *that* they inform it is beyond doubt. Included in this structuring are three very broad factors which, as we shall see at length, have a special relevance to the visual arts. These are

- *The tacit enabling conditions of immediate perception*—based on phenomenal items and relations which are present, and give order to the perceptual field but which are not noticed directly, or which are hidden. *These constellate around the body's present positioning*, and, through it, function as a back-drop to immediate perception. Such a tacit dimension is necessary, insofar as without some sensibilia remaining in the background only, any immediate object of perception would be lost in an overwhelming plethora of stimuli.

- *The constitutive role of imagination*—imagination allows the quasi-sensory projection of items or states of affairs which are not present in the perceptual field. It is deeply involved in our sense of the re-encounterability of both physical objects and the self. Through it we can project the possibility of things and persons occupying places, times, and situations other than those in which they are presently located. (Without such a capacity, it would be difficult to see how language could be learned.) Imagination is also deeply involved in associational meaning, where imagery arising from the cultural or personal connotations of an item or state of affairs strongly influences how it is perceived.[5]

- *Understanding of the basic structure and scope of self-consciousness and agency* knowledge of this kind involves the basic recognition of ourselves and other subjects as creatures of both reason and sensibility, i.e. as *free* beings whose freedom is, nevertheless, inseparable from the brute necessity of physical and organic processes. Through this, what we think and do is informed by a sense of what is possible and what is not possible for us. And, in response to the latter, we sometimes seek symbolic compensations for the constraints placed on us as finite beings.

It should be emphasized that whilst these phenomenological depth factors can be demarcated with some clarity in philosophical analysis they are *not* so easily demarcated in the immediate subject-object experience. And this is true also—albeit in a different way—of how they are embodied in the creation and aesthetic appreciation of art.

Visual art centres on the creation of enduring, aesthetically significant spatial artefacts. In contrast to the generalities of philosophical description, such works are *sensible particulars* whose meaning is only fully emergent if directly perceived *qua* visual (a point which I will return to in Chapter 1, and, indeed, throughout this book). In the visual artwork, features that are basic to the reciprocity of subject and object of experience are *made to exist in a heightened and enduring form*.

The criterion of 'heightened and enduring' here is the relation between the visual artwork's basic ontological status as a material artefact with virtual properties, and the particular style in which this structure is embodied. This relation is constitutive of phenomenological depth in art, and takes on different forms according to the visual medium involved, as well as through the artist's individual contribution. In this book, I shall be concerned, primarily, with what these media allow the individual artist to create.

Of course, it might seem that, since visual artworks are finite self-contained wholes, their meaning *must* be sufficiently expressible in equivalent linguistic terms. But whilst this may be true of their factual aspects (e.g. what kind of object the particular work is, or what kind of things it represents), it cannot be true of the relation between how the particular work looks and its self-contained wholeness.

As I will show at length, this *aesthetic* relation is not only inseparable from the particular way in which the work has been made as just *this* painting or sculpture (or whatever) but is also the basis of visual art's distinctive embodiments of phenomenological depth.

It could be said that visual art *shows* different aspects of phenomenological depth, but does not *speak* them. Such aspects are experienced *intuitively* (a term again explained at length in Chapter 1) in ways which exceed sufficient comprehension through analytic modes of thought.

A phenomenological approach (in the sense described earlier) takes account of this. It is attentive to the concreteness of both the artwork and to our experience of it, through trying—as far as possible—to find a descriptive vocabulary which is adapted to this concreteness.

Some thinkers—including Heidegger, Adorno, and Merleau-Ponty—have attempted this through strategies of elliptical address, which adapt description to the irreducible concreteness of the art object. This approach has its merits, through emphasizing that artistic meaning can never be sufficiently paraphrased in discursive terms, i.e. that it *shows* rather than says.

At the same time, however, this must not be allowed to eclipse the demands of descriptive clarity. More elliptical approaches risk a paradoxical denuding of the artwork's concreteness—through failing to acknowledge its *aspectual* being. A work's different aspects, for example, might not exist apart from the aesthetic whole, but if they can be identified, this suggests that they play some distinctive role in relation to that whole. Indeed, the very fact that such identification is possible, and the particular character which it takes in different cases, can tell us something about the nature of both art and its individual works.

To understand visual art involves, therefore, (at least in part) a description of such distinctive aspects and how these relate to one another. Done carefully, this can enhance our understanding of the whole, since, through it, one comprehends the aesthetic unity's power to contain and direct its aspectual dimensions.

This mode of description is not, in itself, a distortion or reduction of artistic meaning. It only takes on *that* character if we take it to be a sufficient re-creation of such meaning.

My approach takes these points into account. It uses a non-elliptical descriptive strategy focused on the creation of visual art, and on the phenomenological depth embodied therein, and disclosed thereby.

Overall, the book offers a sustained *revision* of contemporary philosophy of the visual arts. It is a phenomenology which describes how key cognitive and metaphysical factors are embodied *in* the creation of art, in its ontological structures, and in our aesthetic responses to it.

Those visual media (such as film and video) which centre upon temporally realized *word/image* relations are not addressed, since their linguistic aspect necessitates a somewhat different investigative approach. I shall, however, consider temporally realized digital works which have a visual (rather than a textual) emphasis later on in this volume.

It should be emphasized that the book does not pretend to be encyclopedic in exploring the relation between visual art and phenomenological depth. However, it does have an important degree of *comprehensiveness* by virtue of its detailed investigation of all the major idioms in which visual artworks are usually created.

The basic structure of argument is as follows. Chapter 1 considers the limitations of reductionist approaches to visual art, and offers a general account of the intrinsic significance of the image based on phenomenological depth. Chapters 2 and 3 focus on phenomenological depth as embodied in key relations between the ontology of pictorial representation, the unity of self-consciousness, and the objective and subjective dimensions of cognition. In Chapter 4 this is explored further through a critical development of some ideas from Merleau-Ponty concerning the significance of painting. Chapter 5 characterizes key aspects of sculpture's distinctive phenomenological depth, through exploring it in relation to the notion of transcendence.

Chapter 6 extends the approach through detailed analysis of the complex structures of phenomenological depth that are at issue in abstract art. A general theory of meaning for such works is proposed. (This involves showing the sense in which they too are images, with intrinsic significance.) In Chapter 7, attention is focused on an idiom that has been extremely influential in recent art practice, namely Conceptual Art. (I understand 'Conceptual' in a broad sense, to encompass performance-based works, also.)

In Chapter 8, the distinctive phenomenological depth of photography is discussed, through a development of ideas from Roland Barthes and Susan Sontag. Chapter 9 offers a detailed analysis of the key structures of digital art and the implications which these have for the development of art *per se*. Finally, Chapter 10 offers an extended analysis of the phenomenology of architecture in relation to the body.

As a Conclusion, I consider the broader implications of my arguments, for the future of art history and the practice of the visual arts.

1　Against Reductionism
The Intrinsic Significance of the Image

Introduction

Discussions of visual representation sometimes begin with an indication of the sheer variety of artefacts in question. The clear implication is that this diversity in itself casts doubt on any attempt to define such representation.[1]

I argue otherwise. There is much work in aesthetics which converges on a pertinent shared position. The position holds that visual representation *per se* is based on a convention whereby resemblance between the image and its subject-matter (in terms of salient shared visual characteristics) is the basis of the referential function, without being a sufficient condition of it.[2]

In the present work I operate with, and to some degree expand, this shared account—most notably in Chapters 2 and 3. A complete phenomenology of visual art, however, needs to be based on additional and rather more challenging material. Specifically, it must negotiate the *formative aesthetic power* of visual art.

This consists of the artist's distinctive visual handling of the medium and compositional factors. Through the *style* in which a work is created, our cognitive relation to what it represents is altered in ways that are distinctive to the visual arts, and, indeed, to the specific medium involved. This is artistic *formation* in the fullest sense, and to comprehend it is to engage with the *intrinsic significance of the image.*

As we shall see in due course, this significance converges on issues of phenomenological depth. Such depth is shown through ways in which the creation of visual artworks embodies complex relations between the human subject and its objects of perception, knowledge, and action.

Of course, in an age of global consumerism, it may seem that image-theory should concentrate on photographic or electronically generated imagery, primarily. However, it should be emphasized that the great bulk of western art and visual representation in most non-western cultures is primarily pictorial or sculptural.

Indeed, *qua* visual representation, photographic and electronic images share many logical and stylistic features with traditional idioms, and in key respects are derivative from them. This being said, the new idioms also have distinctive phenomenological depth of their own, which will be explored at length in Chapters 8 and 9.

A further worry should be noted. It centres on the claim that there are as many theories of the image as there are 'sites' and contexts of image-production and reception. To talk of the image's intrinsic significance, accordingly, might seem an 'ahistorical' abstraction. However, (as I shall show in detail further on) objections of this kind are not viable. Indeed, *theories of the image's intrinsic significance, have been of the most decisive importance for art history itself.*

In this respect, for example, the development of German art history from Hegel, Robert Vischer, Conrad Fiedler, through Hildebrand, Riegl, Worringer, Wölfflin, early Panofsky, and even Edgar Wind, offers many important (if somewhat scattered) insights concerning the image's intrinsic significance.[3]

These are made possible because the tradition in question focuses on art as a *formative* aesthetic power rather than as a surface presented to the sensitive observer for contemplation (an approach which restricts much Anglo-American formalist art history and criticism).[4]

More recently in the English-speaking world there has been a revival of art historical studies informed—albeit in very different ways—by a sense of the intrinsic significance of the image. Here I am thinking specifically of work by Michael Podro, David Summers, James Elkins, and Yves-Alain Bois.[5]

Podro's recent writing has a brilliant sensitivity to pictorial detail, and to the perceptual expectations which the reading of such details sets up in the informed viewer. Summers has offered the basis of a reconfiguration of art historical method through his profoundly searching phenomenological analysis of the distinctive structures of pictorial space, and their historical and transhistorical vectors.

Elkins' contribution is more complex still. For whilst much of his work addresses the diversity of visual imaging and the different ways in which it can be understood, what is ultimately decisive for his approach is a sense that visual images have some meanings which can never be sufficiently analyzed in words.

The distinctiveness of Bois' work is in its productive interchanges between an enriched, *genuinely* pluralist notion of theory, and the concreteness of specific artists and art-practices. He is one of the few contemporary art historians I know of who has addressed what I call 'phenomenological depth' in a sustained and searching way.

All these thinkers clarify the intrinsic meaning of the image at different levels of its formative aesthetic power. My approach extends this. For it focuses on the ways in which such artistic formation involves factors which are fundamental to our knowledge of self and world. In particular, it is interested in *the conceptual basis and implications of structures that are fundamental to the ontologies of visual media*—rather than (as with the other thinkers just mentioned) the historically diverse ways in which these structures have been exemplified.

Now this renewed interest in the intrinsic meaning of the image faces a significant problem. It is the challenge of contemporary art history's widespread and sometimes aggressively *reductionist* orientation. This orientation is—by intention or, more often, by exclusion—generally antagonistic to the idea of the image's intrinsic significance. In the remainder of this chapter, therefore, I will attempt to meet the reductionist challenge, and then set the scene for the main arguments of the rest of the book.

Part One of the present chapter critically analyzes the basic structure and limits of reductionist art history and theory. In Part Two, some possible counter-arguments to my critique are dealt with. Part Three presents the outline features of an adequate theory of the image's intrinsic significance, and the key role played by phenomenological depth is identified. In conclusion, some qualifications to this main direction of argument are made.

Part One

First, the reductionist strategy. Griselda Pollock asserts that

Understanding of what specific art practices are doing, their meanings and social effects, demands . . . a dual approach. First the practice must be located as part of the social struggles between classes, races, and genders, articulating with other sites of representation. But second we must analyse what any specific practice is doing, what meaning is being produced, and how and for whom . . .[6]

Cashed out in more specific terms, this reading of visual 'production' emphasizes such things as the immediate material, social, and institutional circumstances in which the image was produced, the stylistic and cultural sources it draws upon, its conscious and 'unconscious' modes of displaying them, what audiences it addresses and creates, and its modes of reception and transmission amongst various 'constituencies'. The overriding tendency, here, is to reduce all questions of meaning to issues of socio-historical contexts of production and reception.

The social history orientation has dominated recent art history. In addition to Pollock, key thinkers such as John Barrell, Carol Duncan, and Albert Boime, among many others, have all—in different ways—emphasized the social conditions of production and reception in the understanding of art.

As one method of art historical analysis amongst others, the social history approach is of great importance and has had the salutary effect of emphasizing the role of broader societal and political factors in explaining how specific bodies of work come to be made and received. The problem is, however, that most social historians of art operate as though their approach provides a *sufficient* characterization of meaning in the image. This has the effect of reducing the image to its informational content and persuasive effects, and to the social and other circumstantial elements which enable these. Apart from the occasional discussion of technique and artists' materials—it is consumer and historical-context orientated.

Social reductionism of this kind is combined often with a tendency to assimilate art's visual dimension on the basis of models derived from literary analysis. This *semiotic reductionism* characterizes, especially, the work of Rosalind Krauss, W. J. T. Mitchell, and Norman Bryson. Bryson even proposes, for example, that pictorial naturalism should be understood in terms of the denotation/connotation relation. In his words, 'denotation results from those procedures of recognition which are governed by the iconographic codes. . . .'[7] It is the 'minimal recognition schema'.[8] Connotation is primarily bound up with secondary effects of meaning. In relation to this, Bryson notes that

> Whereas the viewer can consult an iconological dictionary to determine the precise meaning of the attribute carried by a particular saint, with the crucial codes of connotation—the codes of the face and body in movement (pathognomics), the codes of the face at rest (physiognomics), and the codes of fashion or dress—no equivalent lexicon exists, there is no dictionary of these things that we can consult. Knowledge of these codes is distributed through the social formation in a diffuse, amorphous manner . . .[9]

Hence,

if the naturalism of Western painting is persuasive, it is so not only because of a logic internal to the image and existing solely in the enclosure of the frame, but also because mundane experience so associated the subtle body of signs with the material body of practice that the codes of pathonomics and physiognomics, of dress and address are fleshed out at once . . .[10]

On these terms, whilst it might be thought that pictorial idioms achieve 'naturalistic' status by virtue of detailed consistency with reality, Bryson's point is that this effect is actually achieved through the viewer's perceptual/imaginative filling out of the work's connotative cues on the basis of social awareness. As he also observes,

the realist image disguises or conceals its status as a site of *production*; and in the absence of any visible productive work from within, meaning is felt as penetrating the image from outside.[11]

On these terms, the picture is reduced to a kind of visual text, with its own distinctive made qualities (*qua* drawing, painting, sculpture, photography, or whatever) marginalized. In particular, the rich consistency between a work's visual texture and its subject-matter's appearance is made into a function of social reception skills, rather than the artist's handling of the medium. Again, reductionism and the role of the consumer displaces the significance of making.

It is important to emphasize that the theoretical standpoints just described are not mere reflections of attitudes current in the late 1970's or 1980's, rather they involve analytic structures that have been continued and, in a sense, *naturalized* as a dominant orthodoxy by the next influential wave of scholars (including, for example, Jonathan Crary, Kevin Moxey, and Mark Cheetham). The only major difference is that this second wave of reductionism tends to legitimize itself by reference to the authority of Foucault's 'genealogical' approach to knowledge (a topic that I will address a little further on).

Reductionism in its individual or combined varieties faces the following central problem. Its dominant notion of 'production' is a composite phenomenon emergent from a broader field of meanings. Within this, *the process of artistic formation is dealt with as a function of 'production's' component factors rather than as a unifying principle which directs those factors*. The upshot is that what is distinctive to the creation and meaning of visual images *per se* is either repressed or distorted.

Now to think of artistic creation as involving the 'production' or 'construction' of 'meaning' or 'identity' is to use analogies or metaphors derived from artifice *per se*. However, this actually involves a surprising and hitherto unnoticed reversal of significance.

In another work I have described what is at issue here as follows:

> Ironically, whilst the 'production' metaphor has its origins in artifice, its application to the semantic domain actually distorts our understanding of the artefact. Far from assimilating meaning on the model of artifice, the strategy has the [reverse] effect of re-contextualizing artifice as a variety of signification . . .
>
> [In this respect] it is clear that the metaphorical linking of 'production' and meaning is driven by a contemporary western interest. For if meaning is understood as something which is 'produced' or 'constructed', then it seems close to middle-class fantasies of natives and workers, fields and factories. It appears earthy and real, and far removed from the despised ivory towers of pure knowledge. Meaning, in other words, is here articulated through a metaphor whose political correctness is highly congenial to contemporary western relativism.
>
> Unfortunately this fantasy engenders an even stronger reverse dynamic. For to understand meaning on the metaphor of production or construction, is to reduce it to the means-end model of western instrumental reason. But at the same time, through this reduction, it now *appears* that artifice and meaning amount to very much the same kind of thing. They can, accordingly, be analyzed on a common methodological basis as modes of signification. Ironically enough, *by linking artifice to signification the latter is able to dictate the terms in which the former is understood.* Complex forms of making are thus reduced to the status of signifying practices, and adapted, thereby, to the special interests of western academic relativism.[12]

The point is, then, that the strategies of reductionist art history and theory (and related feminist, postcolonial, and poststructuralist critique) interpret the visual image as a means to an end or, better, as a text meaningful only in terms of its informational or persuasive functions in the site of class, race, and gender struggles. This involves an almost exclusive concern with the image's relation to modes of consumption. Its *aesthetically formed* basis—its created status in the fullest artistic sense—is reduced to a mode of signification which counts as just one element amongst others in the 'construction' of meaning.

In effect, this approach allows the western art management structure—historians, critics, curators, and administrators—to redefine art on the basis of their own professional interpretative interests.

This approach is an unconscious expression of the consumerist mind-set of neo-conservatism—a mind-set which characterizes all things fundamentally in terms of their use-value.[13]

Of course, the irony is that reductionist cultural theories in general take themselves to have 'oppositional' significance. However, this is often a rhetoric of pose and fashion. It subconsciously internalizes, and thereby, extends, the market model of reality based on the idea of an unstable field of contesting forces which continually reconfigure the desiring subject.

Any notion of artistic formation which slips into this framework is immediately reduced. Reductionism assimilates the making and reception of images to western instrumental reason's model of *commodity production, distribution, and consumption.*

It adopts the glossy jargon of political activism—'struggles', 'interventions', and the like—so as to achieve market dominance over rival interpretative brands, most notably 'Modernism'. The quotation from Pollock at the start of this section is a prime example of this unrecognized market mentality. We will also encounter a slightly more abstract case of it a little further on. Reductionism's true status, in other words, is that of an unwitting academic expression of global consumerism.

I will not develop this critique any further at this point. However, a further worrying feature of reductionism must be noted now. It is the way in which its consumerist mentality tacitly degrades non-western art. Griselda Pollock notes that 'Modernist protocols' affirm

> the proper concern of the artist with the nature of the medium or with human experience embodied in painted or hewn gestures.[14]

The implication is, of course, that these interests are mainly the concern of (western) Modernism. However, although Pollock does not remark upon it, aspects of such 'protocols' also extend far before Modernism in complex ways, and far after as well. They are even more central to image-making practices in Indian, African, Chinese, and other non-western cultures, and have been so for, at least, several thousand years.

In these cultures, indeed, the process of creation is often the very core of meaning. It focuses beliefs concerning the magical or cosmological *efficacy* of making. To treat works from these contexts as informational or persuasive visual texts is, accordingly, a suppression of the intrinsic significance of the image, on the basis of western visual consumerism.

It could be argued that this is not true, and that non-western idioms simply require analysis in terms of 'different histories, territories, identities and concepts', *etc.* However, this reductionist rhetoric would merely extend the distortion. Mapping the beliefs and social contexts which inform the creation of a work does not explain *why* the forming of material in this way can be taken to embody cosmic forces or be a vehicle for magic or whatever.

Suppose, for example, it is said that a certain way of carving is believed to affect good harvests because of its likeness to the energy of the Corn God. This again simply invites the question of *why* the creation of such likeness is taken to have such results. What enables the leap of faith from representation to real effects?

It could be argued further that such beliefs are based on the image's presentation of ideas in a vivid public form, and its giving of control over that which the image is of. But this is, again, a continuation of the consumerist mind-set of reductionism.

In fact, an analysis of this kind solves nothing. For whilst vivid public presentation enables the image's object to be a focus of collective attention, this does not, in itself, explain the belief in the act of making's ritual efficacy. And if making the image is taken to give control over the object, this leaves the problem of explaining *what* factor sustains the belief that making a likeness should have this effect.

There are some circumstances in non-western cultures, of course, when—despite being the product of human artifice—an image is taken to be identical with that which it represents, and thence a bearer of the same range of powers. Since, however, the image is also known to have been made, the question still remains of *what* sustains the belief in its capacity to transform into another kind of being?

This leads us to the visual image's intrinsic significance *qua* artefact. For it is clear that the factors which enable the beliefs just described cannot be clearly articulated by a reductionist approach. There is an active aesthetic fascination at the basis of image-making's formative power which cannot be explained away by consumerist reductionism. It is true that the concept of the 'aesthetic' is a modern western one, but it is, in large part, derivative from the more universally distributed concept of *beauty*—in the sense of that whose visual appearance is found fascinating in its own right.

The problem of reductionism's limited scope extends equally to western art. For whilst, in the west visual images serve a massive amount of informational and persuasive functions, the question is rarely asked as to what enables this.

Qua visual, images are extremely efficient ways of communicating information about spatial relations and individuals. However, the so-called persuasive or rhetorical functions of the image clearly go far beyond the transmission of information. The image is able to characterize what it represents.

But why does this carry persuasive power; what is it about image-making which is able to sustain the rhetorical function? Mere descriptions of these functions and their historical contexts of occurrence do not begin to answer such questions. Neither do they explain why the making of representations has been able to develop as a distinctive social practice in its own right, i.e. in the form of *art*.

Reductionist art history might attempt to answer as follows. Art is a privileged form of representation which reflects and consolidates the interests of white male middle-class Eurocentric patriarchy. Its informative and persuasive power arises through representing visual reality from the viewpoint of this dominant and *controlling* power group. Art's privileged status is due to its provision of luxury commodities which can set their consumers apart from others in terms of social kudos.

Again, however, we must ask what it is about the visual image which supports these and other functions, and, especially, what it is about art which *enables* it to sustain the privileged social status assigned to it. Why should it be taken to be worthy of such kudos? If the kudos is based on aesthetic pleasure being regarded as superior, what is it about such pleasure which allows it to be so regarded?

It may be that it distinguishes the individuals who enjoy it from those who are satisfied more by coarser pleasures, but to suppose that it is, therefore, *only* a signifier of difference is to fetishize differentiality and to *foreclose arbitrarily* on the possibility of aesthetic form and pleasure having a deeper cognitive significance.

The problem is here, that when all the social and semiotic functions of art, and standard questions of iconography and iconology have been mapped out and analyzed, the fundamental question remains unanswered, namely what is it about the visual image which enables it to sustain such breadth of meaning? What is the basis of its formative power? We are left, in other words, with the problem of the intrinsic significance of the image.

As we have seen, in non-western art this dimension is especially to the fore. This is not because of some Modernist myth of such art's closeness to the throbbing primal rhythms of the universe or whatever, but because it more manifestly recognizes, and acts upon, a very straightforward truth. This is the fact that, *in the very act of creating an image (irrespective of one's practical intentions and subsequent uses of the image) one literally acts upon the world, and in so doing, changes one's cognitive relation to both the represented object and to oneself, and to existence in more general terms.*

To put this more technically, *to create a visual image involves acting on reality in a way that changes the existing relation of subject and object of experience at all levels.* This, in the barest outline, is the intrinsic significance of the made visual image.

If, therefore, we can identify the factors and implications involved here in more detail, we will have a worthwhile explanation of what is distinctive to the creation and enjoyment of visual images. We will have a genuine *phenomenology of the image*, rather than a mere history of its uses and social meaning.

The decisive issue then, is whether this intrinsic formative significance can be further articulated. Before considering this, however, it is worth disposing of some potential reductionist objections to my strategy. They centre on the claim that the very idea of the image having significance over and above its social uses and contexts is wholly impossible. I shall now consider a few ways in which this latter mistaken claim might attempt to justify itself.

Part Two

A first approach would be to appeal to the *authority* of anti-foundationalist epistemology. It could be claimed that the work of Foucault, Derrida, Deleuze, and co. has wholly discredited that idea of a stable world of fixed categories, subjects, and objects of experience, in which the property of 'intrinsic significance' might find justification. Consider the following passage from Jonathan Crary:

> Whether perception or vision actually changes is irrelevant for they have no autonomous history. What changes are the plural forces and rules composing the field in which perception occurs. And what determines vision at any one moment, is not some deep structure, economic base, or worldview, but rather the functioning of disparate parts on a single social surface. It may even be necessary to consider the observer as a distribution of events located in many different places. There never was or will be a self-present beholder to whom a world is transparently evident. Instead there are more or less powerful arrangements of forces out of which the capacities of an observer are possible.[15]

In a deconstructed world of disembodied subjectivity such as this, there would, indeed, be no room for intrinsic significance. However, despite his overt disavowal of economic factors, Crary's own position embodies, inadvertently, exactly what a market-driven consumerist model of reality (of the kind described earlier) is like, in outline. In it, the relation of subject and object of experience is reduced to the passive consumption of signs in a field of forces.

However, the anti-foundationalist epistemology which sustains this fantasy logically presupposes the very subject-object relation—centring on the stability of embodiment—which it is rejecting.[16]

To put this another way, deconstruction is intelligible only as a function of an undeconstructible context. This consists of a unified spatio-temporal continuum of causally interacting particulars, events, relations, and embodied subjects. Without this stable experiential continuum, no language or perception of any kind—let alone deconstruction—would be possible.

There is a related epistemology which might, at first sight, seem to justify reductionist scepticism. 'Genealogical' critique (of the kind associated with Foucault) holds that conceptual schemas are relative to power, race, and gender relations and the society which produces them. On these terms, to talk of universally significant 'intrinsic meaning' is merely a culturally specific 'power-play'. It reflects hierarchies and territories based on the striving for socio-cultural hegemony.

Such arguments are self-contradictory in two respects. On the one hand what they formulate is a supposed truth about the supposed relativity of all knowledge, but one from which the formulation tacitly exempts itself (through the generality of its claim); and on the other hand, what the formulation posits is actually in conflict with the possibility of language *as such*.

This is because the phenomenon of language—in terms of its learning and application—is only possible on the basis of networks of shared belief which intuitively *internalize* (even if they do not explicitly acknowledge) the stable experiential continuum noted above.

Languages differ, and so do the classificatory schemes they employ; but the very fact that a culture can develop language and classify things *at all* is because of a stable ontology (correlated with the body) which enables such competencies. The very existence of language-use, in other words, entails a non-relativist conceptual scheme.

Now one might offer a softer version of the sceptical claim by holding that knowledge and categories are mere tools to establish the hegemony of one social group's interests over those of others. Hence, the idea of the image having 'intrinsic significance' is one small aspect of this power-play.

However, whilst what *this* position claims is not, in itself, self-contradictory (i.e. does not exempt itself from what it is affirming), it runs up against the kind of problem encountered in the previous section. If knowledge enables the enforcement of hegemony, how is it able to do this; what enables it to achieve its effects? Why are some cognitive frameworks more efficacious than others?

The answer to these questions remain incomplete and unsatisfactory, unless, at some point, it acknowledges compelling factors in our conceptual schemes which—by virtue of their grounding in embodiment—are fundamental to any cognition. The intrinsic significance of the image, as we shall see later on in this book, connects with such factors in sustained ways.

On these terms, then, the idea of intrinsic significance cannot be refuted by using a body of doctrine which is itself manifestly self-contradictory or otherwise incomplete. There is, however, another possibility.

Reductionist art history tends to legitimize itself through a familiar binary opposition between the 'historical' and the 'ahistorical'. The former involves the understanding of events, persons, and activities in their original contexts of enactment, on the basis of institutional, cultural, social, economic, racial, and gender factors. The 'ahistorical' attempts to formulate 'timeless' truths based on its object of investigation being analyzed without reference to the litany of factors just noted. It goes without saying, of course, that 'ahistorical' is seen as a methodological flaw to be avoided at all costs. (The term 'essentialism' is a related sneer.)

Now it might be argued that the idea of image-making having an intrinsic significance over and above its historically specific uses is something ahistorical, and thence an empty abstraction. Images cannot be understood except by reference to the conditions under which they are created and transmitted. However, against this, it must be emphasized that the distinction between the historical and ahistorical *per se* is itself an even greater abstraction.

The problem here is that historically specific phenomena always constellate around more constant elements in human experience, most notably those connected with the conditions of embodiment. This is also true of many cultural phenomena, including visual images. In Chapter 2, I will offer a detailed analysis of pictorial representation, but clarifying a few basics now can illuminate how the historical/ahistorical distinction should be overcome.

Pictures are artefacts which refer by virtue of visual resemblance between marks or incisions on a notionally plane surface and the visual item or state of affairs that is the intended referent. The resemblance in question can be created so as to delineate individual visual items or to render such items in definite spatial relationships with one another. These simple points are *conceptual truths* about pictorial representation. This is because they describe an ontological structure that is constitutive of picturing as a distinctive mode of visual reference. They identify factors that cannot be analyzed away as mere functions of other idioms of reference. The historically specific dimension arises through the different ways in which this structure can be visually realized and the many different cultural uses to which it can be put.

But even here, however, matters are not quite so simple. Mathematical perspective, for example, is a convention for rendering spatial relations between things that is established as a major factor in picturing from the Renaissance onwards. However, it is linked also to conceptual truths concerning both pictorial representation and the embodied subject's relation to the visual field.

In this respect, for example, if a viewing subject changes his or her position, then the whole field of perceived relations changes in strict accordance with this, on the basis of physical laws. Perspective renders the systematic character of this relation in pictorial terms insofar as the items that it represents diminish in exactly calibrated proportion with one another the further away they are from the notional viewer.

On these terms, perspective is not *just* a historically specific development, but is actually the most logically developed and complete expression of one of the factors that constitute pictorial representation's ontological structure—namely the presentation of items in spatial relations with one another. Other pictorial conventions can express absolute regularity, and systems and hierarchies of spatial arrangement, but only perspective can present—within the internal resources of the picture—the systematic and consistent way in which the mobile embodied subject inheres in a *unified field* of visual items and relations. Perspective exemplifies a structure that is basic to perception.

Now it might be objected that to talk of picturing in terms of 'planes', 'notional viewers', and 'perspective' is, itself, to adopt an analytic framework that is historically specific to post-Renaissance western picturing, rather than to pictorial representation *per se*. However, whilst such a framework is historically specific in terms of its emergence, what it describes is not. This is because the features that the framework identifies are conceptually connected to what pictorial representation *is*, rather than just a set of empirical observations about it.

People may not have discussed picturing in terms of planes and the like before the Renaissance, but all that follows from this is that they were pre-occupied by other issues. The validity of the framework as a conceptual truth, in other words, is not all restricted by the fact that it was first theorized under historically specific conditions.

The centrality of such conceptual truths cannot be emphasized enough. To describe picturing in any detail necessitates that, at some point, *one identifies those features that make it distinctive as a mode of reference.* Such concepts as the 'plane' and the 'notional viewing subject' are logically inescapable in relation to this, and if one asks questions about the logical scope of picturing's referential distinctiveness in presenting the interconnectedness of spatial *relations*, then the notion of perspective is conceptually entailed also.

Such conceptual truths are not at all 'ahistorical'. They identify, rather, those transhistorical *ontological* structures that are basic to individual kinds of cultural phenomena, and form *conditions* which enable their more historically specific transmissions. The conditions in question here are not 'timeless' and inert essences. As we have just seen, the 'invention' of perspective engages directly with one of the ontologically constitutive dimensions of picturing. Many, many other factors that are conceptually connected to the ontological distinctiveness of individual visual art media present artistic possibilities that are realized through historically specific innovations. Reductionist art history lacks the analytic resources to negotiate such conceptual truths in relation to the distinctiveness of visual art media. In this book, the relation will be a major focus of attention.

Far from being 'ahistorical' then, my approach actually overcomes the one-sidedness of the distinction between the historical and the ahistorical by introducing a mediating factor—namely conceptual truths concerning the intrinsic significance of the image. However, my conceptual orientation, might raise a further objection (related to the foregoing).

It holds that an approach such as mine is one which conceals the conditions of its own historical construction. Given my earlier points concerning the logical independence of conceptual truths from the historical conditions under which they are formulated, this is, in analytic terms, irrelevant. However, as a matter of empirical fact, the present work is all too aware of the exact historical conditions of its emergence. It is explicitly intended as a critical alternative to those reductionist appropriations of art that are intimately connected to late twentieth-century neo-conservative consumer fetishism, and its continuations.

The book's particular phenomenological orientation draws on a number of other traditions of philosophical and art historical analysis which have been made available by technological and societal transformations in the way information is distributed in the postmodern era. My analysis is both of its times, and looking to change them.

This being said, I do not accept that meaning is 'deconstructed' through the aforementioned transformations. As we have seen, there are always dimensions of meaning which exceed the historical circumstances of their production. By virtue of the factors indicated earlier, these meanings feed into recurrent issues in the diachronic development of culture.

Interestingly, this is just as true of reductionism itself. For whilst it is very much a product of its times, it has established the importance of social and semiotic issues as a vital and recurrent aspect of our understanding of art history. Of course, to be consistent, reductionist practices must deny this, and hold that they are valid only for the current historical situation. But this surely involves a contradiction. For they tend to present themselves as *the* authentic approach to art history, rather than a historically relative phenomenon (a point which I will return to).

My approach, ironically enough, frees them from this contradiction by emphasizing their significance as one recurrently important aspect of the understanding of art. It should be emphasized, however, that the alternative which I offer does not see itself as *the* 'answer' to everything about art. Rather, it wants to highlight another especially significant *recurrent* aspect which needs to be taken cognizance of, rather than dismissed out of hand as 'ahistorical'.

One important qualification should be made, however. For whilst visual artworks have intrinsic significance bound up with the conditions of embodied subjectivity, the terms in which this significance emerges are, indeed, bound up with specific historical and cultural contexts.

For example, Modernist art tends to emphasize the significance of form, colour, and gesture at the expense of 'finish', narrative, and perspectival organization. In so doing, it makes use of structural factors (connected with phenomenological depth) which are always present in art but which, hitherto, were not objects of aesthetic interest in their own right.

This emergence is connected with specific societal conditions such as the stifling effects of mass markets in visual *kitsch* and the inability of academic art to satisfy socially transformed sensibilities. These—and related historical conditions—mean that specific aspects of phenomenological depth now assume an explicit importance which they did not have before.

However, what allows them to emerge in these terms are their intrinsic connections with the ontology of certain visual art media. They relate to factors which *have to be negotiated* in making art—irrespective of how they are explicitly understood at the time of making. (I shall explore this in more detail in the next part of this chapter.)

A final objection might be raised. If something is intrinsically significant, this surely means that it cannot be analyzed further. But if this the case, then of what explanatory use is the notion? Are we not, in effect, saying that what enables belief in the visual image's power to produce extraordinary effects, is an extraordinary hidden power to do so? This, of course, would not be a significant answer. Hence it might seem better to stick with the exclusively reductionist approach—which at least tries to analyze its object in rigorous terms.

Fortunately, the objection does not hold. This is because whilst no qualitative whole is the sum of its parts, these parts are nevertheless conditions which enable that unity. It is, accordingly, possible to analyze and explain how the constituent parts or aspects facilitate the unity in question, even though the analysis cannot, in itself, exhaustively explain the character of the whole.

In fact, *vis-à-vis* the intrinsic significance of the image, such explanation can be done in great detail. It will form the major subject of this book. At last, therefore, we can begin to give the notion of intrinsic significance more substance.

Part Three

I will first offer an overview of how phenomenological depth—bound up with how conditions of perception, knowledge, and agency (described in the Introduction to this book) are embodied in art.

The account will constellate around two terms, the *aesthetic*, and the *intuitive*. The former notion requires an especially detailed discussion, since it is of the utmost complexity despite it having a simple basic structure which is then modified through its many varieties.

Put simply, an aesthetic whole is one present to the senses (or which is imaginatively intended) whose particular phenomenal unity cannot be fully understood without us having had direct cognitive acquaintance with it and its constituent aspects or parts. In the visual context, this means that we must have *seen* the whole in relation to its parts. The unity of these two factors cannot be paraphrased in logically equivalent linguistic terms.

With the visual arts, such aesthetic unity has implications which are not found in other art forms. These stem from the fact that visual art media are necessarily spatial.

Now the basic condition for saying that something exists is that it occupies space. And in the case of human beings, this occupation is based upon the body and its gestural activity. There are, of course, senses in which language and music in their performed and written forms involve gesture, but it is difficult to keep track of the gestural aspect within their broader, temporally realized, communicative functions.

With the visual arts matters are different. We know that even the most technically 'finished' work—simply by virtue of being a drawing or painting or sculpture or whatever—has been brought forth through gestural manipulation of aspects of the physical world.

This is by no means a one-way process. For in both working the medium, and responding to the character of the emerging structure, the artist's gestural orientation will be reconfigured.

In key respects, this models the human perceptual situation *per se*. Even though we rarely remark upon it, the world's aspects and contours reconfigure in strict correlation with the body's coordinated movements and activity in relation to them. Likewise, we are compelled to change our bodily orientation in response to what the world thrusts upon us.

Vis-à-vis the completed visual artwork, one knows that the final form has come about precisely through such correlation, activity, and response. In contrast to other forms of consciousness, *such visual works directly exemplify the reciprocal interaction of body and world at the very ontological level which is most central to it, namely that of space-occupancy.*

There is a second aspect to this. An embodied subject's present perceptual field does not just happen; it has a unity and structure which is a function of the relation between the immediately given, our current bodily position, and our experience of the past and anticipations of the future.

Now to follow the meaning of a literary or musical work involves reading or listening, i.e. accessing its parts in a temporally successive linear way. This means that, in the process of reading or listening, parts which occur before, and enable one's immediate sense of the work's unity, are *present in memory only*. And our anticipation of how that unity might develop in parts yet to come is, at best, only manifest in imagination.

However, *qua* spatial object, *all* the parts of a visual artwork are, in principle, accessible in the present (dependent only on perceptual orientation). The role played by past and imagined gestures and positions in creating the phenomenal unity of the work is here completed and manifested *at the level of immediate perception*, rather than filled out through memory or imaginative anticipation, primarily.

The created visual artwork displays many of the factors involved in its own *physical* causal history; and, in so doing, directly exemplifies the dependence of present states of affairs and perceptual givens upon their past states, by preserving those states in the work's immediate phenomenal presence.

There is also a third aspect to be considered. The unity of any event in time (including, as we saw earlier, the literary and musical work) involves its components being perceived in an exact temporal order. The unity in question is rigidly linear. The unity of a visual artwork, in contrast, *qua* spatial object, allows the factors which comprise the finalized unity of the work to be perceived in any order.

This freedom exemplifies why space-occupancy is the decisive factor in existence. Spatial items and relations preserve their identity without necessary reference to exact orders of succession in time. By enduring through time in this relatively open way, they allow themselves to be perceptually encountered under many different aspects. The visual artwork exemplifies this fullness and plenitude of spatial being.

It must now be asked as to why these phenomenological factors are not exemplified by just *any* spatial object. A first answer concerns the 'twofold' character of visual art. The gestural activity which brings about such works does not create just a spatial artefact, it creates an *image*. (Indeed, as we shall see in a later chapter, this character even extends in complex ways to abstract works.)

To create a visual image is to configure physical material so as to represent some state of affairs other than the material itself, using isomorphism in terms of such things as shape, colour, texture, volume, and mass, as the major basis of reference. A convention or code of projection is involved, but one which constellates around a *natural* phenomenon—visual resemblance.

The visual image, then, is twofold in the sense of having a material base and a referential content. This simple structure exemplifies some complex phenomenological factors. For example, it is a conceptual truth that two different material bodies cannot share the same spatio-temporal position simultaneously. And the picture, sculpture, or abstract work is, in the most *literal* terms no exception to this. But such works at least give the appearance of overcoming this truth insofar as the work's physical body *and* that of what it represents appear to occupy the same spatial coordinates simultaneously. No matter how we rationalize it, there is something magical and fascinating about visual art at its basic level of appearance.

There are also some related but even more complex levels of phenomenological depth involved. This is because the life of consciousness in large part involves mental representations where we literally imagine our bodies being located at other positions in space or time, or where we imagine what it would be like to see the world from another person's perceptual viewpoint.

All these complex virtual 'elsewheres' are, of course, projected from the body's actual immediate position in the here and now. It is, indeed, only insofar as we know what it might be like to occupy other positions than our present one that we can become conscious of our personal identity across time.

In its projection of a virtual content from a material base, the visual artwork exemplifies this. It shows how alternative virtual places and times can be projected within, and thence coexist with, immediate 'real' physical coordinates.

Indeed, this has a more general significance still. For the images of visual art also show—in a vivid way—that cognitively significant states (the work's representational content) can be engendered from, and sustained by, material bodies. This means that the image not only represents its content but at the same time exemplifies something of the most general structure of the human condition itself—namely consciousness's correlation with, and emergence from, a physical body.

All these considerations show why visual art has an intrinsic significance which spatial items and mundane artefacts, *per se*, do not. Their twofold character feeds into, and activates, the points noted earlier concerning the visual artwork's significance as a spatial unity.

There is also a final issue which must be noted. Again it is a simple point with far-reaching implications. The visual artwork is created through physical making, or, in some of the more conceptual idioms, assembly, configuration, or juxtaposition. This means that such a work's visual appearance will be characterized from the viewpoint of the creative artist or ensemble. It will have some element of *style*—as an interpretation, rather than a reproduction of reality.

Of course, the style may not amount to much. It may be no more than an example of a commonplace way of creating. If, however, a work or corpus of work is *original*, our interest in its style as the exemplification of a distinctive way of doing things will be engaged.

Originality is an aspect of uniqueness, and uniqueness of all kinds is, in phenomenological terms, a profound factor in how we occupy space and time. Art discloses many aspects of this in both its making and aesthetic appreciation, and the visual arts do so in the most perceptually direct terms, insofar as they are *autographic* in nature.

These originality and uniqueness style-factors, then, are of major importance in drawing attention to the aesthetic aspect of the visual work. And since artistic creation and aesthetic appreciation are directed towards the part/whole structure of phenomena, it follows, accordingly that in the case of the visual artwork this must centre on attentiveness to spatial unity and twofoldness, and, as a consequence, to all the cognitive factors which converge on them and their relation. The aesthetic unity of visual art has, necessarily, a *distinctive* dimension of phenomenological depth.

This should not be understood hierarchically. Each art medium has its own special way of exemplifying cognition's relation to the world. In the case of the visual arts, their aesthetic distinctiveness flows out specifically from a privileged relation to human embodiment and its modes of visual perception and space-occupancy.

Now it is vital to emphasize that the phenomenological depth involved in art is not negotiated at the level of ideas alone. It is engaged by means of its role in enabling the aesthetic object. We are concerned with both how—in terms of the relation between whole and parts—phenomenological depth is involved in the work's aesthetic unity, and how this unity is further developed by illuminating such depth. Everything focuses, here, at the level of immediate aesthetic perception. Philosophical and other descriptions of art cannot have the same effect.

Within this aesthetic matrix, many phenomenological depth-factors related to the ones just cited can be involved. These include treatments of virtual content which overcome contradictions between the organic and inorganic; painterly clarifications of the reciprocal relation of gesture and the conditions of visibility; the reciprocity of freedom, contingency, and necessity in processes of creation; image-making as a purification or celebration of Being; and many other factors which I will describe in the course of this book.

In the creation of the image, these and other phenomenological depth-factors are exemplified within the work's basic aesthetic structure, and thence come to exist as something more than mere ideas. They give the image its deep-seated intrinsic significance.

Sadly, in recent times phenomenology has been somewhat neglected in favour of that fashionable but—at times—dogmatic anti-foundational epistemology which I criticized earlier. However, even if such relativism were valid, it would only involve the rejection of rigidly systematic philosophy.

This would leave a more modest notion of the phenomenological relatively unharmed. For *whatever* one's philosophical or theoretical standpoint, this—by definition—involves general conceptions of the nature of perception, knowledge, and agency, and the problematics of our experience of these.

When, accordingly, we engage seriously—by whatever means—with factors which enable the specifically human character of our cognitive and metaphysical inherence in the universe, then the objects of our engagement can be described quite legitimately as having *phenomenological depth*. It is phenomenological depth in this modest—but supremely important sense—which informs the making and appreciation of visual art, and which is at the basis of its distinctiveness.

At this point, however, an important question must be asked. If phenomenological depth is so intimately bound up with the visual artwork as aesthetic object, then why do we have so little *explicit* conscious awareness of it in this context? Indeed, the very fact that a work such as the present text is required in order to explain what is involved might suggest that phenomenological depth has no pressing relevance for visual art at all.

If this sceptical objection were true, however, we would have no way of explaining why 'significant form' in art was significant, or why visual art is the kind of thing which can be so powerfully expressive in emotional or persuasive terms. Our only resort would be to assign these effects to 'aesthetic properties' or 'expressive properties' *per se*.

But this would tell us nothing unless we could explain what sort of things, phenomenologically speaking, enabled such properties to have their profound effects. In the absence of such an explanation, the way would be clear for reductionism.

Fortunately there is a viable answer to the sceptical objection. To understand it, we must now consider the much neglected notion of the *intuitive*. In some usages this means various kinds of unanalyzable or even ineffable insight.

However, not all intuition involves this. There is a more commonplace sense which I shall call *explicable intuition*.

Consider, for example, the way in which our dealings with the world is informed by the knowledge that no material body can occupy two different sets of spatial coordinates simultaneously, and that to move from one point in space to another can only be done through the continuous traversal of spaces in between.

We may or may not have explicitly learned these *as* facts at some point, but these—and many, many, other related *conceptual truths* about the conditions of space-occupancy—inform all our behaviour as embodied subjects without us having to have them in mind each time we deploy or recognize them.

Indeed, we may have become *so* habituated to them (through their simplicity and/or familiarity) that we actually find it hard to explain them in formal terms. It may also be the case that we respond to the implications of something intuitively, even though we have not actually followed the entire chain of inferences which warrant that response.

The larger part of our knowledge exists most of the time in this intuitive form, and aesthetic considerations especially so. What separates ineffable from explicable intuition is that in the former there is a dominant element which, *of its nature,* cannot be put into words adequately, whereas the latter—whilst not usually noticed in explicit terms, can, in principle, be given *some* explanation, given the right context of understanding (such as through a philosophical text).

The aesthetic has both these intuitive aspects. The unity of an aesthetic whole is ineffable to the degree that its unity can only be fully comprehended through direct perceptual acquaintance. However, if we are called upon to explain *how* this aesthetic unity is possible, and why we find it so powerful, then we can begin to analyze the constituent phenomenological depth factors which enable the emergence of the whole and which are intuitively engaged with in the creation and appreciation of aesthetic objects. We can offer some explanation of a work's unity and its ramifications—as long as the explanation always constellates around direct acquaintance.

What is involved in this explanation is *the unpacking of complex series of explicable intuitions concerning the relation of parts and whole.* And the more complex the aesthetic object, the more complex the intuitions. In the case of visual art these will embrace the phenomenological factors concerning embodiment, perception, and space-occupancy, which I described earlier.

These factors are, in a sense, quite straightforward, but—unless one is used to philosophical thinking—are rather difficult to put into words. For example, in creating a visual artwork, the work is formed on the basis of an interpretation in a physical medium produced by (in the most literal terms) a unique finite agent or creative ensemble. This means that through this new addition to the world the world is transformed, however slightly.

By creating this transformation, the maker adds to his or her consciousness of both the represented item and the medium of representation and is thence put in a new relation to both factors, to himself or herself, and to the world in general. He or she is centrally concerned to negotiate the spatial unity of the work and its twofoldness.

To make a visual artwork just *is* to do all these things, in concert. Hence, whilst it might be unusual to think of the creative process and its aspects in such explicit terms, we *must* have some intuitive understanding of them and of their ramifications insofar as they are logically constitutive of the making of visual images.

Making or enjoying a visual aesthetic object *just is* a cognitive negotiation of part/whole relations that are becoming, or are already charged with, complex phenomenological depth on lines described earlier. We somehow feel that the aesthetic object is important, and, as it were, trying to tell us something, even if we cannot put it into words.

My point is, then, that this intuitive sense of importance arises because the aesthetic unities of visual art are not only harmonies of line or colour or whatever *per se*. They also exemplify and clarify factors which are fundamental to embodiment, perception, and space-occupancy.

The artist's creative fulfilment and our appreciation of his or her work are intuitive recognitions of complex meanings which are focused in the process of creating images. We take the image to be significant, because *it already aesthetically exemplifies factors which are basic to our cognitive and metaphysical inherence in the world*. It involves consciousness of phenomenological depth in an intuitive way.

On these terms, even before it is used for any practical purpose, the image has already empowered us, experientially speaking, in relation to Being. It has an intrinsic fascination which sustains our belief in its broader efficacy.

If this theory is correct, it explains the origin of visual art. The image's intrinsic fascination facilitates its practical deployments, and these employments may well wholly preoccupy us. In such cases the agent acts only on the basis of simple repetitions of formulae and procedures, and the work's aesthetic aspect—whilst intuitively recognized—does not stand out in its own right.

In other contexts, however (and most notably those connected to the recognition of originality and style), making and looking at the artefact may be found pleasurable for their own sake, and, in some cultures, indeed, the enjoyment of such intrinsic significance may become the major reason for making visual images.

When this occurs, we need a term to name the relevant practice. In the west, of course, the term is 'art'. 'Art' as a label is a western construct, but what enables and demands its 'construction' is the transcultural and transhistorical intrinsic significance of the image. The creation and enjoyment of such significance is, in the most general terms, the conceptual basis of visual art. Such art, in other words, is the practice whose meaning is *constituted* by the image's intrinsic significance.

I am arguing, then, that the making and aesthetic appreciation of visual art centres on the image's intrinsic significance, and that this is constituted by the intuitive negotiation of phenomenological depth in the terms already described.

It should be reiterated, however, that this does not reduce artistic meaning to the expression of philosophical generalities. The key thing is the aesthetically distinctive way in which phenomenological depth operates in specific works or bodies of work.

What is decisive is the way in which it enables individual achievement, and, through this, further illuminates our shared embodied condition. The artwork exemplifies phenomenological depth, but does so in intuitive terms which philosophical understanding cannot adopt except insofar as it uses elliptical, quasi-poetic—that is to say, artistic—idioms of expression.

Conclusion

I shall end with some important qualifications. First, (as noted earlier) various kinds of phenomenological depth are implicated in the logical distinctiveness of each major art medium, and I have explored this diversity in another recent work.[17] There are also some important overlapping factors which I also treat of in detail there. The present book, in contrast, will confine its attention to phenomenological depth in its specifically visual expressions. This concentration is warranted insofar as even within the visual domain, issues of great complexity are involved.

It should also be emphasized that such depth will be analyzed primarily at the level of intrinsic significance. Art history, of course, also relates to it in other ways. There are, for example, iconographical and iconological/genealogical approaches which centre upon the way in which images are linked to specific texts, or are created within a cultural milieu of metaphysically significant ideas. In this respect, for example, one thinks of the huge literature on such topics as the Neoplatonist context of High Renaissance art, or of the rich theoretical manifestoes and intellectual influences which are involved in the development of abstract art.

Such factors are, of course, a vital aspect of art historical analysis *qua* historical. However, as I have already argued, they do not enable us to negotiate the intrinsic significance of the image. I shall not, therefore, advert much to these alternative interpretative approaches.

This leads directly to the most important qualification of all. It would be a gross error to treat my critique of reductionism as if it were a critique of art history *per se*. To reiterate a vital earlier point, I freely acknowledge the importance of reductionism, but my worry is that it has become increasingly imperialist and exclusionist in its ambitions—as though other approaches are ahistorical distortions. It is this methodological authoritarianism which the present critique is directed towards.

The irony is, of course, that (as we have seen) reductionism takes itself to be rather inclusive *vis-à-vis* finding a voice in art history for women, and marginalized minorities and the like. But, as I also argued, the voice in question is only allowed to sing in the western instrumentalist key of meaning-as-documentary-or-rhetorical-content. It is excluded from participation in the image's intrinsic significance, because—even when acknowledged at all—reductionism caricatures that significance as no more than 'Modernist protocols'.

And this is the substance of my qualification. I am not offering some *system* to replace reductionist approaches. Rather I am offering a theory of meaning for the visual arts with substantial implications for art history. Specifically, these involve the need for an *inclusive revision*, which can begin to theorize what reductionism represses or mistakenly identifies with Modernism. This revision embraces all the factors which justify the idea of the history of *art*, as opposed to histories of representation.

The formulation of such a theory is a formidably difficult task, but it may be that what is needed at this point is an approach which is philosophical. By elucidating the image's intrinsic significance *qua* phenomenological depth, art's claim to high cultural status, and a source of historical interest in its own right, can be justified.

2

Figure, Plane, and Frame
The Phenomenology of Pictorial Space

There is a major shortcoming in the existing literature on pictorial representation. It is the tendency to reduce pictures to sources of visual information, and to emphasize what is involved in their *recognition*, at the expense of addressing what is achieved *in their making*.[1]

By the latter, I do not mean questions of aesthetic merit or the physical aspects of picture-making as such, but rather the way in which the appearance of some visual item or state of affairs (and our cognitive relation to it) is transformed when it is rendered *in* a picture. This *formative* rendering, of course, cannot be considered in isolation from the recognitional viewpoint, but, given proper emphasis, it can change the way in which that viewpoint is understood.

A second major shortcoming is the existing literature's tendency to separate sharply the problem of what is distinctive to pictorial representation from the features which enable pictures to become art. The possibility of *intrinsic* connections between these two aspects has not been explored in significant detail.[2]

In this chapter, I will negotiate these shortcomings through a unified theory which embraces picturing as a formative activity as well as a source of visual information, and which links the picture's distinctive ontology to the possibility of visual art itself.

The focus of this unified theory will be a phenomenology of *pictorial space*. Some tacit references to this space are found in most discussions of picturing, but, again, it has scarcely been addressed as a topic in its own right in any extended way.[3]

This is unfortunate, for it is only by considering pictorial content *and* its embeddedness in broader, formative visual structures, that both the ontological distinctiveness and the correlated phenomenological depth and artistic potential of picturing emerge. Pictorial space is the inclusive concept which encompasses these factors. By addressing its four major aspects, the narrow (observer-based) focus of much current theory can be compensated for.

Part One of this chapter, accordingly, considers the figurative content of pictorial space, by emphasizing its interpretative character, and the extraordinary modal plasticity which is implicated in this.

In Part Two, attention is paid to a neglected feature in which all figurative content is embedded, namely the planar structure of pictorial representation. It is shown that this involves a virtual immobilization of the relation between the subject-matter and the picture's notional internal viewer. It is also shown how this planar structure is decisive, also, for more marginal forms of picturing.

Part Three shows how the recessional structure of planarity is unified through relational foreshortening and linear perspective. These features make manifest that systematicity of spatial relations which is usually taken for granted in the course of our normal visual perception.

In Part Four, consideration is given to the way in which framing devices symbolically complete pictorial space's formative activity.

As the argument in each part proceeds, important connections between the structure of pictorial space and the origins of art will be emphasized as they emerge. The Conclusion will gather these points together.

Part One

Language can (and mainly does) posit things which are not themselves linguistic. In contrast, pictures can only refer (in distinctively pictorial terms) to other visible things.

Of course, what pictures represent, and the way in which they are represented, can denote or connote broader symbolic meanings which exceed the visual. A lion, for example, can be depicted so as to symbolize national courage or natural ferocity. However, in strictly pictorial terms, we see a lion. The broader associations are dependent on the context of the picture's creation and use for their recognition (or through the use of accompanying linguistic descriptions). They arise from the relation between the picture and logically external factors, rather than from that which is distinctive to picturing itself.[4]

Given the tie-in between picture and subject at the level of vision, it is hardly surprising that so many have taken the recognition of shapes and coloured masses as pictures *of* things, to involve the same broad cognitive principles which inform the recognition of those kinds of things *per se* in ordinary visual perception.[5]

However, this has to be squared-off against the fact that whilst language can communicate sufficiently through bodily expression alone (in speech), picturing *always* involves the use of at least some material which is independent of the body's own organs. It issues in artefacts which, once made, exist outside the body, and, almost always, independently of it.[6] Language, of course, can be embodied in an independent medium such as writing, but this embodiment is not a condition of its character *qua* linguistic, in the way that such embodiment is necessary in order for something to be a picture.

In characterizing what is distinctive to pictorial space, then, it seems logical, at the outset, to focus on the ramifications of this formative, artefactual dimension. The most decisive factor here is that the picture does not mechanically reproduce its subject-matter, but is, rather, an *interpretation* of it.[7]

Pictorial interpretation operates between two complementary vectors—the schematic and the particular. If something is pictured, this entails, at the very least, that the picture presents it as a recognizable instance of such and such a kind of three-dimensional item. It has a *schematic content* which presents characteristics sufficient to identify the relevant kind or kinds.

In visual terms, such schematic characteristics can be analyzed as *constructs* from specific solid shapes (such as cylinders, spheres, cubes, cuboids, pyramids, polyhedrons, and irregular variations of these) or combinations of such figures modified by the full array of two-dimensional geometric forms (notably regular and irregular lines and curves), and the use of colour-based media. *Qua* visual, any particular three-dimensional item can be regarded as a construct of these factors, in varying combinations, and varying degrees of complexity.

Now at the recognitional level, the picture's viewer will mainly negotiate its figurative content without taking account of the constructed dimension. However, not only can this dimension be *logically* analyzed as a construct from more basic geometric forms, it is an active factor, also, in how pictures *tend* to be made in practical terms.

Painting a figurative image, for example, involves more than just applying irregular shaped dabs, etc., to a surface. The brushstrokes are accumulated to delineate basic forms—notably geometric lines and shapes—which, using further regular and irregular forms—are then given broad accents suggestive of three-dimensional bodies. Finally, these are filled in with more specific details.

In some cases—such as stick figures—the constructive process results in particulars which do no more than present the schematic form of a specific three-dimensional kind in the most general terms. In other cases, the particular will be developed through further details which define it, not only as a particular, but as an *individual* (i.e. a particular instance of the schema with enough characteristics to allow it to be distinguished qualitatively from other such instances). In many forms of picturing, this dimension of individuality will be to the fore as a basis for more complex communicative functions.

It is, of course, in picturing's constructed character, and especially the articulation of individuality in the sense just described, that some origins of the artistic impulse can be found. For the constructive activity involved does not just mix basic geometric forms, but rather blends them in complex ways on the basis of the individual creator's stylistic interests and expertise. It allows for invention, and it is the exploration of such inventiveness for its own sake, that, in part, facilitates the development of specifically pictorial art.

However, there are also some rather more unexpected factors involved. To understand them, we must emphasize, first, some of the broadest features of picturing.

In this respect, for example, the schematic aspect is decisive. For whilst many images do not have individuality in the sense described above, they must *always* have a schematic *core* of three-dimensional, kind-individuating visual aspects. This core may be overtly schematic (as in the stick figure) or it may be embedded in a network of more individual details. In the absence of such a schematic core, there would be no grounds for calling something a picture rather than a two-dimensional configuration *per se*.

With this in mind, two important conclusions can be drawn. The first is that whilst pictures can be created so as to depict individuals who actually exist, or who did exist, there is no necessity that they should be created with this *denotative* end in view.

It is possible to simply make a representational schema, as such, or to fabricate the appearance of an individual through constructing it from combinations of the basic three- and two-dimensional geometric forms mentioned above. All that is required are forms which individuate a specific *kind* of three-dimensional item by constructing a sufficient quantity of relevant visual aspects from the more basic forms.

The second important conclusion is that the possession of schematic aspects means that (once the convention of picturing has been understood) the image is always pictorially intelligible at a basic level without it having to be 'decoded' by reference to external circumstances bound up with the context in which it was made or is used.

For example, whilst most western viewers will recognize pictures of the crucifixion of Christ, through relating the image to religious tradition, someone from another culture might not know this context. But, even so, if such a viewer is familiar with picturing as a practice, he or she will at least be able to identify a human figure hanging from a cross-shaped structure. Such recognition is achieved without having to refer to any circumstances external to the picture itself.

These conclusions—derived from picturing's constructed core—are indicative of pictorial representation's *relative semantic autonomy*. However, this logical property has a correlated ontological feature in terms of how figurative content structures pictorial space. This feature is *modal plasticity*.

Pictures can be created, of course, so as to denote actual existents. However, as we have just seen, by virtue of its *constructed* figurative content, pictorial space is intelligible without reference to such existents, or to actual or supposed contexts of use. This means that it presents visual possibilities.

Indeed, pictures can even present the *nomologically impossible*. For example, humans can be represented as having wings, flying over a landscape, or as being alive in the midst of a fiery furnace, even though at the level of empirical actuality such things are not possible for humans. More generally, pictures can represent *any* visual item as possessing characteristics or being in spatial relationships which, in actuality, are not physically available to it.

The extreme reach of picturing's modal plasticity is its capacity to present metaphysical impossibilities. Masaccio's *Tribute Money*, and Van Dyck's frontal and profile *Portrait of Charles 1st*, for example, show temporally distinct events or aspects next to one another in a shared plane, as if they were present to the observer at the same time. The figures or aspects recognizably common (in visual terms) to each event or viewpoint are presented, literally, as being in three different times simultaneously.

An interesting spatial variant of this is in such things as the duck/rabbit figure and Necker cubes of gestalt psychology, where—in effect—two different material bodies are represented as co-extensive simultaneously in the same exact spatial coordinates. A syntactic variant is M. C. Escher's many representations of such things as staircases which seem to end at their beginning, or, alternatively, seem to have no beginning or ending.

Now the normal perceptual world is governed by physical laws. What is actual, possible, and necessary in terms of the visible, and the changes which it can or cannot undergo is determined by this nomological framework. In making a picture, the creator is also bound by physical laws, but these same physical laws do not regulate pictorial content.

Pictorial space's constructed aspect evokes actuality, possibility, and nomological and metaphysical impossibilities in ways which symbolically transcend what physical space allows. In terms of phenomenological depth, pictures can exceed the usual constraints which embodiment places upon cognition. They can present radical perceptual alternatives to the visual given.

This provides the second vital connection with the origins of pictorial art. For, through modal plasticity, *pictorial space allows the creator to symbolically reorganize and re-make visual reality itself.* It is, in other words, not only a kind of creative release from the constraints of the reality principle *per se*, but one, indeed, which allows the creation of an alternative reality shaped by the individual creator's will. (The power of this, psychologically and aesthetically speaking, is of the utmost importance, and I will return to it in the Conclusion to this chapter.)

It should be noted, of course, that literature also allows such alternative creation. However, it operates mainly through imaginative realization, rather than at the level of what is presented directly to the senses. Picturing, in contrast, works its creative 'magic' not only at the immediate sensory level, but through vision—and it is vision, of course, which provides our main cognitive orientation towards that ultimate criterion of the real, namely space-occupancy.

Now it might be objected that in linking modal plasticity to the constructive aspect of figurative content, I have been using a 'thinned-down' notion of construction which is unduly tied to what is recognizable from within the picture's own internal resources. But in an account which is supposed to be stressing picturing's *made* aspect, this might be regarded as unacceptable. Picturing is an activity where the making of the image is inseparable from the network of intentions and purposes and practical contexts in which the work is produced. 'Constructed' as used by me (the objection continues) is an unwarrantably abstract notion.

The objection is, however, not compelling. There is no doubt that the modal plasticity of pictorial space connects with the practical contexts and intentions in which pictures are made. In fact, the question of whether or not a picture denotes an actual or previous existent can only be determined *conclusively* by taking account of circumstances external to the picture itself.

However, the frailty or absence of these circumstances also throws us back to the work's internal resources and its constructed aspect. For in making a picture, *the maker knows that it will not remain in exact correlation with any actual individual which it is created to denote.* That individual's appearance will change, at some point it will cease to be; if the picture is of a landscape, the landscape may be built over in time.

More generally, the picture may be moved to a place far away in space and time from that of its referent, and may still be around long after the referent has ceased to exist. Whatever the case, it is intrinsic to picturing that the character of its denotative relation to a depicted actual individual will be obscured or erased by time.

But despite all this, the picture, in its construction, still presents the visual appearance of a possible individual, irrespective of our being able to identify the actual referent. Indeed, it is this ambiguous interpretative hovering between an actual visible possibility and the strong suggestion of a possible former visual actuality that is one of the most fascinating aspects of picturing's modal plasticity.[8]

This provides a third important connection to the origins of art. Picturing's modal plasticity means that whilst positing recognizable visual states of affairs, pictures also, as it were, *suspend our natural attitude* to them. The picture fascinates by virtue of its striking independence from, or ambiguity in relation to, the constraints of the real—a fascination which need not, as has been shown, involve any directly practical considerations. This suggests that there is something about pictorial space itself which is conducive to that disinterested viewpoint which is integral to the *aesthetic*. (Again, I will address this in more detail in this chapter's Conclusion.)

I turn now to a second key aspect of pictorial space's separation from the 'real' visual world. It centres on an often misunderstood, and thence neglected, aspect of pictorial space, namely its planar structure.[9]

Part Two

Dominic Lopes and other major theorists tend to emphasize the link between pictorial planarity and Albertian-type perspectival pictures. As Lopes puts it, in such works

> a picture's surface should be treated as equivalent to the line of sight between artist or viewer and subject on to which the subject is projected. Given the

rules of optical projection, pictures so treated will present shapes on the visual field similar to those presented by their subjects seen from some point of view.[10]

Now it is true that a specific formalization of spatial relations in recession from the frontal plane is distinctive to 'Albertian' picturing (and I will consider it in the next section). The role of the plane, however, is equally decisive for the notion of picturing *per se*.

This is because picturing involves placing or inscribing marks on a surface which has the appearance of being two-dimensional (even though, in the strictest physical terms, it is not). Such virtual two-dimensionality means that figurative content, of necessity is projected between two notional planar boundaries.

The first consists of a background plane against which the figure is defined. This can be entirely neutral in the sense of being left blank; or it may consist of secondary figures whose main role is to provide visual surroundings of relevance to the fuller recognition of the main subject. Even in the extreme case of the figure being a cut-out shape, its three-dimensional appearance utilizes the surrounding physical context as a kind of proxy background (unless, of course, we mistake the cut-out for an example of the thing which it represents).

A second plane is involved insofar as a represented three-dimensional figure sets up a virtual distance between those edges of the figurative content which appear to be furthest from the viewer (and which 'touch' the background plane), and those which appear to be nearest. The nearest edges here constitute a notional *surface plane*. The distance between the background and surface plane define the scope of pictorial depth—in terms of both individual foreshortened figures and spatial relations between them.

This is even true of highly schematic 'stick figures' where three-dimensional forms are rendered through the conjunction of lines alone. Here, a familiar frontally presented shape allows the two-dimensional forms to be seen *as* three-dimensional by virtue of the way in which the frontal aspects-shape forms a crude surface plane defined against an immediate rather than gradually emergent background plane.

It should also be emphasized that the more fully modelled a three-dimensional form is, and the more it is pictured in spatial relations with other items, the more likely it is that secondary planes will be suggested through their parallel or oblique relation to the frontal plane.

We now reach the decisive point. By being rendered in a planar format the picture's subject is cognitively enhanced. In the first place, insofar as the pictorial figure is defined against the background plane (whatever content that plane may have), it is, in effect, a simplified but, thence, clarified presentation of a figure/ground relation which is basic to perception. The relation is basic because if we did not focus on a 'figure' area of immediate intentional interest to the exclusion of surrounding 'ground' contexts, our cognitive capacities would not be able to take even the first step towards knowledge.

Picturing not only visually foregrounds this basic perceptual structure, but offers an important augmentation. This is due to the fact that, generally speaking, the optimal conditions for visually perceiving an individual item or state of affairs involve the viewer and object both being stationary, with the object perceived from a frontal viewing position not too near and not too far away from the object.

The picture embodies these relations in a distinctive way. Even if the object is obliquely placed, its virtually immobilized character and the stationary frontal viewing position just described allow it to be scrutinized individually, and in its relation to surrounding items and states of affairs.

Now in ordinary visual perception, the viewer is mobile. Even if the trunk of the body is in a physically stationary position, such a viewer will have slight head and eye movements, however small. In fact, the adoption of an entirely stationary viewing position is actually hard to achieve, and even harder to maintain over any length of time. Indeed, whilst visual perception in general involves attending to a figure defined against a ground, this relation is *constantly* shifting and directed towards new contents on the basis of our cognitive and broader practical interests.

In making a picture, in contrast, the artist fixes the figure-ground relation on the basis of the planar structures described above. Through these structures, the artist presents the subject-matter from *an absolutely stationary frontal viewpoint* vis-à-vis any notional viewer.

And even if the represented subject is meant to be in motion, its rendition in a planar structure invests it with virtual immobility. The planes, as it were, *hold* and stabilize the subject and present its selected aspects in a fixed way that is not available, normally, to ordinary visual perception. Pictorial space intervenes on such perception by creating immobile figures which are isomorphic with selected aspects of the shape and mass of the subject-matter. In this way, the subject-matter is referred to, but is also, in symbolic terms, as it were 'bracketed off' from the phenomenal flow of real time.

43

My use of the notion 'virtual immobility' should not be understood as analogous to the way in which a photograph arrests a moment of visual time. In the photograph, we know—by virtue of what a photograph is—that the image presents a momentary cross-section from a spatio-temporal continuum. A causally specific actual past subtends the photographed scene, and the scene itself undergoes a quite specific set of causal changes after the photograph is taken. We may not have much—if any—knowledge of the events leading up to the subject being photographed, or what happened to it afterwards, but we know that these events actually did happen, and in a determinate causal sequence.

The item or state of affairs represented in pictorial space, however, is not connected to this rigid horizon of actual visual time. It is an interpretation of the subject which does not exist before the artist makes it.

This contrast with the photograph extends also to the picture's virtual content. Looking at a depicted scene, we may imagine, playfully, how it might have appeared before this specific 'moment' of representation, or of the different ways in which it might appear subsequently, but this really is no more than an exercise of imagination (though it is one with its own very special importance in relation to painting, as we shall see in a subsequent chapter). All that the picture does in the strictest ontological terms is to present an appearance of its subject-matter where the passage of time is not a condition of presentation—even though the subject itself may be represented as in motion.

I take this 'presentness' (as I shall call it) to be a key feature of pictorial space. It centres on *consistency* between the subject-matter's appearance and the frontal viewpoint of a notionally stationary observer. A picture can recognizably allude also to temporal motion in its figurative content, but it does not use such motion as a structural feature of representation (either explicitly—as in the case of film and video, or implicitly—as in photography's 'grabbing' of a momentary feature of the actual space-time continuum).

In terms of virtual content, pictorial space releases its subject-matter from the constraints of mutability—from necessary positioning in a rigid horizon of past and future causal actualities. The only active temporal factors involved are those bound up with the physical act of making the picture in the first place, or of perceptually scanning it.

Before considering some apparently difficult cases for the link between picturing and planarity, it is worth dwelling, briefly, on a couple of intriguing associated factors. As mentioned earlier, no plane surface is, *qua* physical object, flat in absolute terms. Pictures may appear to be flat, but under close examination their physically three-dimensional nature (no matter how attenuated) will emerge.

Interestingly, the nearest we get to such flatness in nature are the surfaces of frozen, fossilized, or super-cooled liquids. These can, of course, often contain foreign matter whose appearance (if not substance) is preserved beneath the transparent or opaque two-dimensional surface of the solidified liquid. It may be that there is an echo of this visual preservation in our more primeval responses to pictures, but for present purposes there is a rather more important dialectical contrast to be emphasized.

We know that solidified liquids are the main natural manifestation of flat appearance. Hence the picture's virtual flatness—which is manifestly not the flatness of a solidified liquid—is indicative of the fact that pictorial space is beyond natural constraints. The insistent *appearance* of flatness—over and above other markers of the picture's artefactual status—is of the utmost importance in presenting pictorial space as something different from the natural space occupied by those thing(s) which the picture represents.

On these terms, then, the absolutely stationary orientation of the picture plane and the virtual two-dimensionality of the physical medium are mutually complementary. They *separate* the subject as presented from the conditions under which it is normally perceived. This separation is of the greatest phenomenological depth, insofar as it enables the embodied subject to comprehend key aspects of the objective world at the immediate sensible level, whilst at the same time, enjoying some release from the cognitive constraints which normally determine that level.

Now it might be objected (by one such as Lopes[11]) that, even if my account is not tied to 'Albertian' perspectival representation specifically, its emphasis on the frontal viewpoint privileges unduly what might be called 'conventional' picturing. But if planarity is so central to picturing as such, it must also encompass more 'difficult' pictorial idioms such as maps, pictures in reverse perspective (where, in contrast to the Albertian mode, the size of component elements diminishes as they get closer to the viewer), 360 degree images, semi-decorative pictures such as those split-images made by the Kwakiutl Indians, and marginal pictorial styles such as Cubism.

Of these idioms, maps are admittedly different in the sense that they adopt an aerial viewpoint, but even here, the planar structure is overtly in play insofar as the maps involve markers (such as contour lines) which import a defined sense of some surfaces being nearer to the notional viewer than those at ground level.

The structure is also in play tacitly, insofar as—like the stick figures discussed earlier—the creator operates with linear schemata which set up a notional sense of three-dimensional presence. In this respect, for example, the outlines on a map without contour lines present land masses which are taken to be above sea-level. This means that even here, there is a background *and* a notional aerial-viewing plane which constitute pictorial space.

The other aforementioned putatively difficult idioms not only involve planar structure, but do so in a way which shows its active, formational character, even more dramatically than conventional forms of picturing do. Consider, for example, the case of reverse perspective. Here, features from the distance are clarified through being placed closer to the frontal plane. The order of both perceptual space and pictorial recession is reversed so that distant objects can be made amenable to the stationary frontal viewpoint, rather than being lost in the distance.

Similar considerations hold in relation to single 360 degree pictures. In these images, the artist compresses the full visual appearance of an item or state of affairs into a single stationary frontal viewpoint, which makes it accessible for viewing without any change of physical position being necessitated.

Kwakiutl split-images are even more instructive in this respect. For here, something's visual appearance—say a bird's—is reconfigured so that a few of its salient visual aspects such as beak, eyes, claws, and wing-structure serve to present it as a partially abstract structure which is symmetrically divided in terms of the stationary frontal viewpoint. Here the subject-matter is, in effect, *re-made* in even more thoroughgoing virtual terms for the benefit of that viewpoint so that its essence can be comprehended in spatially compact terms. Perhaps the most fascinating case of all in this respect is Cubism. Whilst Picasso and Braque are its great representatives, it is an idiom which has been developed by many other artists in many other different cultural contexts.

The meaning of Cubism in the broadest sense, accordingly, involves complex issues of art historical interpretation. However, it is noteworthy that *all* the major interpretative standpoints emphasize two complementary features which are of special interest to the present discussion.[12]

First, Cubist works actively adapt their subject-matter to the surface picture plane in a way which multiplies the aspects accessible to the stationary frontal viewpoint. The subject is, as it were, visually distended or 'unpacked' for the

Fig. 1. *A Kwakiutl Indian split-image of a bird motif.* From Franz Boas, *Primitive Art* (New York: Dover, 1955). Courtesy of Dover Publications.

benefit of that viewpoint. Second, in some works, the complexity of this adaptation gives rise to a secondary organizational principle which, in visual terms, complements the formative dynamics of the picture plane. This is the much-discussed Cubist 'grid'.[13]

Its origins are in a tendency to render the subject through facets (i.e. local planes, often with a gently oblique emphasis) a tendency which already characterizes much of Braque and Picasso's work by 1908. In the next few years, the facets gradually lose their individual integrity, and are increasingly rendered in partial and open terms. Through this, they gradually shift towards the appearance of a grid structure which, in compositional terms, gives clarity and visual stability to the virtual three-dimensional substance of the subject-matter by integrating it with the two-dimensionality of planar structure.

As in the case of the Kwakiutl split-image, the subject's appearance is here reconfigured through being adapted for presentation to the stationary frontal viewpoint. The exact character and broader significance of this adaptation differs from the Kwakiutl works, and, indeed, there are differences between individual Cubist artists themselves, but the basic pictorial strategy is the planar emphasis which I have described.

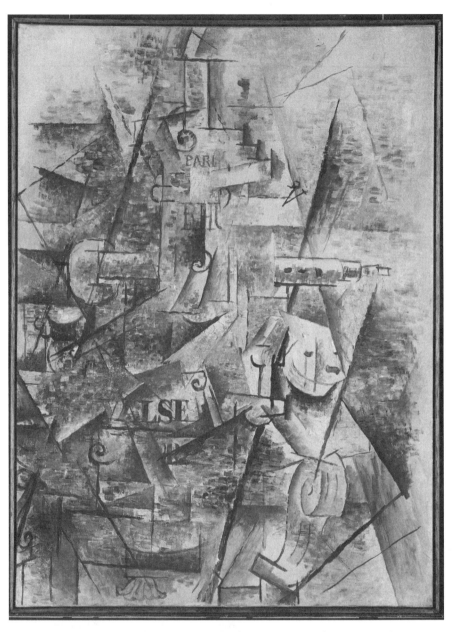

Fig. 2. George Braque, *Clarinet and Bottle of Rum on a Mantelpiece*, 1911. Oil on canvas, 93.5 x 72.3 cm. Tate Modern. ©Tate, London 2008, ©ADAGP, Paris and DACS, London 2008.

Now it is true that in much work of the so-called 'Hermetic' Cubist phase of around 1911 to 1912, it is difficult to identify what kind of subject-matter is being represented. However, without exception, they all contain details which explicitly retain a recognizable three-dimensional character, or which use two-dimensional motifs (such as newspapers) to suggest at least some virtual continuity with the broader socio-physical world. Such devices act as visual catalysts enabling the subject to be recognized as a three-dimensional body or state of affairs which has been radically adapted, and thence transformed, on the basis of the demands of planar presentation.

Given, therefore, the sustained connection between planarity and so many supposedly difficult examples, an important point must be reiterated. It is the formative character of planar structure. Through it, the represented subject is spatialized in a distinctive way in accordance with the demands of an absolutely stationary frontal viewpoint.

It should be emphasized that this adaptation is highly creative, rather than a mere technical exercise. The very fact something basic to pictorial space opens up this inherently creative avenue of development, is, therefore, another point of intrinsic connection between such space and the origins of art.

The main argument in this section, then, is that through its absolutely stationary 'presentness', the picture actively separates the subject-matter from the conditions under which things of that kind are normally perceived.

Now planarity, as we have seen, sets up basic depth relations. However, pictorial space in the fullest sense involves not only the plane and its contents, but *unified* recessional structures linking these. I shall now consider the two major varieties of such linkage.

Part Three

Sometimes, in the same picture plane, different items are depicted in proximity, but without any intention to represent them as having a similar relation in terms of 'real' physical space. If there are no connecting visual factors within the work's pictorial space we take such multiple images to simply share a plane whose function is entirely neutral. Objects are simply juxtaposed against a common background.

The first major step beyond this occurs when objects presented in the same plane have differences of size whose correlations suggest different positions within a *shared represented spatial location*. Of decisive significance here is when these correlations enable relations of *in front* and *behind* (in terms of the represented items' position in relation to one another) to be distinguished from those of *below* and *above*, respectively.

Sometimes this *relational foreshortening* (as I shall call it[14]) will not be entirely consistent, but will carry enough relevant visual cues to establish the idea of representing a single recessional space within the limits of the individual work.

Such is the case, for example, in much western pictorial representation from classical antiquity (such as the Pompeiian frescoes) and in those modern and avant-garde tendencies which radically diminish perspectival accents. It is also a feature of much oriental art, where, even though the recessional space tends to be flattened out for panoramic effect, there are enough cues to establish the representation of recession and distance relations within a single continuous pictorial space.

Now the significance of differing sizes between figures in a representation can also be determined by non-visual factors (e.g. in some Byzantine pictures such differences express the figures' respective importances in the theological hierarchy), but in these cases, syntactic meaning is a function of external contexts rather than the structure of pictorial space itself. When the distinction of in front and behind from below and above is systematically expressed *within* the work itself, then we are justified in regarding this as the basis of a distinctively pictorial 'syntax'.

The most developed form of this is linear perspective, where all orthogonals converge on a single, shared vanishing point, and where the sizes of objects diminish in strict proportion with one another, the nearer they approach this point. There has been much debate about the significance of this, in terms of whether such perspective is truer to our visual perception of spatial recession than other pictorial idioms. However, perspective's claim to privileged status has, in fact, nothing to do with this.[15]

The real issue concerns its significance in the systematic visual presentation of possible positions in three-dimensional space. For any viewing subject in 'real' physical space, spatial appearances reconfigure as the subject's position changes, and do so in systematic correlation with these changes. The key term here is 'systematic'. Our immersion in the spatial world is governed by physical laws which apply just as much to the visual perception of space as to physical bodies themselves.

Linear perspective is the most complete pictorial expression of this systematicity. As well as presenting its immediate visual content in terms of systematic convergence on the vanishing point, the exactly calibrated gradual character of this convergence is such as to indicate the possibility of unlimited systematic continuation beyond the edges of the picture, and beyond the horizon. The suggestion is that, if the viewer entered into the image, a new set of exactly calibrated spatial relations would constellate around this—and so on, *ad infinitum*, reconfiguring with each change of position.

As well as this absolute expression of mathematical perspective, an apparent variety is used also. Here, an artist may use multiple vanishing points if they allow his or her subject-matter to be interpreted in more interesting ways, compositionally speaking. However, it must be emphasized that this taking of subtle liberties with perspectival structure does not generally disrupt our sense of the systematicity of the represented space. If anything, it enhances our sense of the complex nature of spatial system.

Now in ordinary perception, this systematicity is not explicitly presented— we are immersed in it through binocular vision, responding to it intuitively in our moment-to-moment repositionings. However, linear perspective makes the immanent systematicity of space explicit. It involves a monocular planar immobilization of spatial items and relations *and* of the observer's viewpoint. This separates the systematic aspect of such relations from their fluid embeddedness in normal visual perception. Linear perspective does not 'correspond' with our ordinary perception of spatial relations, in other words; *it invests spatial systematicity itself with the character of visual presentness.*

On these terms, then, just as basic planar structure *per se* separates pictorial space from physical space, so too do its main principles of syntactic unity— namely relational foreshortening and linear perspective. They stabilize and present the systematic unity of visual space in a way that is not available to ordinary visual perception.

Now it is true that relational foreshortening and linear perspective are massively useful for conveying visual information *per se*. But the fact that they are also separate from normal perception also accentuates their potential for creative use and exploration in its own right (including the nomological and metaphysical impossibilities described earlier). Again, therefore, we have a connection between a formal syntactic structure of pictorial space and the possibility of art.

All the separating functions which I have discussed so far are completed by an additional radical feature which has featured little in the analytic literature.

It concerns the role of the picture's edges. I shall call this feature *circumscribed planarity*. It is by reference to this that the distinctness of pictorial space from physical space becomes a symbolic factor in planar structure itself.

Part Four

Circumscribed planarity involves some sort of framing device defined by the picture's physical edge *per se* (a kind of notional 'frame'), or by being marked out on the surface of the picture, or (in its more familiar three-dimensional physical form) through a cloth, plastic, ceramic, wooden, or metal frame constructed around it. This physical frame will usually be, in part, co-extensive with the physical edges of the picture, but it does not have to be.

Interestingly, Derrida notes that the frame stands out from the pictorial work and from the surrounding milieu 'like a figure on a ground'.[16] It also merges into each of these grounds—either to define the picture itself, or to indicate where the milieu outside the picture begins.

In empirical perceptual terms, the frame clearly has the effects which Derrida describes. But its major symbolic importance is better indicated by Georg Simmel. He claims that the pictorial artwork is a self-contained aesthetic whole, and that its boundaries

> are that absolute ending which exercises indifference towards and defence against the exterior and a unifying integration with respect to the interior in a *single* act. What the frame achieves for the work of art is to symbolize and strengthen this double function of its boundary. It excludes all that surrounds it, and thus the viewer as well, from the work of art, and thereby helps to place it at that distance from which alone it is aesthetically enjoyable.[17]

I will address these effects *qua* aesthetic in the Conclusion to this chapter, but two cognitive factors involved in them need remarking on now.

The first concerns the integrating function of the frame. Simmel rightly comprehends a factor which is made more explicit by Wolfflin, namely that the edges of the picture offer a structure which allows the pictorial content to be arranged with reference to the edges regarded as a limit, or as something to be continued, notionally, beyond (so-called 'closed' and 'open' form, respectively).[18]

Similarly the spatial depth within the work can be given clarity through being organized in a recession of planes in parallel with the main picture frame, or which recede more dramatically—often using devices which appear to cut through the main picture plane at oblique angles. In all these cases, the circumscribed planar structure guides and elucidates the internal pictorial organization.

Simmel is also right to emphasize the way in which the frame separates the image from the external world, thus emphasizing it as an aesthetic whole. But this has much broader ramifications.

To see why, it is useful to speculate on the origins of pictorial framing. The first recorded pictorial images are on the walls of caves. Here the individual representations do not inhabit any clearly defined space over and above the rock surface. In some cases, indeed, the pictures incorporate physical features of this surface as an illusion-creating feature.

This suggests that whilst the parietal artists were making pictures on the basis described earlier, they did not regard pictorial space as something ontologically different from real space. Indeed, it seems reasonable to assume, also, that the relative inaccessibility of the caves where the pictures were made is indicative of the images being regarded as embodiments (or at least markers) of some privileged physical portal between the real and the spirit worlds.

On a more old fashioned interpretation, it may be that the making of these images was meant to create magical power which would be efficacious for hunting purposes. But, in either case, the point is that *pictorial space and that of the three-dimensional world were probably regarded as not clearly distinct from one another.* What happened in the one was taken, in some respects, to be causally related to the other.

This situation does not remain static. In a great deal of Sumerian and Babylonian line engraving and shallow relief carving, horizontal margins and then enclosed four-sided borders appear around individual pictures. Indeed, in the west (at least by Minoan times) individual pictures on walls and pottery are often clearly defined through framing devices drawn around them. Even if intended decoratively or to emphasize the subject's special significance, this is achieved by separating the image from its surroundings by circumscription of the picture plane.

The very fact that images should be separated thus rather than left in a common plane, is indicative of some basic recognition of the formative separateness of pictorial space, i.e. the fact that it presents the subject in a way that is significantly different from the circumstances of ordinary perception.

Literally, the framing devices define and emphasize individual planes wherein specific items or states of affairs are clarified visually through selective presentation of their key aspects. Pictorial space becomes explicitly separate from the visual space of the physical world precisely through its role in this cognitive enhancement.

Framing devices, then, have the practical effect (intended or not) of clearly demarcating pictorial space, and signifying its difference from ordinary perceptual space. This difference is further accentuated through the development of media such as paper, wooden panels, and eventually, easel painting where the physical boundaries of individual works—framed or otherwise—are clearly understood as marking out a distinctively pictorial mode of space.

Surprisingly enough, whilst it might seem that framing devices function so as to declare the picture's physical edges, in both historical and conceptual terms it seems likely that the reverse is true. The physical edges radicalize a framing structure which was probably already in use before free-standing pictorial media were developed, and which can also operate *within* the picture's physical limits (although in recent western art this is somewhat rare).

Before moving to a Conclusion, it is worth deliberating on why framing devices take characteristic shapes. Why, for example, are rectangles, and to a much lesser extent, squares, ovals, and circles favoured as framing devices, in a way that triangles, polygons, and irregular shapes are not?

The answer to this must be speculative, but can be extremely instructive as well. Matters hinge, surely, on both negative and positive considerations. In negative terms, irregular and polygonal forms are of potential perceptual interest in their own right, and could distract from the framing of pictorial content. Triangular frames are also like this to some degree, and, in addition, tend to visually compress the space in at least one of the corners.

Circular and square frames achieve a satisfactory directedness towards the content of pictorial space, but they enclose it rather too completely by dint of their absolute regularity. Circular forms have the additional problem of being difficult to draw or construct by hand.

With rectangular formats (and to a lesser extent, ovals) this directedness is also achieved, but with the signal advantage of appearing to extend outwards in two equal directions, either horizontally or vertically. This dynamism suggests the virtual extendability of pictorial space left, right, and above the stationary viewer as well as in front of him and her. Its framing function is thereby one which focuses on the main represented subject but which situates it in a relatively open space. It is also one which can be augmented for more specific symbolic purposes through, say adding a triangle or semi-circle to the top of the work (as in many works of Italian Renaissance art).

The visual dynamics of the rectangular format is important not only for the representation of visual states of affairs and 'scenes', but even for the depiction of individual items. For since the picture presents its three-dimensional subject aspectually from one fixed viewpoint, it is important to frame it through an active format which makes the given aspect suggestive of hidden ones which might emerge to the viewer if he or she or the object changed position. Through its virtual openness (in the terms just described) the rectangular format provides this.

Conclusion

I have, then, described what is involved in the creation of pictorial space *vis-à-vis* its structural components. These are figurative content, planarity, recessional unity, and circumscribed planarity. They centre on a formative power which adapts the subject-matter's three-dimensional appearance to the demands of two-dimensional media.

Whilst the perception of this pictorial space has some kinship with our normal viewing of the world, it is also radically separate from it. Normal perception is mobile, whereas the relation between the notional viewer and subject-matter in pictorial space is absolutely stationary. Through this, *it suspends our natural attitude towards the visual world*. Instead of the subject-matter being present to perception as such, it has the character, rather, of what I have called *presentness*.

In each section, I have pointed out how the structural features of pictorial space are connected with the possibility of art. I shall end by bringing these points together.

The concept of 'art' as something more than specific idioms of artefact making *per se* is, of course, mainly western in origin, and this might suggest, at first sight, that both art and related concepts such as the aesthetic have no legitimate application beyond the western cultural context.

However, the points made in this chapter suggest otherwise. In this respect, the key factors in pictorial space which I have described, prove decisive. Rendered in pictorial space, the visual world is virtually amenable to the power of the human will to present it or transform it.

Such power is surely at the heart of why image-making in so many cultures is taken to give some sort of control over that which it is an image of. To be fascinated by this is not simply to take pleasure in some imagined control which the making of the picture will give over the subject-matter. For the very fact that it can be taken to have such power in the first place suggests, surely, that *it has already been experienced as something, the making of which is special in its own right.*

This special significance converges, in the first instance, on what in Part One I called 'modal plasticity'. Pictures *transform* the appearance of reality. Indeed, by symbolically transcending the constraints of the real *per se*, the picture is able to engage, inventively, with some of our deepest spiritual needs by giving symbolic compensation for the limitations of our finite being.

Indeed, this modal plasticity means that, in terms of content, picturing is enormously fecund. As we saw, its scope encompasses visual actualities, possibilities, and even some impossibilities. Modal plasticity, in other words, is not just some dry ontological property of pictorial space. It exemplifies, rather, *an horizon of infinite creative potential* in terms of representational content.

Some cultures may choose to focus on only a restricted aspect of this horizon. But this is a cultural fact only—and one which can be challenged if the maker expands his or her sensibility to consider the possibility of alternative contents. And even in terms of quite specific kinds of subject-matter or individuals, picturing still allows many different ways for such content to be articulated. The picture-maker may be happy to repeat formulae, but, again, this is a cultural factor rather than something intrinsic to picturing, *per se.*

When understood as an intrinsic feature of pictorial space, then, modal plasticity can be understood as an horizon of creative potential which exceeds any limits placed upon it by specific cultural contexts. It follows, then, that to realize this is to be placed in a position wherein the exploration of pictorial possibilities for their own sake becomes an option. It is to realize the *possibility of art* itself.

Such realization is strengthened by a correlated insight. For just as there are no limits on the kinds of visual thing or state of affairs which can be pictured, pictorial style, also, has extreme plasticity in terms of how it is realized. Even if a culture's style of picturing is entrenched and unchanging, this unchanging character is culturally determined only. How pictures have been made hitherto does not circumscribe further possibilities of stylistic creativity.

There are, in principle, as many possible styles as there are individual makers. These can range from the most minimal schemas to the most illusionistic *trompe l'oeil*; or from the thinnest use of contours to levels of expressionism where the pictorial content is scarcely perceptible.

This means that to understand picturing's intrinsic modal plasticity and its stylistic correlate is to comprehend the extraordinary scope for creative invention which is intrinsic to picture-making as a practice (over and above its culturally specific functions). It is, in other words, to comprehend the possibility of becoming a creator, i.e. an *artist*, as well as a maker.

Earlier on I emphasized how the presentness of pictorial content is achieved through organization in terms of planar structure and relational or perspectival recession. These are not just transparent means of presentation. They actively change the appearance of the subject-matter in relation to the demands of the medium.

This change has the greatest intrinsic creative potential in its own right. The disposition of content in relation to the pictorial structure and style is one of the most important sources of *compositional invention*. Again, whilst picturing in some cultures may follow rigid formulae in terms of how presentness is achieved, the nature of pictorial space allows the aforementioned structures to be realized in many different ways—determined by the nature of the particular subject-matter, and the creative preferences and skills of the maker.

These points, in themselves, show further how the possibility of art is intrinsic to the nature of pictorial space itself. However, to understand the depth of this intrinsic feature it is important to emphasize another dimension. It centres on the way in which all the factors just described, actively separate pictorial space from the conditions of ordinary visual perception. By thinking this through, *the link between pictorial space and the possibility of art can be extended from the maker's viewpoint, to that of the observer.*

In this respect, it will be recalled that I have given great emphasis to the way in which picturing adapts its subject to the background and surface planes, and presents it in terms of virtual immobility to a notionally stationary observer with a frontal viewpoint.

This goes beyond the ordinary—highly mobile—conditions of perception, and sets pictorial space apart from that of reality. It offers a cognitively enhanced visual presentation of the subject, through a rendering which suspends (in virtual terms) that subject's necessary positioning in time. Suspension of this kind enhances the separateness of pictorial space from that of the practical world.

The techniques for unifying planar structure in a single pictorial space are embodied in these factors. Relational foreshortening and linear perspective are significant not through corresponding to the perceptual mechanisms whereby we see things, but precisely because they go far beyond such mechanisms by investing the (normally taken-for-granted) systematicity of visual space itself, with the character of *presentness*.

Again there is a decisive separating off here—of the pictorial as a fascinating exemplification of spatial systematicity which is consistent with the way in which we perceive space but which is also significantly separate from it.

Now the fact that pictorial space is radically separated from ordinary visual space in all these ways does not of itself realize a picture's artistic potential. We may simply attend to the visual information which it is conveying. Alternatively, one might look at it in terms of technical issues alone.

However, if we link the earlier points about the intrinsic creative potential of pictorial space to its separateness, another possibility emerges. For when a picture's idiom of making present (using all the creative factors already mentioned) embodies some element of originality, then it can fascinate, in its own right, through opening up aspects of the visible world and a human relationship to it which we had not been aware of before.

The fact that this creative vision is rendered in a space which is 'of' the visual world, but, at the same time, so separate from it, involves a special cognitive orientation. Specifically, *the pressures and constraints which might arise in a 'real' visual experience of the kind of subject-matter depicted, or in response to another person's verbal characterizations of it, are removed when encountered at the level of pictorial space.*

Through such space, we can explore another person's selective interpretation of the visible. It is a vision which has been made at a publicly accessible level and is liberated from immediate existential pressures, and from the vicissitudes of time.

Pictorial space experienced *as pictorial*, opens up a distinctive *freedom* of access to how the world is visualized. This positive experience is not directed by practical demands, and has, accordingly, a disinterested and aesthetic character. From the viewer's as well as the maker's standpoint, therefore, the experience of pictorial space, in its own right, embodies the possibility of art.

This artistic significance of the picture is, of course, made overt through the use of the picture's edge and correlated framing devices. These act as organizational factors in terms of figurative content's recessional relation to the plane, as well as emphasizing the limits of the particular pictorial space.

The two factors are highly complementary in artistic terms. For how content is disposed in relation to the picture's limits is another important source of *compositional invention*. It opens up, thereby, aesthetic possibilities as well as purely virtual ones.

In this respect, the actual character of the frame, also, can play an interesting role. As we have seen, it can be purely notional—as in those cases where the physical edge of the picture is apparent without any physical material being used to emphasize it. In other cases, it can be no more than a margin or border drawn, painted, or inscribed on a surface in order to demarcate one particular pictorial space from another. In other cases still, it is a physical frame whose individual character must be carefully selected in relation to the picture which it is meant to declare.

Whatever the case, it is clear that as well as drawing attention to what is contained within the frame, and affirming also the separateness of pictorial from 'real space', the frame has a profoundly aesthetic function. For *it invites appreciation of the way in which the picture is composed as well as a purely recognitional relation to its contents and planar structure.*

Indeed, the character of the physical frame itself—in terms of the material it is made from, and sophistication in the way it harmonizes with the picture's content—can be a kind of explicit symbolic affirmation that this is an artistic image rather than just a piece of pictorial information.[19]

I have argued, then, that pictorial space has a complex and distinctive structure based on the four key aspects which I have analyzed at length. I have emphasized how this is not just a space of visual information, but one of phenomenological depth—arising from the subject-matter being adapted, virtually, to the demands of circumscribed planarity. It has also been shown that this complex adaptation generates enormous aesthetic potential under each of its aspects. Through it, pictorial space clarifies basic structures in our perceptual relation to the world at the level of perception itself. When this aesthetic potential is realized, meaning takes on an *artistic* character.

I have argued at length, then, that the possibility of visual art is, in key respects, embedded in the very nature of pictorial space. Whether this possibility is developed or not is a function of the particular cultural, historical, and personal circumstances in which the individual artist makes his or her pictures.

3   Pictorial Representation and Self-Consciousness

Introduction

This chapter will offer some important further explanations of the pictorial image's intrinsic significance through linking it to key cognitive factors that bridge the relation between subject and object of experience at several different levels.

Self-consciousness is not simply given, rather it is acquired gradually, and, once acquired, can be developed further. In ontogenetic terms, the child gradually learns to co-ordinate its senses through bodily interactions in reciprocity with the world and through socialization and initiation into language. At the phylogenetic level, the species progressively evolves more complex and sophisticated modes of bodily co-ordination correlated with more complex patterns of socialization, and communicative gesture.

The term 'correlation' needs remarking upon. For given some creature which has grown or evolved to a specific state, one can identify sets of behavioural traits, dispositions, and competence, which define that state. Now, if we seek also to explain how that state came to be (i.e. account for the process of its growth) matters become much more complex. Some of the identified traits, disposition, and competences, will be functions of similar or more primitive sets of qualities, but the evolution of these into their higher forms may also involve asynchrony, i.e. one trait or disposition (or whatever) achieves its higher phase before other forms do.

Matters are also made more complex by the fact that whilst a creature's given state may be resolved into logically distinctive elements, its growth involves all these elements functioning in an undifferentiated unity. In these circumstances it becomes correspondingly more difficult to explain the particular patterns of interaction between the elements, and to identify specific points of origin.

Given all these considerations, the best approach is to say that processes of growth, the development of specific elements, are *correlated* with one another in both logical and causal terms. On logical grounds we might see some elements as primary, but the causal story of their growth into higher forms and the conditions which facilitate this are at best speculative.

However, whilst speculation cannot be decisive, it can be informative through laying bare structures which are common both to an element or elements in a process of growth, and to other specific phenomena. These links might be so strong as to suggest that the growth of the said elements is correlated with the presence of the phenomena in question; i.e. the latter influences the former in crucial respects even if we cannot give an exact causal story of how this comes about.

This, I would suggest, is the nature of the relation between self-consciousness and picturing. To show this, Part One of the chapter outlines the structure of consciousness and self-consciousness in terms of the basic cognitive and affective competences which they presuppose. I then consider some specific aspects of self-consciousness in more detail, paying particular attention to the notion of the present moment and its relation to the projection of alternative perceptual possibilities.

In Part Two, I outline some aspects of the ontology of the picture and suggest that they have a key correlation with the consolidation of factors that are necessary conditions of self-consciousness.[1] This is a key dimension of phenomenological depth.

Part One

Consciousness involves rather more than mere capacity to respond to stimuli. It involves also a capacity to adapt alternative patterns of response to them. Such an ability logically presupposes at least four basic competences.

The first is *attention*; namely, a creature's ability to perceptually scan and follow changes in its environment without at the same time being necessarily propelled into active response. The second capacity is *comprehension*. This centres on the ability to perform at least rudimentary acts of subsumption and discrimination, for example, the recognition of prey or predator, or the distinction between material which is edible and material which is not.

The third capacity is the most interesting (in many respects). It is the capacity for *imagination*. In its most basic sense, this allows past or possible perceptual encounters to inform a creature's present behaviour. Through this, it can perform the acts of comprehension just noted, and anticipate—from cues within the environment—the imminence of factors associated with its physical needs or survival.

Such anticipatory functions also link up with the final element in consciousness—namely the search for *gratification and replenishment*. One presumes that all organic life forms need such gratification and replenishment; but in conscious creatures these experiences are actively sought out, rather than enjoyed purely on an *ad hoc* basis in chance encounters.

Now to be self-conscious, by definition, involves the capacity to ascribe experiences to oneself. Such a capacity would not be intelligible without reference to the four factors just cited. However, it also entails that the factors are used in a quite specific way—namely, to articulate four further (and closely related) insights.

The first of these is *reversibility*—the fact that the one who perceives is an element within a broader world which is more than the sum of the subject's perceptions and projects. To put this another way; the subject must also recognize its status as object of perception for another. Related to this is the insight of *species-identity*, which consists of the recognition that the world of which one is a part also numbers other subjects who perceive and respond to the world on the same structural principles as oneself. The third insight is that of *freedom*; namely, the awareness that one has the capacity to inaugurate action on grounds other than mere determination by natural impulses.

This also relates to the final insight which concerns *existential belonging*. In this respect, one can assume that the reason why a conscious creature adopts specific patterns of behaviour in relation to procuring the means of its subsistence and survival is purely biologically determined. Here the structure of consciousness is very closely tied to the realization of physical need. In self-conscious beings, matters are different, and this is not just because of the awareness of temporal continuity which is involved in personal existence. For it can be asked why it is that any such sense of continuity is possible.

And what is presupposed here is an experience of time composed from interrelations between the themes and rhythms of our own personal history.[2] This entails that what happens to us *matters*; experiences signify emotionally and take on different values in relation to one another.

There is, of course, a basic synthesis of this sort wherein the unified operations of the body subsume and discriminate at the level of perception; but this can only function insofar as the syntheses of immediate perception draw upon and play off against memories of and responses to the past and expectations of what might be, or of what might have been. This perceptual synthesis links up with memory and desire so as to form a unified field of meaning and value which defines our particular mode of existential belonging.

The texture of immediate momentary experience also has its own tacit satisfactions and frustrations which are determined by relations of unity and diversity between the individual's present and his or her sense of past, future, and counterfactual alternatives. It is a texture whose complex relations have an intrinsic emotional and existential value. The unity of self-consciousness is, in other words, that of complex *aesthetic narrative structure*. The deeper aesthetic structure subtends and sustains the immediate network of current interpretations in terms of which an individual understands the 'meaning' of his or her life.

I am claiming, then, that the four primary factors in consciousness—attention, comprehension, imagination, and gratification—need to articulate four further correlated factors in order for self-consciousness to be achieved. In reciprocal concert, the primary and secondary factors, allow a point of reflection where the 'I think' of self-awareness becomes possible. Now before considering the role of picturing in relation to this, I want to look in more detail to an element that focuses all the many different factors I have mentioned. Let us call it *corporeal imagination*.

First, then, we can only be explicitly conscious of a present by virtue of reference to a past. Bergson has usefully brought out something of what is involved here in his distinction between 'habit' and 'fact' memory.[3] Habit memory is simply the outcome of repetition. In learning to say, ride a bike, or acquire skill in snooker, countless experiences of these activities are undergone, and the upshot is that one can ride a bike and has skill in playing snooker.

Now the key point is, that whilst all these past experiences inform our capacity to carry the present activities, their presence is for the most part subconscious; indeed, the dates and minutiae of the relevant past experiences are irrelevant, and/or beyond specific recall.

In this context, the effect of past experience is to habituate us to the correct performance of a specific activity. This mode of habit memory is something common to all conscious life. What is distinctive to human beings, however, is the experience of factual memory. This is simply the ability to recall that at such and such time in our lives such and such a thing occurred. Such an ability arises from the acquisition of language, but the following factors are also central.

Between habit and fact memory is a considerable space of phenomenological ambiguity. One may, for example, know that William the Conqueror won the Battle of Hastings in 1066, but have no recollection of the circumstances under which the fact was learned. This space, however, is of no great philosophical interest. What is of such interest is, as it were, the gap between habit and fact memory. For here is an element which may have a decisive relation to the acquisition and sustaining of self-consciousness.

This element consists in corporeal imagination deployed as *a medium for fact memory*.[4] Through such means, the past can be recalled in virtual as opposed to merely abstract terms, i.e. in terms which invoke a sense of the recollected fact's original sensory vividness—its presence-to-body.

Now, of course, one cannot recapture a moment from this past in its full sensible immediacy. This is because the immediate quality is a function of intentional orientation rather than raw sensory vividness alone. At its point of occurrence, an event in the past is a surface of a particular segment of the body's total physical and psychological relation to the world at that time. It is, phenomenologically speaking, *vast*.

Even the most familiar memories involve complex elements of this kind, such that, the more they go into the past, the more difficult they are to realize in corporeal terms. They require imaginative *interpretation* of the highest order. Perhaps in much of our thinking on this topic we have been bewitched by the wrong picture. The memory-image is not akin to the photograph, it is more akin to the painting. To realize a memory in corporeal terms is to create something like a Kantian 'aesthetic idea' on a factual basis. One 're-models' experience.[5]

This corporeal or virtual aspect of imagination is also important in two other related respects. First, as well as defining itself against the past, the present moment can only be individuated by reference to alternative perceptual possibilities to the present and by reference to the future. Again, the further away these are in existential and/or temporal terms, the more in the way of imaginative interpretation or, indeed, fabrication, they require. It is through corporeal imagination, in other words, that we can make general sense of times and places which are not immediately given to us in perception, through being able to imaginatively project what they might be like.

Similar considerations hold *vis-à-vis* our sense of identity with or alienation from other people. Every human being can form an idea of what it is to be another human being, but this idea can only fully develop if it is accompanied by some corporeal realization of *what it might be like* to perceive the world as another perceives it.

Central to the factors which inform self-consciousness, then, is the exercise of corporeal imagination. This occurs when imagination is employed in a semantically specific mode—so as to individuate specific events or states of affairs (from our own past or more generally) in a way that has, at least, the overtones of immediate perceptual experience.

Such an employment is always interpretative; it exaggerates, idealizes, understates, diminishes, omits, precisely because the individual is seeking to grasp what is not perceptually present on the basis of the interests which define his or her present. It is a free but not arbitrary act of interpretation. In its reaching from present to past and future it is able to be informed by the concrete totality of our existence.

We can, of course, project past, future, and counterfactual states abstractly in thought, but in corporeal imagination we realize them interpretatively as virtual presence-to-body, i.e. in the form in which things matter most to us. Corporeal imagination, therefore, is the very flesh of the aesthetic structure of the self.

Given these points, the corporeal imagination seems an especially fecund concept *vis-à-vis* explaining the acquisition of self-consciousness. For it is profoundly implicated in our consciousness both of self and of places and times which range beyond the immediate perceptual field. Perhaps, then, we can speculate that the stabilization and articulation of corporeal imagination is a decisive element in the growth and structure of self-consciousness.

We are now in a position to consider the function of picturing in relation to this issue.

Part Two

The task that faces us is to explain how the making and reception of pictures might involve a more stable and public exercise of corporeal imagination. There are many approaches one might take in relation to this. Consider the following.

To make or perceive a picture involves connective activity, as do all acts of self-consciousness. Indeed, it has a further thing in common with them at a basic level, insofar as it posits a specific semantic content. For to count as a picture 'of' something, the artefact must refer (by virtue of resemblance *and* convention) to some specifiable *kind* of thing other than itself.[6]

This visual semantic specificity has many important ramifications. At the heart of these is the fact that for human beings cognition has a profoundly visual emphasis. The reason for this is that space-occupancy is a primary property of any form of existence. It follows, therefore, that if a creature is to evolve and survive it must negotiate the conditions of space occupancy.

Vision and visual imagery are the optimum means for doing this in that they facilitate the perception of things and states of affairs as totalities, *from a distance*. Other senses such as smell and hearing can register a stimulus before it becomes necessary to negotiate it in direct physical terms. What they cannot do, however, is to offer the simultaneous and highly determinate readings of shape, extension, spatial interrelations, and the overall cohesion of these factors, which are the basis of visually grounded cognition.

These considerations are a basis for key aspects of pictorial representation's phenomenological depth. It is, of course, possible that there are self-conscious beings elsewhere in the universe whose major cognitive orientation is towards another sense—such as touch or sound. Beings of this sort might, accordingly, have a special relation to music or sculpture respectively. Their 'form of life' in the broadest sense would be *very* different from ours.

However, this is (arguably) to their disadvantage. For it might be that a culture whose form of life is steeped primarily in music or sculpture lacked (in the case of the former) an ambience of cognitive specificity and (in the case of latter) semantic depth and diversity. The visual emphasis, in contrast, facilitates these very qualities.

In this respect it is interesting to introduce the idea of a progression—involving the transition from sculpture, to picture on a surface; to picture on a delimited surface; to picture on delimited *plane* surface, and finally to the easel-based picture—the image which is, in physical terms, totally detachable from its context of production.

This transition is (although the exact empirical order of elements might be contested) a *logical progression*. One would also expect it to mark the general stages in which picturing itself has chronologically developed. If this were disputed, one could at least say that these are decisive developments in the growth of pictorial representations. For they all involve refining and developing both the basic techniques and conventions which give the semantic structure and scope of picturing.

These centre on a complex dialectic between content, style, and the physical limit or edge of the representation. The explorations and greater control achieved in relation to the medium (through the progression just noted) enable it to articulate more semantically determinate and fecund conventions, such as foreshortening and mathematically based perspective. Greater attentiveness to nuance of medium, convention, and work are involved here. Human gesture (of which language is the most complex aspect) becomes at once more focused and yet more diverse in its scope.

There is a further crucial aspect to this. Earlier on I alluded to the cognitive primacy of the visual. This has important links with judgements of magnitude and position. The greater durability and diversity of particular items at the level of the visual means that it provides a stable and fecund network of relations whereby measurements (which, in the final analysis, are always determined comparatively) can be made.

Picturing involves specifying kinds of visual things, the relations between their parts, and their inter-relations with other visual things. Vision has the power to comprehend a complex of such factors simultaneously. It also involves a highly developed capacity for reading the presence of hidden visual aspects as a kind of inference from those which are immediately given.

The creation of pictorial representations involves sustained attentiveness to both these dimensions. As the picture projects its subject-matter—and especially if it goes beyond schematic representation—it makes them more cognitively specific in both qualitative and quantitative terms, i.e. enables us to recognize qualities of 'whatness', detail, aspectuality, and position.

Indeed, to visually represent the real is to orientate oneself in a sustained way to the most decisive features of space occupancy at a concrete rather than abstract cognitive level. And whereas the function of vision *per se* is to scan and comprehend these features, the picture allows them to be both fixed in an enduring medium, and to be interpreted and revised and built upon on the basis of the artist's own distinctive way of handling the medium. (I shall return to these features in more detail a little further on.)

Picturing, therefore, is an activity which embodies at a public, learnable level, factors which inform a key element in the 'inner life' of self-consciousness. Like the corporeal imagination, it *exemplifies* (in Goodman's sense of possession plus reference)[7] something of the sensible structure of its referent in a way that ordinary uses of language do not.

In a sense, the picture objectively clarifies and, as it were, *accomplishes* corporeal imagination. It offers a publicly accessible vision of things, in a way which declares vision to be inherent in the world. The picture is, in other words, a mode of seeing whose essence is to be seen. It thus reflects that dialectical interdependence of subject and object of experience ('reversibility' as I have termed it), which is a necessary feature of self-consciousness.

The relation between picturing and corporeal imagination is also profoundly significant in another sense. In the previous section I argued that it is the imagination which enables the full comprehension of time through enabling the projection of what it might be like to occupy spaces and times other than those of the present. However, in its pictorial form, the image also offers us a surprising *release* from the constraints of time.

At the root of this is a profoundly phenomenological characteristic which picturing—as an art of spatial realization—also shares with sculpture. It is that correlation of the virtually immobilized subject-matter and stationary observer of it (which I discussed at length in the previous chapter).

This amounts to a kind of *suspension of tense*. Iconographical analysis may reveal that a picture is intended to represent a quite specific and dateable event or moment in time. However, the picture *qua* picture does not disclose this meaning through its own internal resources (i.e. at that fundamental logical level where, simply through knowing that it is a picture, we can identify what *kind* of item or state of affairs is being represented).

It may be, indeed, that we cannot identify any temporal reference in the work at all. The picture is simply of such and such a kind of thing. And even where there are visual cues sufficient for us to recognize that we are, in fact, dealing with a picture of an event there is no way of knowing—without further *non-pictorial* information—whether the event is intended to be past, present, or future.

There is, of course, the possibility that the pictorial content of a work might contain characteristic historical reference material—such as period dress, or culturally familiar themes (such as the Crucifixion of Christ). But even here it may be that the image represents people acting out a scene from the past or an event of indeterminate historical location which happens to look like the Crucifixion.

The basic convention of pictorial representation does not, *in itself*, involve the distinction between past, present, and future as a structural feature of the code. If an event is depicted in a work, then that event is, as it were, *eternalized* by virtue of being indeterminate *vis-à-vis* whether it is meant to be occurring in the past, present, or future.

This aspect of picturing's phenomenological depth has, of course, the most profound psychological and cultural significance in relation to commemorative and other ritual uses. However, rather than develop these, I shall now consider some further connections between picturing and the corporeal imagination.

In this respect, we will recall from earlier that when the past or other perceptual alternatives to the present are projected in imagination, they are necessarily structured and interpreted on the basis of the present interests of one who imagines. They do not occur raw; they are stylized.

Now in a picture this dimension of stylization is to the fore. Particular nuances of handling a choice of subject-matter enable us to determine the kind of, or specific cultural context in which the work was produced and, in the case of pictorial *art*, the specific individual or social ensemble who made the artefact.

Recognition of the particular has a more general significance. For, as we have seen, a key function of the corporeal imagination is to facilitate our sense of species-identity through identifying with others. When a child learns what a picture is and how it is made, he or she is able to recognize that other people see the world in roughly the same terms as they do.

With maturity it then becomes possible to comprehend both sameness and difference in the way pictures represent. We are able to identify with the way the artist sees, whilst still retaining a sense of what is distinctive about our own personal outlook on the world.

This trajectory is augmented by the transition to easel-painting (noted earlier on in this section). The transition to this final stage corresponds with two facts—the development of oil-painting and printing techniques, and the changes in status of the producer from craftsman or artisan to *artist*.

These (together with other factors) create the conditions for a *plethora* of pictorial representations. The image finds formats and rationales which enable it to become detached and thence existentially discontinuous from its context of production and intended uses. Pictures are where *we* find them; we are surrounded by them; we exist *in* the pictorial.

This means, on the one hand, that (through being detached from the causal context of production) the picture is viewed primarily as an embodiment of a personal vision—rather than as an epiphenomenon of localized historical context and circumstances. Yet on the other hand, this release from the point of origin means that we can identify with what is special about the picture on very much our own terms. It is this dialectic between these two aspects—over and above empirical functions of persuasion, dissuasion, or the transmission of information—which determines the life of pictures in our own culture *qua* pictures.[8]

The two remaining links between corporeal imagination and picturing are perhaps even more fundamental. In this respect, we will first recall that our sense of the present draws upon our responses to the past, and perceptual alternatives to the present (whether counterfactual or futural). The life of self-consciousness, in other words, breathes in an atmosphere of virtual presence. The picture offers an objective mode of this in both its material and semantic being.

On the one hand it is a *made* thing. What results in the work could have been made differently. It was made for a *reason*. This means that it has a use-value—a destiny; a route into the future. On the other hand, whilst the represented content resembles and has visual kinship with aspects of the world of perception *per se*, it is also discontinuous with that world, most notably (as we saw earlier) through the suspension of tense. It offers a virtual *alternative* to the immediate world; indeed it is an objective *exemplar* of virtual presence.

All these points meet in one final consideration, the picture is an artefact, which (at the level of making, at least) has been freely brought forth. Now in most mundane artefacts, any sense of the work as an exemplar of freedom is obliterated by our orientation towards use-value. However, pictures have the power to be different in this respect precisely because they are haunted by those overtones of visual specificity, stylization, species-identity, and virtuality, which I have discussed. To articulate the self through making a picture is to draw upon the deepest roots of self-consciousness *per se*.

This is also the case for the viewer. For the complex aura of meaning which I have outlined is intuitively present in even the humblest picture. Free creation here becomes the focus of free existential belonging. The contingent and transcendent world of otherness has been fixed in contours, which simultaneously engage and allow us to explore the structures of our own being. Whether or not this exploration is undertaken is determined by both the character of the particular work, and its relation to both tradition and the personal and general experience of the viewer.

Two conclusions can be drawn from the approach which I have taken. The first is that picturing is correlated to the advance and deepening of self-consciousness. It is not a case of 'trivial pieces of magic'; rather the picture draws upon fundamental constants in experience, with a directness that is—arguably—more profound than any similar tendencies in literature and music. Pictures exemplify characteristics of the kind of thing which they resemble and also structures of self-consciousness itself. There may also be room for arguing that specific styles, or technical innovations in pictorial art—such as perspective—link up to these constants in a more direct way than other styles and innovations.

For present purposes, it is worth arriving at a more speculative conclusion. The key point in this respect is the publicly accessible and multi-layered meanings of the picture. It can be played with; it fascinates; it is a more stable mode of imaging than that of the corporeal imagination in personal experience. This suggests that the picture is not simply an objective realization of corporeal imagination, but may even be correlated with the growth of self-consciousness in the most *fundamental phylogenetic sense*.

It would be easy to say that the corporeal imagination which informs all the necessary factors in self-consciousness is fixed and stabilized through the acquisition of language. However, the conventionalization and inflection of vocal gesture which makes language itself possible, has, as I have argued, an intimate link with the visual. This suggests that pictures (through their links with corporeal imagination) are profoundly implicated in the process. How far one can take this is a function of the sense or senses which one can attribute to the phrase 'ascribe experience to oneself'.

In this chapter, then, I have described key aspects of the intrinsic significance of the image in its pictorial mode.[9] Through its conceptual connections with key factors in self-consciousness, it manifests phenomenological depth *intuitively* (in the sense described in Chapter 1). It is this richness of complex intuitive meaning which gives the image some of its intrinsic aesthetic fascination. I shall now explore this further in relation to the specific character of painting.

4   The Presence of the Painter

Introduction

As we have seen, picturing is an art of *spatial* realization. This means that in order to understand what kind of thing is being represented, we do not need to scan the work's parts in a specific chronological order of succession. With literature and music, in contrast, we have arts of *temporal* realization. Here the recognition of meaning is dependent on comprehending specific parts in an exact, linear, temporal order.[1]

From this basic contrast, many interesting effects arise, most notably the fact that what pictures represent is orientated towards a single item, scene, or moment of action, whereas literary narrative can encompass action spanning unlimited periods of time.[2]

Another fascinating difference is that literature and music are based on tokens which instantiate—through reading or performance—a work which is, ontologically speaking, a type. The fact that temporal realization is necessarily involved means that such works are imaginatively intended. How we 'read' *Mr. Pickwick*, or perform the *Hammerklavier*, involves the creative and imaginative interpretation of descriptions or a notational score.

In painting, however, whilst an image may provoke imaginative associations, it already has the character of a particular image. It is based on natural resemblance conventionalized as a means of visual reference. The pictorial image presents visual characteristics which are sufficient to individuate a specific kind of visual item(s) or state of affairs, over and above the marks, lines, or colours, which embody these characteristics.

A picture of a landscape, for example, involves features set out for us already in visual terms rather than achieved through imaginative realization alone. The picture has an isomorphic relation to the visible things which it represents.

(Abstract works are a special case here, and I will address them as a topic in their own right in Chapter 6).

Now whilst these contrasts enable the identification of pictorial (and, indeed, sculptural) representation's distinctive features, they do not, in themselves clarify what is unique to painting *per se* as an art form. We need to probe further and clarify painting's distinctive role *qua* gestural activity in modifying the relation between subject and object of experience. By investigating this, the extraordinary scope of painting's phenomenological depth will begin to emerge.

One avenue of approach is through an account of *the presence of the painter*. This means an account which stresses the significance of painting as a creative gestural act which interprets and changes visual reality. At the heart of this is the reciprocal interaction between the painter, the ontology of his or her medium, and the visible world.

A useful introduction to this *formative* sense of painting is the work of Maurice Merleau-Ponty. He is one of the few philosophers whose explanation of visual art gives due emphasis to the distinctiveness of painting. However, whilst Merleau-Ponty philosophizes the ontology of the painted image, there are many respects in which his ideas are incomplete and need sustained further development.

In this chapter, therefore, Part One interprets and develops Merleau-Ponty's theory of painting in terms of the relation between painting and the visible world. Part Two then moves far beyond what Merleau-Ponty himself offers, through an account of the further significance of painting in terms of how it realizes that reciprocity of mobility and stationary frontal viewpoint which is fundamental to vision. In Part Three it is argued that painting has a deeper significance still, through its relation to the holistic core of experience.

Part One

I will begin by outlining some important ideas from Merleau-Ponty's last published work 'Eye and Mind' of 1961.[3] In it he claims that

> Scientific thinking, a thinking which looks on from above, and thinks of the object-in-general, must return to the 'there is' which underlies it; to the site, the soil of the sensible and opened world such as it is in our life and for our body—not that possible body which we may legitimately think of as an information machine but that actual body I call mine.[4]

Merleau-Ponty's point here is that the lived-body—rather than abstract scientific or cybernetic models of it—is the basis of our most fundamental cognitive orientation towards the world. Painting, indeed, is able to draw upon and express this 'fabric of brute meaning'[5] in a way that other art forms and modes of symbolic expression and analysis cannot.

To understand why, we need to look in more detail at this level of 'brute meaning'. In relation to it, Merleau-Ponty observes that

> visible and mobile, my body is a thing amongst things; it is caught in the fabric of the world, and its cohesion is that of a thing. But because it moves itself and sees, it holds things in a circle round itself. Things are an annex or prolongation of itself; they are incrusted into its flesh, they are part of its full definition; the world is made of the same stuff as the body.[6]

Through these points Merleau-Ponty is not just emphasizing the shared material physicality of the body and the world, he is emphasizing how they define one another's character. His approach here might be explained and further developed as follows. The shape, size, position, and perceptual characteristics of physical things are not absolute, but are correlated with the size, and perceptual abilities, of the particular kinds of creature which apprehends them.

In this context, the mobility of the body is of paramount significance, and, most especially, in the way in which it grounds the perceptual process in *depth*. On these terms, the visual field is not some passively registered set of data, rather the juxtaposition and overlap of objects is mapped out by my own immediate position in relation to them, by the positions which I could take up, and by the ways in which I could act upon them, and other factors besides. As Merleau-Ponty says,

> Everything I see is in principle within my reach, at least within reach of my sight, and is marked upon the map of the 'I can'. Each of the two maps is complete. The visible world and the world of my motor projects are each total parts of the same Being.[7]

Each visible item is characterized, then, within a space of possibility determined by what the body can do, as well as being defined by its relation to, and contrast with other visual items. Nothing is, in perceptual terms, simply there. We recognize a visible item or state of affairs on the basis of its position within a complex network of bodily competences and visual relations.

There are two other features of our embodied inherence in the world which need to be emphasized. First, Merleau-Ponty notes that

> The enigma is that my body simultaneously sees and is seen. That which looks at all things can also look at itself and recognize, in what it sees the 'other side' of its power of looking. It sees itself seeing; it touches itself touching; it is visible and sensitive for itself. It is not a self through transparence, like thought, which only thinks its object by assimilating it, by constituting it, by transforming it into thought. It is a self through confusion, narcissicism, through inherence of the one who sees in that which he sees, and through inherence of sensing in the sensed—a self, therefore, that is caught up in things, that has a front and a back, a past and a future . . .[8]

By virtue of being embodied, then, the human subject knows itself through, at the same time, knowing that it is an object of sense for others (a fact which, one assumes, other animal life-forms, are not as distinctly aware of). To conceive oneself as object means that one can imagine oneself occupying positions in space and time which are different from the ones which one presently occupies. The present position is given its distinctive character through being (at least) tacitly contextualized in relation to this horizon of alternative positioning.

From these complex factors, it is clear that the embodied subject's perceptual relation to the world is, in large part, interpretative and creative. How it focuses attention on the visual field, which aspects it scrutinizes, which aspects it overlooks, will be a function of its perceptual history, of different positionings, and reflection upon that history, as well as upon general factors inherent in the human mode of embodiment.

There is a decisive network of reciprocal relationships involved here. These all converge upon the fact that just as the sensible configuration of the world is given its character by human embodiment and personal history, so too, that mode of embodiment and its particular history is called forth by the demands of a re-encounterable sensible world.

This world cannot be arrested and, as it were, fixed or used up, in any one perception or sequence of perceptions. It engages the embodied subject in a profoundly intimate pattern of exchanges. Our perception of things is selective and stylized such that the object of attention is powerfully contextualized by all the various experiential perspectives and history which inform our comprehension of it. Our response, therefore, involves a *characterization* of the object.

Hence Merleau-Ponty's observation that

> Things have an internal equivalent in me; they arouse in me a carnal formula of their presence. Why shouldn't these in their turn give rise to some visible shape in which anyone else would recognize those motifs which support his

own inspection of the world. Thus there appears a visible of the second power, a carnal essence or icon of the first.[9]

Here we have the origins of the picture and painting. The 'carnal essence' referred to is not a faded copy of the world, but, rather, a gathering up and concentrating of the visible. It is the visible stylized from the viewer's particular standpoint. If this carnal essence exceeds introspective orientation, and is created as a painting, then the visible comes to exist in a fuller sense.

This can be shown in a number of ways. First, as we have seen, the selective and stylized dimension of perception means that what we perceive always has a strong subjective loading. The painting exemplifies this. It enables a key structural factor in vision to become visible itself, through the artist's style.

Second, the pictorial image is able to address that texture and tapestry of visual relations which are constitutive of how a particular item appears to us, but which are not usually noticed—insofar as we are usually preoccupied with what kind of thing the item is, or with questions of its practical utility. It focuses some of those latent enabling conditions of visual perception which are central to phenomenological depth. As Merleau-Ponty says in relation to the painter's task,

> Light, lighting, shadows, reflections, colour, all the objects of his quest are not altogether real objects; like ghosts, they have only virtual existence. In fact, they exist only at the threshold of profane vision; they are not seen by everyone.
>
> The painter's gaze asks them what they do to suddenly cause something to be and to be this thing, what they do to compose this worldly talisman and to make us see the visible.[10]

On these terms, the painter interprets, identifies, preserves, and displays the network of visual relations which are constitutive of the immediate appearance of items or states of affairs, but which are generally overlooked in favour of the mere act of their recognition or of their practical utility.

It should also be emphasized (although Merleau-Ponty himself does not) that the means of this visual disclosure, namely the gesture involved in inscribing or placing marks on a surface, is itself a mode of bodily orientation. Just as our visual perception is made possible by bodily orientation, painting thematizes this necessary role of the body, through our knowledge that the painting is something which has been brought forth through the bodily activity and positioning of its creator.

Given this analysis, we must now ask about the status of drawing—which is related to, but not identical with painting.

In relation to drawing, it might seem that, through being orientated towards line, shape, mass, and position, it has a privileged relation to primary properties, i.e. those factors which are centrally involved in space-occupancy, and, hence, which are central to vision. Earlier, we noted Merleau-Ponty's point that scientific models look on 'from above' and only mark out those vectors or dimensions of depth which are amenable to manipulation or description. Primary properties articulate *this* level.

However, the full complexity of spatial depth is actually much more than what is amenable to such manipulation, or, indeed, scientific or verbal description. And, of course, whilst drawing uses line, shape, mass, and position, so does painting. Indeed, its extension of these factors into the dimension of colour means that painting is the more comprehensive medium, ontologically speaking. In a sense, painting incorporates drawing.

The phenomenological depth of painting, then, consists of the following. On the one hand, it reveals how its represented subject-matter comes to be seen and stylized in visual terms through the artist's bodily positioning; and, on the other hand, this revelation is made possible by the painting's auto-disclosure as this specific work, composed from this unique configuration of gestures. Through painting, the virtual and the physical, the world and the body, are shown to inhabit one another simultaneously and inseparably.

It is, of course, possible to describe this phenomenological depth in philosophical terms, but uniquely, painting's formation of visual space exemplifies it at the level of sense perception itself. Other visual media—such as photography—also move in this direction but either lack the gestural dimension which exemplifies the visible as something which is, in part, configured through the embodied subject's positioning. (In the case of photography, the image places rather more emphasis upon the visual singularity of the represented content than on the artist's positioning. I shall discuss this in detail in Chapter 8.)

The differences which I am schematically indicating here are not, of course, of hierarchical import. Painting has a different ontological structure from other visual media, just as they do from it. This means that each medium has a distinctive visuality which discloses the world in equally distinctive ways. (These will be explored throughout this book.)

Part Two

There are some further distinctive features of the ontology of painting which Merleau-Ponty does not develop. These can be approached through a putative critical point.

In his account, Merleau-Ponty emphasizes the mobility of vision, and painting's role in modelling the visible in a way which eludes analytic thought. However, one might claim that the former point is in conflict with the latter. For if vision is mobile, how is it possible for painting to model it—given that by definition it is a static two-dimensional medium? Surely, the best it can do through such static means is to present artificially arrested or 'frozen' configurations of the visible. And if this is the case, then it is not far off the analytic attitude's 'looking on from above'.

Now the very fact that 'it is the act of stylization begun in the least perception which amplifies into painting and art'[11] (as Merleau-Ponty puts it in an earlier work) means that painting's modelling of the visible is also a changing of it. This changing (for reasons which will become clear subsequently) is of interest over and above any analytic informational significance that the image might have.

There are some further considerations which must also be emphasized. They take us far beyond Merleau-Ponty's account (though they are entirely consistent with it). Specifically, these involve thinking through some of Chapter 2's points about pictorial space, in relation to the specific case of painting.

The first relevant point is the fact that whilst vision involves the embodied subject constantly changing position, this does not occur in absolute terms. Indeed, such mobility is correlated with the achievement of *stationary orientation*—in the form of those privileged moments when we are relatively motionless and thence able to comprehend what is given in vision in rather more detail than is possible when we are on the move.[12] The optimum form of this, of course, is when we are facing the object directly, rather than having to peer at it from an awkward viewing position.

Now in the case of free-standing sculpture (and even some reliefs), compositional factors often favour a frontal viewing position. However, the three-dimensional character of such work demands that one must change one's position in order to comprehend its unity in the fullest sense. In the case of painting, matters are rather different. Here a single and stationary frontal viewing position is sufficient for engaging with the work's unity. One's eyes may move in a scanning process, but one's body does not have to change position.

Of course, one might make such a change in order to study some specific pictorial effect, but whilst oblique orientations of this kind can enhance understanding of the work's unity, they do not have to. And they are not presupposed in order to get a basic sense of the work's compositional unity.

This stationary frontal orientation gives painting a very special significance. To start with, it means that painting's static character is not that of an arrested motion (with mainly analytic interest). Rather its stationary frontal viewpoint models an orientation which is basic to vision in the sense described above. However, as I described in Chapter 2, this stationary viewpoint is hard to achieve in ordinary perception. Painting *qua* pictorial realizes it with a completeness which such perception can only aspire towards.

Crucially, painting achieves this in its own distinctive way, by virtue of its active gestural character. At the heart of this is the fact that (as noted at the beginning of this chapter) the unity of a spatial object is, in perceptual terms, a relatively open one. We do not have to scan its parts in a temporally linear order in order to comprehend such unity.

This openness is realized by painting in a kind of notional *recurrence*. The painting, *qua* achievement of sustained gestural activity, is a virtual replay of the achievement of frontal stationary orientation towards the subject-matter. Even if the work represents items in motion our sense of them is a *coming-to-be* in that position. This is because to explore the painter's style (*vis-à-vis* how the image has been created) is to scan freely the open perceptual avenues of its composition and emergence as a visible thing, again and again. We engage with the *achieved* aspect of frontal stationary orientation—the artist's *way of making* the subject-matter of the painting visible.

It is important to emphasize this dynamic aspect, since it is sometimes misunderstood in the literature. Norman Bryson, for example, has claimed that

> In the Founding Perception, the gaze of the painter arrests the flux of phenomena, contemplates the visual field from a vantage-point outside the mobility of duration, in an external moment of disclosed presence; while in the moment of viewing, the viewing subject unites that first epiphany. Elimination of the diachronic movement of deixis creates, or at least seeks, a synchronic instant of viewing that will eclipse the body, and the glance, in an infinitely extended Gaze of the image as pure idea . . .[13]

Bryson is picking up here on the stationary viewpoint aspect of painting. He assumes that those western tendencies which conceal painting's gestural aspect through strong 'finish' strive, in effect, to render a pristine 'Founding Perception' or timeless 'essential copy' of the real. The assumption is false. It fails to negotiate the achieved, *stylized*, aspect of the stationary viewing position.

In this respect, most of the relevant work in the western tradition strives to change reality—through such strategies as idealization or the search for sublime or picturesque effects. Even in art with a naturalistic or realistic orientation, it is difficult to find work which strives to *copy* the real. And those *trompe l'oeil* works which might be linked to this ambition are relatively rare, and more or less declare themselves as exceptions to the painterly rule.

Indeed, the rise of art itself as a specialist activity in the western world is actually built on the prizing of *differences* between artists in how they interpret the real. We look for images whose style does not simply capture some pure visual 'given', or the style of other artists.

This orientation towards difference means that we are interested primarily in how the artist has created and composed the image. And this necessitates attention to its *gesturally achieved* character in the sense described above—no matter how finished, or otherwise, its appearance happens to be.

There is a further and rather more complex significance to painting's circumscribed virtual structure. Again, it is useful to introduce it by way of a contrast with free-standing sculpture.[14] Any example of this dominant sculptural idiom occupies its own self-contained virtual three-dimensional space. And even if elevated on a plinth (or whatever) its virtuality is mainly subsumed within the broader continuum of the actual three-dimensional reality which surrounds it.

The sculpture may present a virtual world which continues, notionally, beyond the work's physical limits, but these limits do not secure this world from being lost in the real three-dimensional physical environment in which the work is located.

Now, of course, a picture can be hung on a wall and—if unexceptional—be treated as no more than that. In this way, it is absorbed in the real three-dimensional physical environment. However, if the painting is of artistic interest, the circumscribed virtuality of its pictorial space tends to resist such assimilation in perceptual terms. If we attend to such a work, it opens up an internal three-dimensional virtual space which is constrained by the picture's physical edges (usually emphasized by a frame).

Such overt circumscription has a remarkable and paradoxical effect. For it does not signify an end to the virtual space within the painting itself, rather it has the opposite effect in symbolic terms. Once we know what pictorial space is, we understand that the scene represented within the work is just one aspect of an, in principle, indefinitely continuing virtual space that extends notionally beyond the boundaries marked by the edges of the picture.

This cannot be exhibited as a feature of pictorial space directly, but it is signified *de facto* through the way in which the painting's physical edges function as *artificial* terminations of the notionally indefinite continuation of its internal virtual space. These termini serve a compositional purpose but they are not literally a factor within the virtual continuum being projected. Hence their artificial arrest of it is taken as a kind of abbreviation. In relation to the painting's virtual space, its physical edges declare, in effect, 'and so on, and so on, indefinitely'.

The importance of this is that it signifies—indirectly, but unmistakeably—the fact that presently viewed visible items and states of affairs are configurations which emerge from an indefinitely extendable background of other such items and relations. Painting's circumscribed virtual structure, in other words, internalizes and models the all-important inexhaustible *field structure* of vision itself.

Part Three

These features takes on even deeper significance when understood in relation to a decisive structure in human experience *per se*. It involves factors of the utmost complexity.

First, the things that a person does and experiences do not simply accumulate in a quantitative whole. Each experience is given its particular character by its relation to those which preceded it, and by anticipations of possible outcomes and new experiential situations. It is an aspect of a *qualitative* whole.

Now the things which happen to us, are, of course, in many respects contingent—in the sense of arising from situations where more than one action or response on our part was available, and in the sense that, in much of what happens to us, we are dependent on circumstances over which we have no control.

However, there is also a fascinating obverse to this. For once an experience has occurred, then its relation to all the experiences which preceded it is now a *necessary* one. If anything in our preceding lives had been different then an exponential wave of change would have been set up, thus leading to an experience other than the one which actually came to pass. This complex of contingencies and retrospective necessity might be called the *holistic core* of experience.

In everyday life, our grasp of this core is at best fragmented. We may understand the salient contours of the things which determined particular experiences but, as finite beings, our understanding of their linkage cannot be a total one. The holistic core of experience can be understood as an idea, but it cannot be experienced as an actuality.

Or at least, not under *introspective* circumstances. The creation of an artwork, however, offers an at least partial fulfilment of this. For insofar as it is a sensible or imaginatively intended particular (or token of a type) it is a finished and self-subsistent item whose conditions of creation are, in a significant sense, preserved.

Painting is perhaps the best example of this. Given a complete painting, one knows that all the individual moments of its creation—the accumulation and re-working of brushstrokes and the like—are all necessarily present as conditions of the identity of this particular completed work. Individually speaking, the moments and gestures of making were contingent—the painter could have done this or done that. And if he or she had done a different this or that, then the resulting work would have been different from the one which was, in fact, created.

But we have just *this* painting. The individually contingent aspects of its making are necessary from the perspective of the completed work's identity as just *this* specific work. The holistic core of experience is exemplified through painting's character as gestural making. It is modelled at the level of visual perception itself.

This gives it an at least partial completeness which is not available introspectively. For in introspection, the flow of one experience into another makes it impossible to identify the whole network of factors which are necessary to the identity of an individual experience.

Now there is, of course, a sense in which the making of any specific artefact exemplifies the holistic core of experience. It was begun at a certain point and such and such a series of actions resulted in just this outcome, and are thence necessarily implicated in the end-product.

If an artefact's purpose, however, is just to serve a particular function then its identity as this individual artefact is of no concern. In the case of painting, however, the work's stylistic individuality makes us attentive to the particular character of how this is manifest in the work. We are interested in *how* it coheres as an individual.

And through this, the holistic dimension is intuitively present in an active way. The painting did not just happen. It came about through the artist taking a canvas (or whatever) and doing many things to it over a period of time, until the work was complete. We cannot see each individually contingent gesture which contributed to this, let alone comprehend their exact chronological sequence, but, given the finished work, we know that all those gestures are there necessarily *vis-à-vis* the work's identity as just this work.

In this way, the presence of the painter has profound symbolic overtones. It models both a truth and aspiration concerning human experience. The truth is its exemplification of experience's holistic core; the aspiration is the fact that this is realized in an enduring form.

Concerning the latter, as finite beings we desire that the things we are and do become meaningful beyond the confines of mundane existence. Through artistic painting, this acquires a modest realization. Such work embodies the traces of another person's gestures which have been configured and brought to completion in an enduring medium with shared techniques of practice.

This means that what is achieved here is personal fulfilment in a form which can be recognized and appreciated by others. Indeed, the artist's trace-gestures inhere in the painting for as long as the work endures—and this of course can be far beyond the creator's lifetime.

There are further aspects still to this aesthetic overcoming of contingency. The holistic core of experience is a structure in which we are immersed whether we like it or not. *Qua* finite beings, this is necessarily how we inhere in the world as self-conscious rational beings.

In painting, however, this structure itself becomes a vehicle for *volitional* creation. It can be explored and developed freely on the painter's own terms. Hence, whilst the completed work involves necessity at the level of its identity (in the terms noted earlier) it is, at the same time, a *free* celebratory transformation of the holistic core from the realm of the involuntary and private, to the voluntary and public.

Again, this is true of the creation of art *per se*. But painting's profoundly autographic nature—its consummation of a body of gestures in a physically singular material body—achieves it an especially direct way.

Sculpture also has this character, indeed, its free-standing three-dimensional being invests it with an insistency of physical presence that is not available to painting. But in another respect, painting's achievement of three-dimensional projection has its own special distinctiveness.

It presents, in virtual terms, a single scene extracted from a continuum of the visible—a continuum which sculpture's free-standing nature tends to be absorbed within, rather than point towards symbolically. In contrast to this, painting's circumscribed virtual structure means that the field character of experience's holistic core is modelled *internally*.[15]

In this respect, we will recall the significance of the edges of the picture. Their artificial termination of the picture's virtual space signifies that the field of visual relations which sustain the represented scene can be continued indefinitely in notional terms.

Similarly with the moment of experience understood introspectively. We know that, it too, is emergent from a complex background experiential whole whose *exact* character (in terms of how it enables this particular moment of experience) can only be understood indefinitely.

In painting, then, we have a medium whose gestural character vividly presents the redemption of individually contingent moments of the creative process (through their necessity *vis-à-vis* the identity of the completed work). But uniquely, painting achieves this through an internal virtual structure which exemplifies the holistic core of experience in visual terms. It's phenomenological depth is of the greatest profundity.

Conclusion

In Part One, following Merleau-Ponty, it was shown how painting discloses key structures of visibility at the level of vision itself. Part Two went beyond this by identifying further factors of this kind which constellate around the reciprocal relation of mobility and the (cognitively vital) achieved *stationary frontal viewpoint* of vision.

Part Three linked these considerations to a factor which is basic to the human condition, namely the holistic core of experience. All art engages with this. In it the individually contingent moments of creation are gathered up in the finished work to take on the character of necessity *vis-à-vis* their role in the whole of the finished work. What is experientially private and elusive is transformed into a public and manifest self-contained model of the holistic core. Of especial importance is the fact that the involuntary nature of the holistic core is here developed on the basis of free-agency.

By embodying these factors in a physical artefact with distinctive virtual properties, the painter's gestures are realized in a publicly accessible, shareable form. The painter's clarifications of the visible become objectively meaningful for an audience which, in principle, transcends that of the painter's immediate circumstances and lifetime. The gestural traces of the painter's presence take on an enduring aesthetic importance.

Whilst all these factors are *logically* separable aspects of painting, in direct perceptual terms, they are experienced intuitively as a unity. Hence whilst all art engages with the holistic core, the distinctive configuration of painting's various ontological aspects mean that this is expressed in a unique way.

In particular, painting's visible gestural character and its internal modelling of the field-character of vision give it special symbolic potency. (Vision, of course, has a privileged informational significance generally in terms of our cognition of the world, and through this, informs all aspects of our physical and psychological dwelling there.)

Finally, it should be noted that, in this account, I have been at pains to emphasize painting's *formative* significance as a way of acting on and changing the visible world. It might, therefore, be asked why this should be of interest to anyone other than the painter.

The answer has already been given. The decisive features of painting engage—at many different levels—what is fundamental to us as visible embodied subjects. We are not instructed in these terms, rather the painter shows certain possibilities which he or she finds to be significant.

In this, the fact that the painting presents traces of the painter's presence rather than actual immediate presence is of the most decisive significance. For it means that we can identify with this way of visualizing things and enhance our own self-understanding. We can, alternatively, find what it offers to be of no real interest to us. In either case, the vital point is that we can make such appraisals without the kind of psychological pressures which arise when an immediately present person tells us about things which interest them.

I will return to this topic as my book progresses, since it is the basis of a distinctively aesthetic form of empathy which art allows us.[16]

5   Sculpture and Transcendence

Introduction

In this chapter I will explore the phenomenological depth of sculpture by discussing it in relation to the notion of transcendence.[1] Part One analyzes the nature of sculpture in general; and then the specific aesthetic conditions under which it is able to attain artistic status. In Part Two, a brief exposition of the various meanings of transcendence is provided, and these are considered in terms of their aesthetic role (using criteria of the aesthetic broached in previous chapters).

Part Three deploys material from both previous sections by using them to clarify aesthetic transcendence in relation to specific works of sculpture. The Conclusion makes some general points concerning what is distinctive to sculpture's embodiment of phenomenological depth.

Part One

The term 'sculpture' picks out a logically distinct form of art insofar as its basic format is that of a physically three-dimensional configuration, which is intelligible without necessary reference to any practical use-context.[2]

Sculpture's fundamental modes of making are carving, modelling, moulding and casting, construction, or assemblage, or, indeed, any permutation of these possibilities.[3] The material used can be natural, artificial, or again a combination of these.

As a three-dimensional medium the basic perceptual effect of sculpture is to solidify organic form, or motion, or to fill out empty space with material. This can occur in virtual or real terms. Figurative sculpture is an instance of the former, and minimal art (such as Don Judd's) is an instance of the latter.

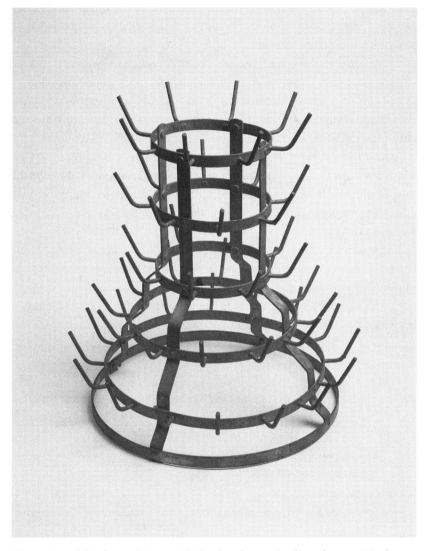

Fig. 3. Marcel Duchamp (1887–1968): *Bottlerack*, 1961 (replica of 1914 original).
Philadelphia, Philadelphia Museum of Art. Galvanized iron. Height: 19 5/8'
(49.8cm); diam. 16 1/8' (41 cm). Gift of Jacqueline, Paul and Peter Matisse in
memory of their mother Alexina Duchamp, 1998. ©2004. Photo: The Philadelphia
Museum of Art / Art Resource / Scala, Florence; ©Succession Marcel Duchamp /
ADAGP, Paris and DACS, London 2008.

There are, of course, hybrid forms where physical material is so articulated as to suggest organic form or process in virtual terms (for example, Henry Moore) or which is rather more allusive and thence elusive—as in the case of Anthony Caro and Ian Hamilton Finlay.

At the other extreme are those found objects associated with Marcel Duchamp—such as the *Bottlerack*. Here, the unexpected recontextualization of a mundane object serves to bring out its associational meanings, and to draw attention to significant qualities of appearance and space-occupancy, which are customarily submerged in our practical dealings with such objects.[4]

Now it is clear that not all sculpture is intended as art, and much of that which is so intended does not actually succeed in engaging our aesthetic attention. In order to comprehend the relation between sculpture and transcendence, therefore, we must first understand the conditions under which sculpture becomes art.

The reason why this understanding is necessary is that the aesthetic appreciation of sculpture is often understood in terms of the 'disinterested' enjoyment of formal qualities, i.e. the way in which the work coheres in terms of shape, mass, volume, and texture. This in itself involves an element of transcendence insofar as, through losing oneself in the configuration, one's capacities for imagination and understanding are brought into a mutually enhancing relationship.

However, an appreciation of purely formal qualities for their own sake does not do justice to the fact that the work which bears them is a product of human artifice; it is not just a formal configuration but one which also embodies a specific way of interpreting the visual and broader world. To attend to the work on these terms presupposes that it stands out in a comparative horizon of other works that we have experienced.[5]

This appreciation of a sculpture has an *aesthetic* character insofar as it is directed towards a sensible configuration and has a relatively 'disinterested' logical ground, i.e. we can enjoy its distinctive style without knowing anything about the immediate historical context of its production or, indeed, the personal circumstances of the artist. What is necessary, rather, is an orientation towards a work's diachronic historical position *vis-à-vis* the development of its medium.

Part Two

Having outlined the key features of sculpture and its claim to artistic status, I shall now link it to the theme of 'transcendence'.

First, 'transcendence' as a term *per se* is used in a very broad fashion in both religious and secular contexts.[6] However, there are a few features which seem to inform all or most of its contexts of use. One of them is the notion of *change of state*. This has a negative use insofar as, through such change, something is transcended in the sense of being left behind (permanently or temporarily).

However, in my use of 'transcendence' there is also a positive element, in that such a state involves movement towards an object (using 'object' in its logical sense) rather than the mere negation *per se* of something that already exists. There is also, in most uses, the strong connotation that such transcendence towards the object is itself a positive thing, or, at the very least, lacks a negative outcome.·

The question arises then as to what the logical objects of transcendence-towards are, and why they are positive. A reasonably comprehensive taxonomy is as follows:

- towards another person or, unusually, another sentient life form
- towards a group or community of sentient beings
- towards physical presence (i.e. that of material bodies or states of affair)
- towards a place
- towards an event or time (past, future, or present)
- towards some conception of trans-physical force or personality

In transcendence towards such objects the human subject enjoys a simultaneous loss and possession of self through psychological identification or joining with the object. This is of positive significance through its evoking of a sense of not being alone, or of sharing something, or of being bonded with something greater. Transcendence, in other words, is not just change; it is change whose dialectic of loss and possession engenders psychological intensity. And it is something which can arise in many experiential contexts.

Now it is a characteristic of transcendent experiences in such contexts that we take their objects to have, or have had, real existence. This is the basis of sincerity or authenticity in our transcendence towards them. However, the reality of the object exerts its own constraints upon us. If it is another person, or a community, or an imagined divinity, then, to some degree we must adapt ourselves to their specific needs. It is not just that we identify or join with the other, but do so on *their* terms.

And this brings with it a significant temptation, namely—and without recognizing that one is doing so—to remake the object of transcendence in the image of what one wants it to be. Indeed, when the object in question is another person or imagined divinity, it is impossible not to remake the other.

The reason why is that by definition no finite creature can break free from embodiment and occupy the exact spatio-temporal position and viewpoint of another being. To identify with the other always involves some element of purely imaginative construction. And the problem is that to be conscious that one is in fact doing this is a very difficult thing in both psychological and moral terms.

The aesthetic experience of transcendence through art is different from this in a highly significant respect. This pertains to the 'disinterestedness' feature noted in Part One. In order to enjoy the distinctiveness of an artist's style we must be able to locate it in a comparative horizon. However, it is not logically presupposed that we have any knowledge of the *immediate historical context* in which the work was produced, nor any knowledge of the personal circumstances of its creator. (Often, of course we will have such knowledge, and it may enhance or even inhibit our enjoyment, but the point is that we do not, logically speaking, *have* to have such knowledge in order to appreciate it in the most basic sense[7]).

Given this, it follows that when we experience transcendence in aesthetic terms reality is suspended in the mode of *possibility*. We know that there was an artist, and, if his or her work has figurative content, that the items or states of affairs which form this content may or may not have actually existed at some time or other. The work as a phenomenal configuration offers a distinctive vision of things but, because it is embodied in an artefact, the psychological pressure and temptation to tacitly idealize are removed. It presents a possibility of experience but one which we can identify with or immerse ourselves in on our own terms.

Here the possibilities of transcendence are realizable on a basis which is qualitatively freer than those which accrue to 'real life' secular and religious contexts. With this important distinction in mind I now turn to the specific phenomenon of transcendence in sculpture.

Part Three

In the most general terms, the possibilities of transcendence in sculpture broadly parallel those towards the logical objects which I described earlier. I shall now consider these in turn on the basis of specific examples of sculpture.

Transcendence towards another person

There is a sense in which all art *qua* art embodies this so far as we identify with the artist's style of articulating form and content. To use a sculptural example, if we consider Michelangelo's *Pietà*,[8] it is quite clear that the artist is evoking the Madonna's relation to the dead Christ in a way that transcends the specificity of the relation. This transcendence is not only towards the universal personal significance of the work's subject-matter. Rather, the artist's affirmation of his own distinctive style, succeeds—paradoxically, through its very distinctiveness—in suspending individuality so as to enable a deep identification with maternal suffering *per se*.

Transcendence towards a group

No matter how psychologically or physically isolated an artist may be, his or her work will always have an *iconological* dimension, i.e. will be informed by styles and thinking which are basic to his or her culture. What makes this into a conceptual truth is that to become an artist *just is* to be initiated into traditions of making and distributing, and specific patterns of use and reception. If the artist transcends these conditions through personal stylistic innovations or refinements, they remain, nevertheless, as the context of reference which is presupposed in order that such innovations or refinements can recognized for what they are.

However, the iconological dimension can have much more than this contextual significance. In certain works it takes on a more thematic role, insofar as they are emblematic of a group identity—be it societal, ethnic, or epochal. Consider in this respect, the sculptural example of a Greek *kouroi* of the Archaic period (i.e. around the 7th century B.C.).[9] Works such as this come with no record of who created them. And this anonymity of authorship seems, as it were, to conspire with frequently noted enigmatic character of the sculpted subject-matter's expression.

The *kouroi* stands as an emblem of both the intoxicating mystery of ancient

Greek culture itself; and of the purity and economy of its sculptural stylistic means. Indeed, this very simplicity itself is all the more startling by virtue of its profound *allusive* power.

As well as directing us to the extraordinary capabilities of Greek visual culture, it also connotes a sense of what might be called *archaic effectiveness*. This means the ability of the distant past to endure through its artefacts and be rediscovered and thence to be a constant formative influence. Again, all great art has this power in principle but the *kouroi*—in its *manifestly* archaic character—makes the power into an emblematic feature of the sculptural image itself.

Transcendence towards physical presence

At first sight it may seem strange to even posit such a mode. However, in this respect let us consider Ian Hamilton Finlay's *Net Markers of the Disciples*.[10] The iconography of this series is based on the fact that four of Christ's disciples were fishermen. Each individual is represented in the series by a net marker. Traditionally such markers were made of wood and cork, and would be carved with the fisherman's initials or monogram. Finlay's markers each carry a specific disciple's initial, but are made from a cast silver-metal.

The iconography just described prepares us for a meaning that ranges beyond the item's physical presence. The simple lump of inscribed metal radiates its own being—its profound and enduring quiddity. For a sculptor, material presence is not a mere fact. He or she will transform the working medium, but no matter how complete the transformation, there is always scope for this to radiate the physicality of that medium.

This is one of the deepest features of sculpture. As organic life-forms, humans come into being and pass away, but this passage is always marked out by the more enduring presence of the inorganic order. This presence is both repulsive and attractive at the same time. We recoil from its cold inanimate nature, but we are also drawn to its symbolic promise—of endurance over aeons. And this endurance also has its more familiar dimension, insofar as the realm of inanimate physical presence is the site of our world-making—through its provision of shelter and physical location.

Now when I referred earlier to the profound and enduring quiddity of Finlay's net marker, I was encapsulating all the factors just described. Indeed, the fact that Finlay's piece is made of metal carries with it its own distinctive range of connotations within the described factors.

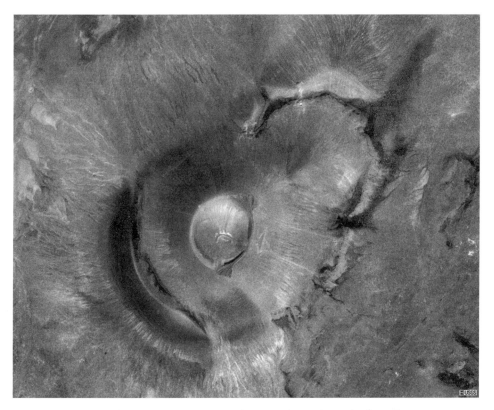

Fig. 4. James Turrell, *Roden Crater*, satellite view, image from the United States Geological Survey.

Transcendence towards place

Rarely are there sculptures—such as those carved from the rock-face at Mt. Rushmore in the United States—which are *inseparably* bound to a specific place. In such cases, the sculpture may well become emblematic of its location as well as its subject-matter. A much more complex example of this is James Turrell's work on the Roden Crater in Arizona, U.S.A.[11] The crater has been physically modified so as to turn it into a sculpture whose function is actually to illuminate Turrell's notion of 'celestial vaulting', i.e. the visual impression that the sky forms a dome over the earth. By modifying the rim of the volcanic crater, Turrell has created a viewing site which will convey just such an effect.

More unusual are those cases where a sculpture made for display at a specific site or simply placed in one, transcends itself to become emblematic of this very site. An interesting example of the former category is Anthony Gormley's *Angel of the North*, which dominates—and thence *announces*—a specific area of landscape near Gateshead in northern England.

Transcendence towards an event

This is a very familiar category, associated especially with the commemoration of heroic events or tragedies (or both) such as great wartime deeds or battles.

Transcendence towards physical powers or forces

A work such as Boccioni's *Unique Forms of Continuity in Space*[12] evokes not only its ostensible subject-matter—in this case a striding human form—but also the dynamism of form in motion *per se*. It is possible to take many perspectives upon what is fundamental to Being, but of these there are two fundamentals, namely time and space occupancy. In relation to the former, it is unintelligible to conceive of any material item except as inhabiting or enduring through time. And whilst—in relation to such things as states of consciousness—it is not entirely accurate to describe them as 'in' space, in the way that a material object is, yet it is unintelligible to conceive them except as functions or effects of space-occupying phenomena.

The interrelation of time and space-occupancy is acknowledged in the notion of *process*. This is precisely what is evoked by Boccioni's sculpture. We encounter the human figure transcended in the direction of that of which, in the cosmic scheme of things, it is an instance, namely process, in the sense just described.

Many other sculptors orientate themselves towards some abstract notion of the 'life-principle' (i.e. the most significant process) *per se*. Whether a work embodies such a factor is not a case of finding evidence as to the artist's intention in this respect. Rather it involves *looking* at his or her work.

And what one looks for is a sense of vitality enjoyed and celebrated for its own sake, through visual transformations of subject-matter, and/or material. In the case of non-figurative works, of course, this involves identifying visual cues, which are suggestive of motion and change. Such cues may even be possible through, as it were, the eloquence of forms alone—for example, through an emphasis on curvilinear features.

Fig. 5. Umberto Boccioni, *Unique Forms of Continuity in Space,* 1913, cast 1972, bronze, 1175 x 876 x 368 mm. ©Tate, London 2008.

Transcendence towards non-physical realities

Again, all art has this evocative power. But let us focus on Bernini's sculpture *The Ecstasy of St. Theresa*.[13] In a contemporary cultural context, it is all too easy to dwell on this image as a metaphor for the female orgasm. This, however, forgets the context of Counter-Reformation spiritual values. That context would of course, emphasize the significance of Church-sanctified religious experience of the miraculous.

There is an especially interesting aspect to this dimension which I will return to in the Conclusion to this chapter. However, the more immediately relevant point concerns the irrelevance of the Christian iconography of the image. For the heightened way in which Bernini animates the drapery of St. Theresa's clothing, and configures her facial expression—mouth open and eyes closed—suggest an explosive loss of corporeality even in its corporal emphasis.

The specific features just identified are ones which affirm the physical reality of St. Theresa's encounter with the Angel. Yet in conjunction with the knowing control of the Angel's smile, these individually corporeal insistencies form a whole which is far more than the sum of its parts. It suggests a reality beyond the corporeal, without, of course, characterizing this reality. Rather there is a sense of breaking free to commune with what is *ultimate*.

On these terms, then, Bernini's image exceeds its iconography and physicality to intimate the transcendent *per se*. And again, such effects are obtainable from other sculptures (as well as other art forms). Consider, for example, Barnett Newman's *Broken Obelisk*.[14] This consists of two parts of a broken steel obelisk balanced on one another—like two pencils joined at their sharpened points. Such a physical juxtaposition is so dramatic and precarious to almost seem unreal.

Yet the means whereby this psychological unreality is evoked—namely the broken metal structure—has an insistently monumental presence. It is almost as though—at the point where the two points of the obelisk are joined—there is a symbolic discharge of energy which exceeds the force of gravity itself. It intimates, thereby, a transcendent realm.

The account of sculpture's modes of transcendence is now complete. I turn finally to some of its most significant ramifications.

Conclusion

As I have noted in the course of the previous section, art forms other than sculpture can have transcendent effects. The final issue which must be addressed, therefore, is whether there is something about sculptural transcendence which is distinctive to sculpture.

An important clue in this respect is provided by transcendence towards physicality of presence. Some sculptures are able to convey a profound sense of this. Indeed, it is an effect which arises from a distinctive characteristic of the visual arts.

In the case of literature and music, the individual work is fundamentally a type of which its particular editions or performances are the token. This means that there is no necessary connection between the meaning of such works *per se* and the particular physical characteristics of the token which embody it. With visual arts, the opposite is the case. Meaning is inseparable from the work in *all* its perceptually accessible physical aspects—even where (as in bronzes) we may be dealing with tokens of a type.

And in this, sculpture offers a more complete physical experience of space. Some works, of course, are free-standing, which in itself allows the work to be experienced in physically very full terms. However, over and above this, any sculptural piece (free-standing or relief) goes beyond painting by offering a physical articulation of depth as well as a virtual illusionistic one.

This feature can also be found in some architectural works, but only insofar as they embody illusionistic depth through the incorporation of sculptural elements. In fact, there is a profound contrast between sculpture's and architecture's relation to depth in general terms. Architecture defines itself as a medium through the physical enclosure of space so as to provide shelter or a site for activity.

Sculpture has the opposite dynamic. It opens up depth by generating it through semantic and physical articulation of a three-dimensional medium. Meaning is created by the emergence of spatial form rather than the enclosure of space.

The physicality of sculpture, then, is fundamental in a distinctive way. It imparts a special character to sculptural modes of transcendence. There is also a further aspect to this distinctiveness—perhaps the most decisive of all.

Sculpture gives form or shape (or some other dimension of meaning) to inanimate material. Painting and architecture also have this character, but in the former the physical character of the image is usually consumed in its virtual structure, whilst in the latter, the functional dimension is powerfully to the fore. It is sculpture which offers the more unambiguous perceptual negotiation with physicality.

This is not just a case of consciousness triumphing over intractable matter. It embodies, rather, the assimilation by life of that which is absolutely *other* than itself, and through this assimilation, a vital 'self'-affirmation. Here, however, we have more than a mere union of opposites. For, in the final analysis, the origins and ground of life itself are in the realm of matter.

In sculpture this secular miracle of life's origins is symbolically re-played and replenished through the material which sustains this style and content. Sculpture dramatically exemplifies the emergence of meaning in the starkest sense. This is the profoundest level of its phenomenological depth.

These factors establish the distinctiveness of sculptural transcendence. One might even say that if transcendence is to be understood in secular terms, it is the creation and aesthetic enjoyment of sculpture which most fully allows the experience.

6   The Logic and Phenomenology of Abstract Art

Introduction

Many twentieth-century artists have written theoretical texts to explain their radical departures from traditional modes of pictorial representation. These departures involve abstract and semi-abstract painting and sculpture, as well as more recent minimal and conceptual art tendencies.[1]

The main focus of discussion in relation to abstract works has concerned the historical and socio-political circumstances in which they were produced, and, in particular, their relation to the artists' own writings and manifestoes and to other bodies of writing. But here there is a problem. Abstract works have established themselves (despite some residual cultural hostility); people enjoy looking at them—and do so mainly *with little or no knowledge of the specialist contextual factors that preoccupy art historians and theorists.*

Here there is a philosophical rather than merely empirical problem—namely, how it is even possible to enjoy abstract art in non-contextual terms. In the personal experience of the present author, many art historians, critics, and curators, take a very condescending approach to those who appreciate abstraction in non-contextual terms. Such appreciation is taken to be some kind of modernist hangover based on (discredited) formalist notions of 'significant form'.

However, whilst the kind of specialist analyzes just mentioned are of decisive importance in explaining how abstract works come to be created, and invested with their specific appearance, this neither explains nor rules out a further dimension of meaning that may explain the possibility of a non-contextual mode of aesthetic appreciation that amounts to much more than formalism. An aesthetic theory of meaning of this kind would identify the abstract version of the intrinsic significance of the image. It would clarify abstract art's claim to transhistorical and transcultural worth.

An important clue as to where we might look for such a theory is provided

Fig. 6. Jackson Pollock (1912–1956): *Number 1, 1948*. New York, Museum of Modern Art (MoMA). Oil and enamel on unprimed canvas, 68' x 8' 8' (172.7 x 264.2 cm). Purchase. 77. 1950. ©2008. Digital image, The Museum of Modern Art, New York / Scala, Florence, ©The Pollock-Krasner Foundation ARS, NY and DACS, London 2008.

by two of the most important contemporary art historians. Consider first an observation by T. J. Clark, *apropos* Jackson Pollock:

> *Number 1, 1948* is thrown. Therefore it is flat, with lines hurtling across the picture as if across a paper-thin firmament. Shooting stars. Comets. Once again, as with Malevich, the high moment of modernism comes when the physical limits of the painting are subsumed in a wild metaphysical dance.[2]

And again, an observation from Michael Fried:

> Caro's abstract sculptures, large and small, grounded and tabled, inhabit another world from the literal, contingent one in which we live, a world which so to speak everywhere parallels our own but whose apartness is perceived as all the more exhilarating on that account.[3]

What is striking about these remarks is that they are made by, respectively, the major social historian of art and a major formalist interpreter. Both ac-

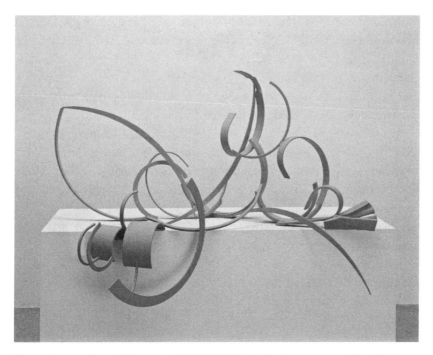

Fig. 7. Antony Caro, *Table Piece LXXXVIII (The Deluge)*, 1969–1970. New York, Museum of Modern Art (MoMA). Painted steel, 100.7 x 158.2 x 90.8 cm. Gift of Guido Goldman in memory of Minda de Gunzberg. ©2008. Digital image, The Museum of Modern Art, New York/Scala, Florence. ©Barford Sculptures Ltd. Photographer: John Riddy.

knowledge that the abstract works that they cite are engaging with virtual factors in excess of what they are as merely physical and/or formal visual configurations. What both Clark and Fried are getting from abstract works are not features based on a knowledge of the historical contexts in which the relevant works were created, but neither are they an appreciation of purely formal qualities *per se*. These quotations, indeed, bring certain dialectical tensions to the fore.

Clark, for example, often makes use of Hegel's notion of an 'unhappy consciousness' in his work. Such a consciousness is divided within itself through being caught between an overt recognition of the transient nature of values, and the need for something more substantial through which enduring self-identity can be achieved.

It could be said that Clark's own work internalizes this same unresolved dialectic. On the one hand, he offers brilliant contextual analyses of the transient historical contexts in which specific abstract works were produced, but at the same time—as in the foregoing quotation—he is looking for something more enduring and substantial in these works. In effect, he is reaching towards a sense of what, in this text, I call phenomenological depth. But his neo-Marxist theoretical orientation is not one that can furnish this.

Again, with Fried, his fundamental analytic concepts—absorption and theatricality—are based on differences in how a subject is cognitively positioned in relation to specific works. However, in the foregoing quotation it is interesting that what we get in terms of cognitive absorption in the object is a function of its apartness from the ordinary contingent world. But what is our *criterion* of this apartness; what are the active features of the 'non-literal world' that Caro's small sculptures inhabit?

What Fried needs here is a mediating term that can clarify the ontology of the abstract work. He needs a theory of phenomenological depth. But his formalism (despite some apparent inspiration from Merleau-Ponty in his earlier work) does not offer any immediately apparent basis for such a theory.

I am noting, then, that two major figures at opposite ends of the analytic spectrum both recognize that there is something more to abstract art than mere contextually determined meaning or 'significant form'. Abstract works connect, somehow, with more fundamental meanings based on factors that are fundamental to how we inhabit the world cognitively and metaphysically.

In this chapter, I will offer a general theory of how this is possible. Part One involves a short logical analysis addressing the conceptual appropriateness of 'abstract art' as a general term. In Part Two, this is backed up through sustained investigation of a 'presumption of virtuality' which orientates us towards the abstract work being 'about' something. It is suggested that optical illusion gives such works a distinctive mode of virtuality.

To set the scene for what this virtuality expresses, Part Three describes a general horizon of possibility which informs the recognition of present perceptual items. The horizon is then explored in terms of its specifically visual aspects. These involve 'contextual space'—a space of possibilities which structures the visible and shapes our interpretation of what is given in normal perception.

In Part Four, it is argued that contextual space forms the basis for abstract art's status as a distinctive form of visual meaning. Some worries about this are considered and answered. Part Five addresses another worry so as to allow a further and most decisive aspect of meaning in abstract art to emerge. In Part

Six, this is consolidated through a comparison and contrast between abstract art's distinctive relation to vision and that of scientific approaches. Some main points of argument, overall, are then summarized in the Conclusion.

Part One

The notion of 'abstract art' *per se* may seem problematic at the outset. Indeed, the very fact that ' abstract' is one of a number of different terms (such as 'non-objective' and 'non-figurative') which have been used to describe the relevant practices, might be taken to underline those practices' historically specific character. They have very different meanings and significance according to the different historical and geographical conditions under which the relevant artworks are created. This means that to even posit 'abstract art' as a category is to invite an essentialist 'master narrative' which can end only in *ahistorical* distortions.

Claims of this kind have been extremely fashionable in recent theory. But whilst such approaches are rightly mindful of the importance of the historically specific, their tendency to dismiss more comprehensive investigative approaches involves a failure of imagination. This is because it overlooks a notion of unity in cultural practice which can be theorized in terms of *functional* rather than essential structure.

On these terms, for example, specific kinds of visual art practice constellate around the physical properties of a relevant medium, and rules for working it which enable the creation of a distinctive kind of visual meaning. The relation between medium and rule defines the practice in question. It is a process of formation whereby aspects of the physical visual world are made into a distinctive kind of meaning on the basis of rules of making and codes of interpretation.

A formative process of this kind should not be regarded as 'essentialist'. Rather, it is a principle of *functional unity* which exists and is transmitted only through its historically specific embodiments. This is not a passive relation, Through these instances, the principle can be repeated, modified, extended, and sometimes even transformed into something wholly new.

There may, of course, be many zones of overlap where it becomes difficult to distinguish one practice from another, but the existence of such zones does not disqualify the idea of a functionally determined core of meaning which is the basis of an individual practice.

With these points in mind consider again the terms 'abstract', 'non-objective', and 'non-figurative'. The terms with the prefix 'non' are historically specific in origin but have been used more generally.

However, there is an awkwardness in this general usage. For it suggests that the basis of meaning in such art is as a negation of expectations based on objective realities and traditional figurative art. However, whilst these negating factors are highly relevant in certain historical contexts, they do no justice to the more active and experimental formative dimensions of the relevant works.

The term 'abstract', in contrast, is rather better suited to general use. For whilst it may seem to connote no more than some vague opposite to that which is clearly recognizable, its use as a verb in the form ' to abstract' is extraordinarily well suited to the functional principle which defines the relevant kind of visual artworks. For in its historical beginnings (with figures such as Kandinsky and Mondrian) we find a process of abstracting from nature so as to present a more spiritually potent form of visual meaning.

As we shall see in Part Two, this is of decisive cognitive significance. For in all the relevant idioms—abstract, semi or partially abstract, minimal and conceptual—there is a dimension of meaning wherein the final work abstracts from factors intrinsic to the visible, and presents them as aesthetic formations in their own right. Indeed, far from such work's expressing 'non-objective' reality, they involve features which are, in fact, basic to our visual perception of the objective world.

To show this, it is necessary to follow up a vital clue. Conventional figuration is based on the expectation that in looking at a visual art we refer to things other than its own properties. Abstract works exploit this same expectation but in complex ways which I shall now address in detail.

Part Two

Abstract works are often very different from traditional idioms, but in order to be even recognized as art, they must follow the presentational or display formats of figurative works. This context for interpretation is not at all neutral. By engaging with it, such works are absorbed within a set of expectations. Specifically, we will look to see what they are 'about' over and above what they are in strictly physical visual terms. There is a *presumption of virtuality* involved.

As a prelude to analyzing this in more detail, it is necessary to consider some problems which might seem to challenge the presumption at the outset.

Consider, for example, minimal idioms in such artists such as Yves Klein or

Ad Reinhardt. Their work sometimes involves insistently monochrome canvases. It might seem, accordingly, that here the presumption of virtuality is not applicable because there is—literally—nothing represented in such works. Similar considerations hold also in relation to minimalist sculpture such as Robert Morris' *Slab* (which is a shallow rectangular block of stainless steel, as simple as its title suggests).

However, against this, we must emphasize that absence, emptiness, and desolation can all be exemplified in visual terms. Hence, to encounter the 'empty' canvas or cognate three-dimensional work in a frame or on a plinth or other display context invites its emptiness to be interpreted in terms of a specific visual articulation of emptiness or absence.

Even if the artist intends no meaning over and above that of the work's bare visual presence, the conventions of presentation and reception in themselves develop its broader significance in associational terms. *Once an abstract work is hung on a wall or placed on a plinth or is presented in some other overt display context, none of its immediately visible properties are virtually inert or neutral.* (I shall return to this and related points in *much* more detail later on.)

A second objection to the presumption of virtuality might be made from a formalist perspective. It would hold that in focusing exclusively on relations of line, shape, colour, mass, texture, and so forth, no presumption of virtuality need be involved.

However, even formal description involves the presumption. The use of metaphors (and thence virtual content) in relation to formal description is almost inescapable. One talks, for example, of 'violent' shapes, and 'heavy' lines, and the like. Descriptions of this kind link formal qualities to those bodily gestures which express psychological states such as calmness, tranquillity, sadness, exuberance, and the like.

We must now consider how the presumption of virtuality works in more concrete terms. This centres on the fact that all abstract art has intrinsic properties of optical illusion—and thence virtual content. Such content, indeed, (as will become clear) even informs the formal structure of abstract works.

A decisive factor here is the figure/ground relation. This is the minimum condition for perception, insofar as to perceive or know something is to perceive or know it 'in relation to' something else.

This applies in the most complex ways to the structure of pictorial art. As we saw in Chapter 2, if something is a picture, it must be a picture 'of' something. This means that it must present a virtual three-dimensional figure in relation to a virtual two-dimensional planar structure. And the more such figures are multiplied and linked in coherent pictorial syntaxes (such as perspective), the more complex their articulations of the figure/ground relation are.

Abstract painting also takes us in similar directions. Relations of colour and shape involve optical illusion—in terms of depth relations, and even motion—when placed upon or inscribed in a plane. Even single lines or dabs of colour in relation to a notional plane, appear to incise or to emerge from it—depending on the character of the specific line or dab. In the case of minimal idioms, the figure of emptiness, absence or whatever, emerges from a ground comprised by the physical edge of the work.

The figure ground relation also applies in more complicated ways to abstract sculpture. Such works exist in a notional cubic, cylindrical, or even irregular column of space defined by the edges of their mount or the physical edges of the work itself. This *notional ground* means that we look at them as things which are there for a visual purpose, and whose individual visual characters are able to constellate or cluster a broader network of visual meanings around themselves.

Most abstract paintings or sculptures, of course, develop figure/ground relations in extremely complex ways. They create virtual spaces where the relation allows some congruence between the familiar perceptual world and the work's virtual space. Of course, optical illusion is encountered in many other contexts, but to encounter it in abstract art is to do so in a context where the presumption of virtuality involves further associational terms rather than mere illusion *per se*.

The abstract work's shapes, colours, lines, textures, and volumes are taken to suggest possible visual modes of three- and two-dimensional space-occupancy other than those of the work's underlying physical being.

But what are these possible modes of space-occupancy? What kinds of items and relations could optical illusion be taken to *represent*?

To answer this question in the fullest terms requires a detailed excursus into the phenomenology of perception itself, and then into its specifically visual aspects.[4] It is to these tasks I now turn.

Part Three

Knowledge—visual or otherwise—logically presupposes reference to factors which are not given in immediate experience. We can only recognize things insofar as they are embedded in a context of expectations concerning how things of that kind behave and are amenable to perception and bodily manipulation. The given is intelligible only in the context of a field of possibilities and relations that are not themselves immediately given.

At a scientific level this can be expressed in terms of explicit laws and rules which govern the structures and transformations of things present in perception. But this is emergent from a more basic level of sensory world-cognition wherein *we learn the character of the objective world through becoming habituated to it in the course of the body's general sensorimotor activity.*

We know, for example, that if we change position, the shapes and sizes of things in our visual field will reconfigure in proportion with this. We know that things are not just surfaces; their solidity means that they are composed of many layers—which would become visible if we were to break them open.

Likewise we know that even the surface of something is not fixed at the level of our normal perception of it, and would look very different if viewed closely and even more complex if looked at through a magnifying glass or microscope. We also know how strange things would appear if viewed from unusual or restricted viewing positions.

Knowledge such as this, of course, is not explicitly entertained every time we perceive a spatial object, but it does inform how we negotiate it. It is at least tacitly comprised in how the object is meaningful for us as a spatial thing of such and such a kind.

It should be emphasized that our ways of recognizing objects of perception is also dependent on psychological and emotional relations to them. We do not merely register things and states of affairs, we *characterize* them in terms of whether they and their properties are reassuring to us or are in some ways threatening. Indeed, the positions into which we put ourselves, and thence the things we find there, emerge through a soliciting or avoidance, on the basis of our interests and our history in relation to the things in question.

The decisive point then is that all perception depends on the object of perception's relation to an horizon of *possibility and relations*. This horizon engages different levels of tacit knowledge and expectation which give the object a specific character. It is the key factor in phenomenological depth.

Now since vision is the most central aspect of sensory-perception, it should be possible to describe the aforementioned horizon of possibility with a specifically visual emphasis. Here is such a description, in summary.

Given any three-dimensional item or state of affairs in our visual field, what enables its recognition in the fullest sense is a contextual space of expectations based on its unnoticed or hidden aspects, or its possible transformations or relocations, and indeed its relation to things not given immediately in the visual field, including those arising from association on the viewer's part.

What we see is not a mere datum. Our recognition of it is based on its fitting in with an horizon of visual expectations, constraints, and associations which are usually not noticed explicitly. Our knowledge of it is given character by this horizon of visual possibility.

In visual terms, there are seven major levels of contextual space involved here.

i) A knowledge of those aspects of spatial items, relations, or states of affairs which, under normal circumstances, are incompletely available or unavailable to visual perception, or are unnoticed by it, e.g. basic spatial relations implicit in the particular, forms at the periphery of the immediate visual field, small or microscopic surface features, internal states, unfamiliar or highly evanescent atmospheric effects and ambiences, and unusual perceptual perspectives (such as aerial viewpoints). This level also includes details of some item or state of affair's visual appearance considered independently of the whole of which they are an aspect.

ii) Visual configurations arising from the destruction, deconstruction, reduction, reconstruction, movement, or variation of familiar items, relations, or states of affairs (including other artefacts, such as buildings or topographic formations). These can include *idealized* realms, where the geometric structure of spatial relations and contents exist is a purified form, apparently liberated from the vicissitudes of change.

iii) Possible visible items, relations, states of affairs, or life-forms which might exist in physical and/or perceptual environments radically different from our usual one.

iv) Visual forms and ideas linked by the imaginative association of elements rather than 'correspondence' with specific states of affairs.

v) Visual forms suggestive of the gestural correlates of particular kinds of states of mind. In this respect, we might talk of such things as 'gentle' lines, or depressing ranges of colour, and the like.

vi) Accidental correspondences or associations where a formal configuration looks like a recognizable visible form other than itself (e.g. when we see shapes in clouds)

vii) Dreamlike qualities and oneiric ambiences.

In talking about things not given in the immediate visual field but which contextualize its full appearance, these seven levels map out the broad logical scope of such contextualization. They comprise a field of broader possibilities and relations that is implicit in the character and meaning of spatial items or states of affairs given in the immediate visual field. Without this contextual space, that field would be no more than an inert screen of visual phenomena.

Now it might be asked how the different levels of contextual space apply. Are they all involved in each visual perception, or is the relevance of one or other of them determined by the kind of thing or state of affairs we are attending to, and by the nature of our interest in it?

The answer is complex. In general terms, we need all the levels as a field of visual competence in negotiating spatial phenomena. But i) and ii) are of especial importance. They describe structures which are inherent in our visual knowledge of both space-occupying things, and their behaviour or potential transformations. If it were not possible, in principle, to relate *any* visible object to both of these vectors—seeing them in terms of what they are, and how they might be transformed in spatial terms—then our relation to the visible would be incoherent.

Levels iii) to vi) do not have the same necessity. This is because they do not describe structural characteristics *vis-à-vis* the *spatiality* of visible things *per se*. However, as self-conscious beings, we inhabit the spatial world as a place of spiritual and imaginative as well as practical exchange. Any visible thing is encountered within and thence characterized (no matter how minimally) in terms of these exchanges. Levels iii) to vii) are the *associational* vector wherein our visual perception of things and ourselves is enriched by the play of imagination and ideas.

These points aside, it is clear that some levels of contextual space will be more relevant to our perception of specific kinds of visual item or states of affairs than will others. If we are exploring the details of a geological formation, the individual parts may seem to take on a life of their own—to be little visible worlds in their own right, irrespective of the whole in which they are embedded. Likewise we may imagine what the form might look like transplanted to a different location or rearranged in terms of its constituent visible elements.

Again suppose we are looking at a dusty table with an interesting shape. We might try to imagine the microscopic visual richness of the dust, or how the interesting shape might look placed in a different context.

The key point is that the levels of contextual space are different interpretative perspectives which we can take on any visual item. We can choose to employ them, or else they can be thrust upon us individually, by the specific visual conditions which are engaging us. Most of the time, however, they will be a field of dispositional interpretative perspectives whose elements are made occurrent with different emphases according to different visual circumstances.

It might be objected, of course, that this group of levels is arrived at stipulatively, and that visual perception can involve many other 'background' factors besides. However, it is incumbent upon the objector to specify what the other factors in question might be. Other logically distinct levels of contextual space may exist, but, as far as I can see, in general terms the list is comprehensive. (That being said, it may, with more detailed analysis, be possible to subdivide these individual levels in more detail. Indeed, such subdivision might be the basis of a wealth of useful research.)

Contextual space, then, is a zone of expectations which constellates around those details and possibilities which inform the character of everyday visible reality (tacitly or explicitly) but without being immediately accessible to normal vision. It draws upon all the phenomenological depth factors described in the Introduction to this book, to varying degrees (dependent on the perceptual context). It also has decisive connections to abstract art, as I will now show.

Part Four

To understand how the connection is made, a useful clue can be found in Merleau-Ponty's notion of the 'invisible'. In this respect, he suggests that painting

> gives visible existence to what profane vision believes to be invisible; thanks to it we do not need a 'muscular sense' in order to possess the voluminosity of the world. This voracious vision, reaching beyond the discrete 'visual givens' opens upon a texture of Being of which the discrete sensorial messages are only the punctuations or caesurae.[5]

The point is that the painter presents those 'invisible' details and effects which are integral to the appearance of some visible item or state of affairs, but which usually pass unnoticed in day-to-day perception. It is this 'texture of Being' which constitutes the fabric and fullness of visual appearance. Our recognition of discrete objects and states of affairs are perceptually abbreviated functions of it.

This notion can surely be applied to sculpture also (though Merleau-Ponty does not do this himself). The sculptor does not produce an object out of nothingness, but either makes it or reconfigures already created physical items in a new distinctive visible configuration. Through this creation we are made aware of the textures and volumes of the work's three-dimensional being, rather than merely recognizing it as a certain kind of spatial object.

To develop Merleau-Ponty's position further, one might say that the 'invisible' takes two forms—the autofigurative, and virtual content. The former consists in viewing structural aspects of spatial appearance (including colour, shape, mass, texture, density, and volume) in relation to the work itself *qua* visible thing. The latter involves such features considered in terms of how they present the work's virtual content.

In figurative art, this virtual subject-matter consists of recognizable kinds of visual items or states of affairs rendered in terms of familiar, frontally orientated aspects (or sets of aspects) presented to a notionally stationary observer in a 'normal' viewing position. In abstract works, the formative powers of visual appearance—colour, shape, mass, etc., issue in works embodying optical illusion.

Because there is no convention of viewing over and above this illusion, abstract works are free from the constraints of fixed and familiar notional viewing positions. They present possible forms of visible existence over and above that of the physical artefacts which are their bearers. (This includes, but goes beyond, those unnoticed details which are the basis of the Merleau-Pontian 'invisible'.)

We now reach a decisive point. Any abstract work opens up a virtual space. If this space does not consist of familiar recognizable three-dimensional items and/or states of affairs, then—insofar as we take the work to be 'about' something—its optical properties *must* be referred to some aspect of the contextual space just outlined. If this reference is not possible, the work amounts to no more than a neutral formal configuration.

However, as I argued in Part Two, the presumption of virtuality which accompanies the conventions whereby abstract works are presented, does not allow such neutrality. Indeed, if form is to have expressive power over and above the merely decorative, then this can only be explained through the evocation of some aspect of contextual space.

This strong claim might be justified as follows: (1) abstract works are always encountered in terms of the convention that they are 'about' something, (2) all such works have properties of optical illusion, however, minimal (3) artists writings and manifestoes are *not* (under normal circumstances) visibly embedded in the work (4) if therefore we are to give meaning to the work within its own internal resources *qua* visual configuration, we must have some internal criterion of 'aboutness' (5) the only candidate for this is the relation between optical illusion and what I am calling 'contextual space'.

Against this argument, a number of objections might be raised. The first is based on descriptive austerity and questions the legitimacy of moving from point (4) to the conclusion drawn in point (5). The objection holds that the optical illusion of abstract works need not be read in any terms other than that of *mere illusion*. In describing such works all that can be said in the strictest terms is such things as 'this dab of colour *appears* to be in front of that one', or 'this shape *appears* to be in motion', or whatever. There are no grounds within the internal resources of the work itself which warrant the further inference that optical illusion *must* be taken to involve contextual space.

However, the austere spatial dynamics described in abstract works are intrinsically more than just that. This because they are presented as *pure visual appearance*, i.e. by and large independently of their usual embeddedness in the spatial being and behaviour of familiar visible things and states of affairs.

In ordinary visual experience, relations such as 'in front of' or 'behind', or being 'in motion', or whatever, are interpreted primarily in terms of practical interests and contexts. The abstract work, in contrast, presents these relations without reference to such interests, and through this *directs attention to the spatial relations in their own right*.

On these terms, to even describe abstract works in terms of optical illusion is to identify key factors in the spatial structure of visual appearance which are not usually immediately accessible. Far from avoiding reference to contextual space, the austere description of abstract optical illusion actually engages with its most fundamental spatial levels.

A second objection might be raised. It holds that surely we cannot say that a work 'must' allude to some aspect of contextual space. It may be, for example, that what is intended is something of personal significance which is not itself visual (for example, 'inner-states' of feeling or other 'dimensions' of reality). Even more importantly, the allusion to contextual space surely cannot be established unless there is evidence that such meaning is intended by the artist. This, of course, involves reference to sources external to the work itself (such as manifestoes or other writings).

In relation to both these claims we must first reiterate the decisive point made above. Insofar as abstract works embody optical illusion, they exemplify key aspects of contextual space. It may be that the artist did not explicitly intend this; indeed, it is very likely that he or she did not have anything like an explicit theory of such space.

However, all humans operate within space and its horizon of possibility without having to have any overt general theory of the structures involved. These are acquired mainly as habitual dispositions arising from practical perceptual and motor activities. Likewise with all art practice, including abstract idioms. The basic conventions involved are learned without necessarily theorizing what these actually involve in more general terms. Indeed, this basic level of meaning will, for the most part, be subsumed within the exercise of the artist's more personal preoccupations.

These preoccupations may be of the greatest historical interest in explaining why such and such an artist comes to create such a work or body of work. But they cannot then be identified as the basic *artistic* meaning of such work.

In this respect, it is vital to emphasize that art—in whatever form—is primarily a social, and only secondarily a private activity. Hence, if an artist wishes to represent some personally significant meaning through a visible configuration, he or she must utilize idioms which draw on a shared visual cultural stock with an associational range which encompasses the intended form of meaning.

This, of course, is precisely what the relation between optical illusion and contextual space offers. In the case of feelings, whilst their visceral aspects may be purely psychological, their behavioural manifestations characteristically involve the visible dimension. We ascribe specific states of mind by virtue of how people look and their behavioural expressions in social and other visual environments. These expressions bring about those correlations of visual form and relevant states of mind which are constitutive of level v) of contextual space.

The general relevance of the artist's intentions in abstract works must also be determined by reference to art as a social practice. It is possible, for example, that an abstract artist creates a serene and tranquil-looking work that generally suggests, say, a seashore, but never actually thinks of the latter association, and actually intends the work's serene appearance to be an *ironic* comment on the unhappiness of his or her existence.

However, if this work is meant for a public audience, then the intention is self-defeating. In publicly accessible terms, the work is tranquil-looking and can be taken to refer, accordingly, to an appropriate aspect of contextual space.

The suggestion of a seashore—even if the artist does not notice it—is also a legitimate association insofar as it is visually consistent (however loosely) with familiar visualizations of tranquil-looking seashores.

Viewing the abstract work in a public context, therefore, we have no alternative except to interpret it in relation to those conventions—such as the presumption of virtuality, and, as a correlate of this, contextual space—which make it collectively intelligible.

The primacy of contextual space here does not rule out positive reference to the artist's intentions or the immediate historical circumstances under which the work was created. However, these can only relate to artistic meaning insofar as they enhance or deepen our appreciation of what is given in the work *qua* visible configuration. If they are made primary, then the work is significant only as an adjunct to theory.

One final objection must be considered. It is a fundamental one which leads us to a decisive positive feature of meaning in abstract art which has not yet been fully articulated in the preceding discussion.

Part Five

The objection holds that even if we allow an intrinsic connection between abstract works and contextual space, there is systematic ambiguity concerning which aspect of that space is actually exemplified in any specific work.

Now it is true that the connection between abstract art and contextual space is not as exact as that convention of resemblance to familiar three-dimensional things on which traditional pictorial art is founded. Abstract art involves more openness—in the sense that the work's meaning can range over more than one level of contextual space.

However, this actually invests the work with *positive ambiguity*. For it means that the work *alludes to*, rather than directly represents, a subject-matter. Contextual space defines a range of possible virtual 'subject-matters' here, but which exact aspect of contextual space is relevant to a particular work is only alluded to.

In this respect, consider Eli Bornstein's *Tripart Hexaplane Construction No. 1* (2005–2007). This work consists of three basic sets of doubled steel planes. They are of equal mass, two being strong light blue on both sides, with the other having a light blue and a purple-blue side. Each of these dominant planes joins the others at an obtuse angle. A host of secondary elongated rectangular

Fig. 8. Eli Bornstein, *Tripart Hexaplane Construction No. 1*, 2005–2007, ©Jacobs University Bremen.

or square planes emerge from, or intersect with, them at right or oblique angles. They offer variations of colour and shape which make the basic structure much more complex.

Some of these secondary planes are of a length which exceeds the upper and lower limits of the main planar masses, thus evoking a sense of the work being, in virtual terms, *self-elevating*. In relation to actual physical elevation, the whole is lifted above ground-level by a mount whose base-area does not exceed the margins of the work's own physical limits.

This work was (in large part) created for the outdoor environs of Jacobs University Bremen, so as to act as both visual and spiritual catalyst for perceptual explorations relevant to both the ethos and layout of the university. However, these broader effects are only intelligible as functions of the distinctive character of the work *qua* individual visible object. The intersecting planar structures at once suggest possibilities of architectural creation, forms of crystalline matter, or spatial elements in motion whose mutual arrest leads to a creative visualization of stasis.

Just by looking, it is not possible to identify the work with any one aspect of these three aspects of contextual space exclusively. *They each apply*—with varying emphases depending upon the perspective of the individual viewer, and—especially—on the overall light conditions which are operative at the time of viewing. The criterion of reference to contextual space is based on loose consistency—that is to say, informal visual resemblance—between the work's optical illusion and those aspects of such space which were described in Part Three.

These alternate possibilities are precisely the virtue of *Tripart Hexaplane*'s status as an abstract work. Because works of this kind are consistent with more than one aspect of contextual space, they have a distinctive power of visual allusion. Their associational power ranges across possibilities which are only tangentially suggested by figurative idioms where our interpretation is severely constrained by the work's recognizable pictorial content.

In figurative art, indeed, the significance of the work's 'invisible' dimension is mainly that of the overlooked or unnoticed. In the case of abstract works, we are often dealing, in addition, with that which is 'invisible' in a literal rather than metaphorical sense, i.e. a space of *alternative visual possibilities* which are suggested by the immediately given and which give it sense.

Abstract art's allusive character is of deep cognitive significance by virtue of its evocation of different aspects of contextual space. Such art creates aesthetic harmonies of parts and whole from a space of possibility which structures vision and the visible. This space is familiar enough to give us a general immediate orientation—even if (as noted earlier) we have not explicitly thought about contextual space and its general structure.

The abstract work, then, is thus able to function between the contextual basis of the visually familiar and its own open—but by no means arbitrary—expression of it. This is its distinctive quality. It is a poignant emblem of both the complexity of our inherence in, and open transcendence towards, the visible world.

Part Six

There is a telling contrast which is worth exploring as a corollary of the fore-going. Science expresses the structure of visible phenomena (and our relation to them) in terms of mathematical concepts and quanta. This involves *models* whose general character is to exemplify the objective mechanisms of vision, and to eliminate vicissitudes bound up with individual perspectives upon it.

Now contextual space can be investigated in these terms—but only insofar as its individual aspects are clearly isolated as a basis for well-defined empirical data analyzed under laboratory conditions or through statistical analysis. But in this something is lost.

This is because vision and its relation to visible things form a complex *open* system. Any whole which is more than the sum of its parts is complex in a minimal sense. But some systems are open, in that they involve highly unpredictable elements rather than circumscribed wholes (the weather would be an example of this). However, complex systems are open in an even more radical sense when they pertain to behaviour and perceptual orientations where free-choice is involved.

Such complexity is correlated closely with a simple, but far-reaching physical truth. No spatial object can occupy the exact same physical coordinates at the very same time as another such object. And when the objects in question here are percipient beings, this means that their interpretative perspective upon the world will always be *unique* to some degree. The horizon of possibility in which their momentary perceptions are embedded will never be entirely congruent with those of other such subjects nor, indeed, with their own previous states. Freedom and uniqueness of physical positioning are mutually correlated. They give the individual viewpoint *qua* individual a necessary role in visual cognition as a complex open system.

It follows, then, that the individual viewpoint is as important for understanding visual cognition as are physical objects, states of affairs, and the causal mechanisms of vision. If such cognition is to be explained in the most comprehensive objective terms, then *the individual viewpoint must be regarded as a constitutive factor rather than a distracting variable*. We must find some idiom of modelling which allows us to express the radical open complexity of vision as a system.

This is provided by the visual arts. Both figurative and abstract art involve a privileging of the individual viewpoint, insofar as the artist's style determines the meaning of what is embodied in the visual work. However, style is not a sufficient condition of meaning, for what is even more decisive is the way in which it serves to *interpret or present* subject-matter and show it in a new way.

Through its character as a spatially realized virtual reality, visual art discloses how things become visible, at the very same ontological level at which that becoming occurs—namely the individual embodied subject's visual experience. The subjective dimension of vision finds an objective model which embodies it, *qua* individual, in a cognitively *elucidating* way. Such a work invites us, in effect, to 'see it like this'.

Figurative works do this in a way that is strictly directed (by the familiar recognizable objects which they represent for a viewer in a notionally fixed-position). Abstract works (as we have already seen) are not so constrained. They can express multiple aspects of contextual space simultaneously. Such works model and thence illuminate individual perspectives upon those aspects of the concealed or peripheral whose possibility structures the visual field. Through the allusiveness of their meaning, they provide objective models which reveal the constitutive role of individuality in the projection of all aspects of contextual space.

This allusiveness—in its far-ranging and complex structures—is, in one key sense, objectively truer to visual perception than the rigid models of scientific understanding. It models the flexibility and dynamism of contextual space's role in visual perception—its existence as a complex open system—in a way that scientific approaches cannot.

From this, two important qualifications should be made. First, there is considerable scope for cooperation between analyses of abstract art and scientific analyses of vision. There is, for example, a massive amount of work to be done on the mechanisms of vision involved in the perception of abstract works, and how far these differ in accordance with the different varieties of such art (e.g. biomorphic, geometric, colour-field). Corresponding questions can be asked also about the neurophysiological bases of such perception.

In broader terms, it may be possible to initiate more far-reaching research into the notion of contextual space itself. This might involve, for example, a reappraisal of the history of abstract art correlated with work in cognitive psychology addressing the relative importance of the different levels/aspects of contextual space *vis-à-vis* the mechanisms of vision. There are also important questions to be investigated in terms of the relation between contextual space, abstraction, and computer-generated imagery.

This leads to the second important qualification. Whatever the cognitive significance of abstract art and whatever the possibilities of combining its study with scientific research, in the final analysis such art is *aesthetic* in character. What counts is not just its allusive presentation of contextual space, but the specific way in which the individual work makes this into a distinctive aesthetic object.

It is precisely this achievement which makes abstract art into something worthy of study. But that being said, it is also this very achievement which highlights the more general significance of contextual space as a fundamental of visual cognition. In abstract art, in other words, artistic achievement does not separate itself off from other areas of scientific interest, but rather *qua* artistic, opens up avenues of connection with them.

Conclusion

I have argued, then, that art which abandons the traditional conventions of pictorial and sculptural representation, but which still follows their conventional formats of presentation, should be described as abstract art. Through adopting such formats it is approached through a presumption of virtuality, i.e. the expectation that whatever is thus presented is 'about' something. In the context of abstract art, this is satisfied through properties of optical illusion.

The presumption of virtuality means that all factors in the work's visible appearance are relevant to such illusion, and will be read in terms of it—if only because they are meanings which are accessible within the internal resources of the work itself.

Now whereas most approaches to this would regard it as no more than a vaguely interesting suggestive or associational feature of abstract works, I have argued that it is of the greatest import. This is because our cognitive relation to the visual field is dependent on an horizon of visual possibility, which structures the objects of our visual attention. The visual given is embedded in a *contextual space.*

Abstract art is able to express this by virtue of the interplay between the artist's individual viewpoint and the *allusive* way in which contextual space is evoked. It is an aesthetic model of vision's character as an open complex system.

7   The Logic of Conceptualism

Introduction

In the previous chapter I offered a general theory of meaning for abstract works, including conceptual idioms (which encompass important aspects of minimal art also). In the last decades of the twentieth century, varieties of conceptualism have been especially influential, often issuing in complex assemblages, site-specific works, and performances.

Some 'Institutional' theorists such as Arthur Danto[1] have argued that all artworks are meaningful primarily through existing in an atmosphere of theory. This approach not only encompasses the non-traditional idioms, but, in effect, privileges the Duchampian 'ready-made' and its more recent conceptual art offshoots as *exemplars of art's essence*. The reason for this *de facto* privileging is that the ready-made's intelligibility *as* an artwork is *manifestly* dependent on its relation to some art theoretical standpoint, and hence reveals the basis of artistic meaning with a directness that other works cannot.

This privileging of conceptual art, however, is not warranted. The Institutional definitions that sustain the privileging are, in the final analysis, self-defeating. *For if a context of theory is taken to be the main determinant of artistic meaning and value, this does not explain what makes art worth theorizing about in the first place.*[2] Any approach which privileges theory must, at some point, negotiate those extra-theoretical factors which justify art as an object of value and concern. If no such extra-theoretical factors are involved, then once we have grasped the 'idea' that the work is pointing towards, then the work itself becomes superfluous.

A more balanced approach sees conceptualism as a primarily western spin-off which is parasitic for its artistic status on expectations grounded in more traditional idioms. However, it has its own distinctive aspects that are worth considering in their own right. Investigating them provides an opportunity for extending the general approach taken in the previous chapter.

The investigation is justified by an even more important point. In this book, I have stressed the importance of the visual artwork's embodiment of phenomenological depth. Now it might seem that this embodiment is challenged by at least one decisive aspect of conceptualism. It consists of the fact that the main feature which defines the tendency is the *designation* of 'found' material as art. 'Found' material is stuff used by the artist but which is neither physically made by him or her, nor 'worked' in traditional craftly ways through carving and the like.

Such material can, literally, be found or acquired by the artist, or it can be made or procured by someone else on the basis of the artist's instructions. It can also be made into constructions or assemblages either by the artist, or by other people on the basis of instructions from the artist. Most importantly, its designation as art constellates around recognition of what the Found material is, in its own right, as well as what the artist actually does or gets done with it.

An important variant of this is the artist's own body. It can be designated 'artwork' on the basis of performing specific actions or inhabiting spaces, without these activities having to issue in some artefact, or instantiate some traditional gestural art form (such as dance or mime). It can also involve the artist directing other people to use their bodies to realize specific or kinds of gestures and acts.

Such work is negotiated more appropriately under the rubric 'conceptual' rather than the usual term 'performance' art because whilst the notion of 'performance' indicates that someone is doing something with his or her or someone else's body or bodies, this applies just as well to dance, mime, or even theatre. But the point of 'performance art' as a term is that it picks out something that is distinct from dance and other traditional performing arts. This extra 'something' consists of a *conceptual loading* that is realized *through* the performance.

Now, it might seem that the central role played in conceptual idioms by Found material and performance means that the link between such art and phenomenological depth is somewhat diminished. Indeed, the fact that in many cases the Found material is mass-produced, or the performance involves mundane bodily activity, may seem to emphasize this diminution all the more. It may even seem that the sheer profusion of anarchic conceptual strategies makes any systematic analysis of it in structural terms hopelessly futile.

However, these worries are unfounded. In this chapter, I will show in detail how Designated Art (as I shall call it) can be understood systematically in terms of its engagement with contextual space, and the expression of phenomenological depth.

To this end, Part One offers a logical geography of basic conceptual formats and strategies which are available for Designated Art. In Part Two, I discuss important aesthetic criteria for assessing the significance of such art, giving special consideration (both negative and positive) to Duchamp's Designated Art. In Part Three, a range of further examples is considered, extending far beyond Duchamp. The Conclusion suggests that Designated Art's conceptual strategies allow it to achieve (sometimes) phenomenological depth with a distinctively existential character.

Part One

As we have seen, in Designated Art, the original character of the Found item itself has to be a recognizable feature of the work—mediated by being placed, juxtaposed, or physically modified (or combinations of these). This occurs, in the first instance, within a space of logical possibilities concerning *format and context*.[3] They are as follows:

1. The unassisted found object—that is, one designated as 'art' through being presented in a display format or context associated with art, and no further physical interventions (if, indeed, any at all) from the artist. This, of course, is the strategy originally instigated by Duchamp.

2. The assisted found object—where the artist or his or her agent alters the found object (though not to such a degree that the object's original or artefactual character ceases to be recognizable)

3. Manufactured objects—where some artefact is made on the basis of instructions from the artist, rather than by the artist in person.

4. Fixed assemblages—where examples of either kind of found object or manufactured object are physically adapted and permanently connected in relation to one another so as to form a complex single work, or a serial work composed from complex individual units.

5. Transient assemblages—namely works which can be physically disassembled into their component found or manufactured parts, and where the manifestation of this possibility is a key element in describing how the work appears.

6. Site specificity—where a work is created for a specific site, or is allocated to such a site on a permanent basis.

7. Site transience—where a work is created for a specific site, but can, in principle, be exhibited in any location.

8. Directional designation—invoked in those cases where an artist intends some real or imagined item, event, or state of affairs to be regarded as a work of art without doing anything other than perform this act of designation. He or she simply directs attention towards the intended object on the basis of instructions or descriptions (or a series thereof)

9. Found bodily activity, i.e. directed towards some purpose other than that of traditional gestural art idioms such as dance or mime, alone. Records of the performance are kept or not kept, on the basis of the artist's requirements. In some cases, the making of such records is made integral to the meaning of the piece. It may be that the work is enacted on the basis of instructions that make it repeatable.

10. Bodily activity or presentation of the aforementioned kind which is intended to solicit and engage with direct audience response.

These formats and contexts describe, I think, the basic conceptual possibilities which are available for creating Designated Art from Found materials. However, what is important is the specific way in which the individual object, or configuration of such objects, is used.

In the previous chapter, I outlined seven levels of *contextual space*, all of which are relevant to abstract works. In principle, Designated Art is able to draw on all aspects of this space. However, there is a difference of emphasis.

Much abstract work involves the exploration of the details and possibilities of visual appearance, *per se*. This means that it will tend to emphasize the first three levels of contextual space—bound up with the visual conditions of space-occupancy, or unexpected varieties of it.

However, the Found element in Designated Art means that we are dealing with material which *already* has a specific identity—the recognition of which is integral to the meaning of such works. In this case, the fourth level of contextual space—visual forms and ideas connected through elements of imaginative association—will have a special importance. Attention will focus on how treatment of the found material shifts meaning from literal recognition of identity into new contexts.

Of particular importance here is the way in which the individual Found object or configuration invokes avenues of association which engage with ideas and values ranging beyond the visual. The Found element is presented or treated in a way which expands its semantic scope.

Conceptual strategies of this kind have four main vectors of operation, as follows:

a) Ad hoc denotation—where some item, event, or state of affairs is stipulated as referring to some other item, event, or state of affairs, or, as not referring to anything other than itself, or, indeed, as not referring to anything at all. In such cases (if the work is to be intelligible to people other than the artist) it is logically presupposed that the nature of the semantic relation being established is explained by means of some accompanying title or text. (Terry Atkinson's and Michael Baldwin's 1967 *Airshow* is an example of this. It involved designating a column of air of indeterminate vertical extent, with a base of one square mile, somewhere on the earth's surface, as a work of art.)

b) Iconic denotation—an unusual idiom whereby instances of format and context categories 1–3 are joined so as to create works that pictorially or sculpturally represent kinds of item, event, or state of affairs other than themselves. (David Mach's and Cornelia Parker's assemblages creating representational sculpture from Found material in the 1990's are striking examples of this.)

c) Metonymy—where a work is presented so as to symbolize some greater physical whole of which it is part, or something with which it is contiguous or has an indexical relation, or something of which it is an instance or token.

d) Connotation—involves a work having loose but familiar range of cultural or biological associations. (Items with phallic overtones are good examples.)

e) Metaphor—when a work's associational meaning is able to suggest a definite kind of item, event, or state of affairs other than itself. In this respect, for example, Robert Rauschenberg's *Monogram*—consisting of a stuffed goat inserted through a car-tyre, is sometimes interpreted as a metaphor for homosexual activity.

f) Allegory—when a work presents an extended metaphor with some narrative element.

g) Irony—where meaning is achieved through the work being associated with some factor that is manifestly at odds with its found or 'ready-made' identity.

Given these complex possibilities of format, context, and associational strategy, I shall now consider their criteria of aesthetic application, and some detailed examples of how such criteria might be applied.

Part Two

If Designated Art is to succeed *as* art, rather than as a mere adjunct to theory, it must surely have aesthetic significance as an individual visual object or state of affairs. This significance centres on three related factors.

The first is *visual pertinence*. This means that *how* the work looks is an integral part of the broader avenues of association which it invokes. It's specific character as just *this* visible thing is not something which can be dismissed as a mere contingency.

One clear expression of this is when the work has intrinsic visual interest in its own right. However, this is not essential to visual pertinence. As we shall see a little further on, there are some Designated Artworks which are visually simple to the point of banality.

In such cases a second criterion comes into play, namely *sufficient paraphrasability*. This is determined by the logical space between two extremes; on the one hand, works where the associated meaning can be sufficiently comprehended by verbal or written description of the relation between the work and its context, and, on the other hand, works whose meaning can only be comprehended adequately on the basis of direct perceptual acquaintance with them—and which cannot, therefore, be sufficiently paraphrased.

There is also a third criterion of aesthetic relevance. It consists of the relation between *originality and nonsense*. It is possible to do things which have not been done before, but which have no significant meaning over and above the fact of not having been done before. It is original nonsense. For it to be original as such, then its newness must actually involve a revelation of associational avenues which lead somewhere in terms of developing the meaning of the found material.

There is an extreme formalist approach which might justify original nonsense by holding that aesthetically significant activity is intrinsically valuable for its own sake without reference to end or purpose. But whilst this may be relevant to aesthetic meaning it is so only with careful qualification and contextualization. And even then, I know of no theories which could establish it as a sufficient condition of aesthetic meaning.

Before looking at works which do satisfy the aesthetic criteria, it is, perhaps, more useful to look at some which fail them. It is, of course, vital to emphasize that applying the criteria is not a matter of simple recognition and labelling. In all cases, the application involves interpretation and argument.

First, then, Duchamp's unassisted ready-made *In Advance of a Broken Arm* of 1915. This consists of a snow shovel leaning against a wall. Here the character of this specific shovel has no manifest bearing on the comical outcome alluded to in the work's title. Any snow shovel would be adequate to the same point. Here nothing is gained by seeing the 'original'. The idea at issue can be perfectly comprehended by description alone. In this case, the work fails in terms of both visual pertinence and sufficient paraphrasability.

A more complex example is Barbara Kruger's *Your gaze hits the side of my face* from 1981. This consists of an idealized semi-classical side view of a modelled female face, overlaid with vertically arranged letraset trumpeting the title of the work. Whitney Chadwick suggests that

> Barbara Kruger's blown-up, severely cropped photographs of women and their short accompanying texts, subvert the meaning of both image and text in order to destabilize the positioning of woman as object. She emphasizes the way in which language manipulates and [she] undermines the assumption of masculine control over language and viewing, by refusing to complete the cycle of meaning, and by shifting pronouns in order to expose the positioning of woman as 'other' . . .[4]

Interestingly, one might just as well argue that the bombastic visual address of Kruger's work achieves the opposite of this. It is actually a *dialectical image* of its opponent's own values, i.e. it is a work whose notional oppositionality is expressed in an aggressive authoritarian visual idiom which actually internalizes, reproduces, and reinforces the very patriarchal mind-set which the work's content is meant to challenge.

However, the most interesting point of all is not whether this interpretation is actually true, but the very fact that the meaning of the work has to be considered in these mainly critical/political terms. There is no room for anything else.

Kruger's work does not open up associational avenues but rather forecloses on them. There is a simple message: 'Patriarchal culture oppresses women. Accept and believe. Do not debate. Do not dare to think, feel, or imagine the complexities at issue'.

In this case, any potential visual pertinence in the work itself is overwritten by its simplistic, sufficiently paraphrasable content. The found elements of image and commercial letraset are merely juxtaposed as adjuncts to theory.

Consider also Vito Acconci's *Step Piece* of 1970. This consisted of the artist carrying out a recorded series of mundane physically tiring exercises over a fixed period of time to a point of exhaustion.

There is no intrinsic reason why just this artist, performing just this activity, should have any specifically visual significance. Certainly, nothing like this had been designated 'artwork' before. But there does not appear any significant reason why it should be so designated. It has no visual pertinence; it is sufficiently paraphrasable in descriptive terms, and has as many meanings as one might care to read into it. This final point means that it is, in effect, little more than 'original nonsense'.

I shall now consider some much more significant examples of Designated Art.

First, Duchamp's *Bottlerack* of 1914. Taken out of context from its practical function, this kind of bottlerack is curiously intriguing in terms of its visual structure—and is so in a way that other bottleracks might not be. It invites avenues of metaphorical association in terms of visual analogies between its shape and both natural and other artefactual formations.

Here there is some genuine element of visual pertinence which means that the work is not sufficiently paraphrasable, and is more than original nonsense—even if it is so only in a fairly narrow way.

A more complex work is the *Fountain* of 1917, which is a porcelain urinal bowl, signed 'R. Mutt'. It is visually quite banal, and falls down on visual pertinence. Indeed, it is sufficiently paraphrasable. However, these restrictions are rather overcome by the simple magic of the relation between the work's material identity as a urinal and its title.

This is not just the irony of a stream of urine being described as a 'fountain'. Rather the more striking oddness is that, in a fountain, the liquid stream emanates from the material base outwards, whereas in a urinal it is imported from the outside. This is a surprising and slyly poetic reversal which plays on associations and contrasts between flow and visual counter-flow, and between that which is ornamental and special, and that which is the mere detritus of biological process, without resolving itself into some simple formula of what a fountain is.

In the case of Duchamp's 'assisted' ready-mades, the artist acts upon the found material in a more sustained way. In many of these works, the aesthetic criteria find a more unambiguously positive application.

An especially striking example is *Why Not Sneeze, Rose Sélavy?* of 1921. This

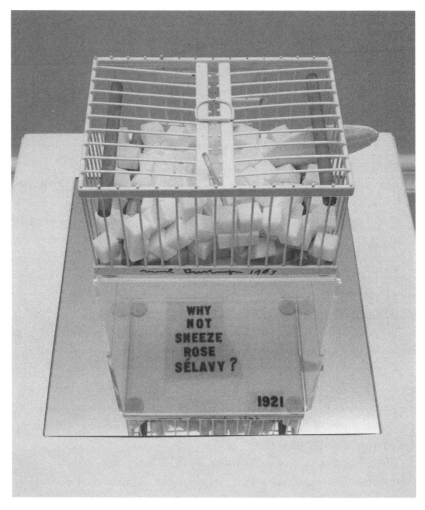

Fig. 9. Marcel Duchamp, *Why Not Sneeze, Rose Sélavy?*, 1921, replica 1964, mixed media, unconfirmed: 114 x 220 x 160 mm. ©Tate, London 2008, ©Succession Marcel Duchamp / ADAGP, Paris and DACS, London 2008.

is constructed in the form of a birdcage, containing a cuttlebone, a thermometer, and 152 cubes—which appear to be sugar but are, in fact, pieces of marble which Duchamp commissioned others to shape as cubes, each one stamped with the legend 'made in France'.

This work has extraordinary visual pertinence, and a wealth of broader associations. The lightness of sugar cubes is contradicted by the heaviness of the marble, and the granular monotony of a sugar cube to the touch is contradicted by the cold smoothness of the marble. This reversal of identity between sugar and marble hints at a kind of creative alchemy wherein things can take on incongruous properties through the power of creativity.

The title is, of course, nonsensical in that sneezing is an involuntary action. However, suppose that it is issued as a challenge rather than as an invitation—to do the kind of thing which cannot be done volitionally. In one respect, this challenge has already been met by virtue of the creativity just noted. The sugar cubes have been 'changed' into marble, or, from another perspective, the marble has been 'changed' into sugar cubes.

Other avenues of association are also relevant. An apparently comical invitation to sneeze would have been rather more challenging and thought-provoking in 1921, so soon after the terrible influenza pandemic of 1918–1919. Indeed, the presence of the thermometer, and sugar to help the medicine go down—but which turns out not to be sugar at all—amplify this possible darker penumbra to the comic title. The final touch in this respect, is, of course, the bird cage—with its connotations of entrapment.

Mention should also be made of 'Rose Sélavy' in the title. It is anagramic of *'Eros, c'est la vie'*. Here, the medical connotations of the work's found elements point to a rather lighter comical interpretation wherein the character of erotic love cages one in, surrounds one with, apparently sweet things that turn out to be neither what they seem nor to be subject to volitional control. No real cure for Eros is available, even if one wanted one. One can see out of the cage, but cannot hope to leave it, ever. One might as well try to sneeze . . .

This work, then, can be interpreted as bringing together avenues of association between medicine, mortality, erotic love, in relation to the power or powerlessness of will.

Some significantly darker elements in Duchamp's aesthetic find expression in his most important late work—*Etant Donnes* (1946–1966). This tableau consists of an old wooden door (completely bordered by bricks), velvet, twigs gathered by Duchamp himself, leather stretched over the metal armature of a female form, lino, glass, an electric motor, and various other items.

The viewer's immediate access is to the door. It has the ambience of a benignly secret place, or one long abandoned. One can only view what lies behind the door by looking through a peephole in it. To fully experience the work, in other words, requires a complex and immediate perceptual relationship with the configuration rather than a perusal of it through photographs and the like.

It is disconcerting to have visual access only through these difficult means. Indeed, the discomfiture of the viewing conditions is an apt preparation for what the interior reveals. The female form is naked and holding a gas lamp. Duchamp's twigs and other background material are arranged as an eerie landscape—like a wooded park in the centre of a city.

The voyeuristic aspect of the work is made both manifest and difficult. Especially disturbing is the question of whether the female form is self-presented as sexually accessible, or is a dead body disposed of in an isolated place. The viewer is placed in the worst position—of having arrived for an assignation, or being the possible perpetrator of a crime, or a witness after the fact, or the discoverer of the crime. Matters are made even more complex by the fact that the lamp held by the woman is still lit.

Whichever interpretation might apply, the reality of this work is to exist as something glimpsed and conjectured upon rather than gathered up complete. And each interpretation carries with it a profoundly different set of moral implications for the viewer.

This brief outline of some of Duchamp's key works is extremely instructive. He may have been extremely critical *vis-à-vis* traditional aesthetic values; he may even have wanted to affirm the importance of art ideas over made objects, but, despite this, his assisted ready-mades and constructed tableaus have a remarkable *creative intricacy*.

Even in their good-humoured aspects they have broader connotations which allow them to locate themselves at the intersection of thoughts about love, death, the uncanny, release, and the like. They engage with contextual space in terms of imaginative associations and insights concerning mortality. Their phenomenological depth, in other words, has an existential as well as perceptual orientation.

Having introduced some key works by Duchamp as exemplars of Designated Art's aesthetic relevance, I shall now consider some interesting examples of it by other artists.

Part Three

A useful starting point is a work by Joseph Kosuth from 1965 entitled *A Four Color Sentence*. It is a sequence of neon lights which present the title of the work with each word in a different colour. In this and many other works from the mid-1960's and 1970's, Kosuth used theory about art—and its supposedly tautologous definition, to create visual configurations of one kind or another. Sometimes these involve texts, most of which tend to fall victim to sufficient paraphrasibilty.[5]

The present work is slightly different. Its basic strategy is sufficiently para- phrasable but the fact that it is, indeed, a sentence in four different colours sets up a visual interest whose full recognition demands that the viewer should have direct perceptual acquaintance with it. In fact, because colour is not usu- ally linked to the function of words, there is a kind of magical transformation of the properties of one thing into those of another—a weaker version of Du- champ-type strategies.

However, given the centrality of visual forms and words (and the relations between them) in human communication, Kosuth's object operates at an exis- tentially serious level in spite of itself. All words *qua* visible do have colour, but as these usually involve variations on black, they usually pass unnoticed.

Indeed, it is vital for linguistic communication that they should. For if we routinely attended to the physical characteristics of the embodying script, linguistic communication would become paralyzed by secondary detail, and would collapse.

Hence, by physically presenting the words in his work's title as the visual ba- sis of the work itself, Kosuth opens up different avenues of associational mean- ing. On the one hand there is the slightly clever game played with self-reference and rather problematic ideas about the nature of art; on the other there is the sheer uncanniness of the work in psychological terms.

In terms of the latter, Kosuth's piece invests language with an unexpected *visual aesthetic power*. This distraction from the function of normal linguistic communication is intoxicating by being both a relief from the commonplace, and yet one which hints slyly at the danger of paralysis through detail, noted earlier.

A rather different angle on Duchamp's legacy is presented by the *Arte Povera* tendency in Italy in the 1960's and 1970's. An *Untitled* work from 1968 by Gio- vanni Anselmo, for example, consists of a vertical granite block with copper wire and a fresh lettuce suspended from the block, with dirt/ashes gathered on the floor directly in front of the work.

Here there is a curious transposition. The configuration of lettuce and stone is reminiscent of a wreath laid upon a gravestone. Such expressions of mourning are commonplace—they are a visual routine which the bereaved go through.

Fig. 10. Giovanni Anselmo, *Untitled,* 1968, granite, lettuce, copper wire. Musée National d'Art Moderne, Paris—Centre Georges Pompidou, ©Anselmo Giovanni, ©Photo: CNAC/MNAM, Dist. RMN/©Philippe Migeat.

However, precisely because Anselmo's work performs a similar visual ritual using incongruous—even ludicrous—material (the fresh green colour of the lettuce is startling in itself), the ritual of wreath-placing is made into something more reflective. Anselmo's work thematizes the fact that such placing gravitates around a relation between organic life and cold stone.

Even more importantly, it makes this into something which cannot be taken for granted—made into a merely observed ritual. This is because if the work is to survive as an artwork, it has to be constantly renewed through replacing the living organic component. Here, there is no room for forgetting . . .

One of the most interesting and complex developments of Designated Art is the complex use it makes of photography and other idioms for mechanically reproducing images.

Consider in this respect, Louise Lawler. Her work in the 1970's and 1980's orientated itself towards the aesthetic potential of the relation between the whole or aspects of selected artworks, *and* their presentational contexts. In photographing these relations, she would give as much emphasis to effects or incidental details arising from the works (such as reflections) as to the actual work itself.

How many pictures? of 1989 is a beautiful example of this. It is a cibachrome photograph of the wooden-panelled floor of a gallery space, inflected by reflections from a Frank Stella abstract painting. In this case, the painting itself is not shown. We have only its glorious reflections.

There is one obvious and mundane avenue of ideas opened up by this work. It is to see it as a kind of deconstruction of the autonomy of the individual visual artwork. On these terms it is 'shown' that the artwork does not exist in complete isolation from the visual context of its presentation. This context blends with it, and may, in part, be responsible for some of the aesthetic effects attributed to the work in its supposedly autonomous being.

There is also a rather more powerful avenue of association opened up. For Lawler deals, in effect, with *found appearances*. There is a sense, of course, in which this is true of a great deal of photography itself. Some works are created from scenes discovered by chance which present great compositional opportunities.

However, Lawler's enterprise is based on searching out the momentary and otherwise lost visual 'fallout' which *accrues to the presentation of art specifically*. What is the general chance basis of felicitous photographic discovery is here pursued in a more focused and intrinsically aesthetically charged context.

There is a complex dialectic involved. On the one hand we are, of course, dealing with well-composed photographs, but these are ones which, at the same time, record the aesthetic ambience of artworks *other than themselves*.

In this latter, manifestly *Found* role there is a further internal dialectic of both sadness and reconciliation. The sadness consists of the fact that every art work has wonderful moments of poignant visual contextualization—the great majority of which are lost without ever being noticed.

Reconciliation arises from the fact that not only are fragments of these otherwise 'lost moments' preserved in Lawler's work, but that—as an enterprise—her projects encourage and guide the viewer in conserving similar moments from their own experience of art's shifting contextualizations. Lawler's found appearances, in other words, are inscribed with edifying potential for the viewer's own activities as well as for immediate aesthetic absorption.

The use of photography by Designated Art extends, of course, in many other directions. Some of the most interesting of these involve records of performance and body art (for example, Carolee Schneeman's important works of the 1970's). However, I shall now consider an example which involves photography used, as it were, to *achieve* performance for an indefinite period of time.

In a piece from 1994, the Canadian artist Cassandra Dam used a near life-size photograph of herself (taken on a timer), nude, addressing the viewer frontally. The pose itself is a subtle combination of assertiveness and an off-key 'matter of factness'.

Significantly, the image was not offered as a photograph *per se*, but was taken so as to be installed in her parents' house, in principle, on a permanent basis. (In this sense it functioned as a kind of permanent possibility of performance.)

The power of the work, of course, depends on the relation between the intrinsic content of the image and its unexpected location. In her preparations for the work, the artist was preoccupied by familiar concerns concerning the female body and the gaze, but *qua* its installational context, the relation of the artist's body and the gaze exceeds the parameters of standard gender issues.

It is especially powerful in its play-off against traditional family structures and values. To have a near life-size photograph of one's daughter in the nude—accessible to both family members and household visitors, provokes ideas concerning both parental authority and sibling responsibility.

For the non-family member of cruder sensibility, these ideas can range over a host of associations, some of them quite prurient. 'What a way for a woman to make a spectacle of herself. Displaying her boobs and bush quite shame-

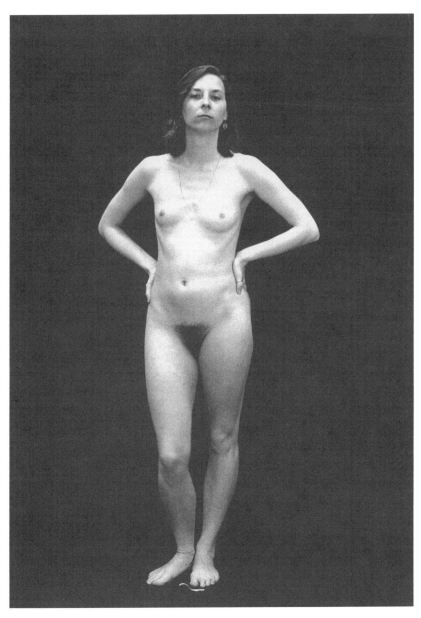

Fig. 11. Cassandra Dam, *Performance*, 1993, photography. By artist/model S. C. Dam.

lessly, not just to anyone, but to her own family! Imagine what her Dad must be thinking!'

For *any* viewer embedded in the norms and values of a patriarchal society, it is difficult to escape at least some initial reactions of this sort. With the male gaze, especially, this response easily transforms into one of direct sexual interest and unlikely fantasy.

In the artistically attuned, however, some further and more reflective ideas emerge. These centre on the recognition that, in Dam's project, ideas of na-ked body-ownership *vis-à-vis* the gaze are projected not only at a psychologi-cally and morally difficult level, but, indeed, at the very *family* level—*usually elided*—where contentious social attitudes concerning the body become en-trenched in the first place. Many *secrets* are submerged there . . .

However, whilst thematizing this zone of repression, Dam's project simul-taneously transcends it. The very fact that she could site the image in her own family home without problems in the first place, shows that issues surrounding naked body-ownership and the family do not have to be submerged. Indeed, if a family has developed mutual trust and respect, then such revelation of body can be taken as a celebration of such values.

The point is, then, that in using and contextualizing her body as described, Dam goes far beyond making some 'statement' about the body and the gen-dered gaze (on the dreary lines of Kruger *et al.*). There are different layers of ideas and associations involved which make the artist vulnerable, but, in so do-ing, render the work itself aesthetically complex by virtue of not resolving into one 'easy' interpretation.

In Dam's piece the photograph plays an essential role, and is not simply a means of documenting a performance. In other works the role played by proc-esses of documentation is more ambiguous. An interesting case of this is the work *Expanding in Space* performed by Marina Abramovic and Ulay (1977). It consists of a naked man and woman standing back to back between two mobile columns and then each walking straight into the pillar facing them simultane-ously. The action is repeated, with the columns gradually being pushed further and further back by the protagonists, until they have reached a point where they cannot shift anymore. Even then, the actions are repeated for a while, until Ulay walks away, and, later still, Abramovic completes the performance.

This work is stark in its evocations of the Sisyphean nature of human projects and, at another remove, relationships of alienation, yet inescapable involvement, between the genders. In this case, the recording of the performance on film has significance beyond documentation. For it means that the futile repetitions at the heart of the original performance can be repeated endlessly, in principle, through mechanical reproduction. The performance itself lasted thirty-two minutes, but its character resonates with connotations of endless continuation.

In providing the possibility of unlimited repetition, in other words, the film perpetuates the work's animating concept as well as providing its physical documentation. It underwrites the blind serial symbolic necessity that determines those individually contingent, willed impacts on the columns that are central to the work. Through this, it becomes a factor in the work's phenomenological depth.

Conclusion

In this chapter, then, I have described the conceptual structures of Designated Art and the ways in which these might be aesthetically tested. It is important to emphasize these aesthetic criteria, because in many respects Designated Art is an easy option. It is the perfect vehicle for the colonization of art practice by the management world of curators, critics, gallery owners, and investors.

Now whilst such art is parasitic on expectations derived from more traditional idioms, it does have its own interesting ways of embodying phenomenological depth. I noted in relation to Duchamp that whereas most abstract works are orientated towards the perceptual dimension of contextual space, his work connects rather more directly to the realm of imaginative association, and in particular to factors that are more than visual.

This is not to say that other abstract idioms cannot do this; it is just that in their case the extended visual configuration itself, rather than the idea which it embodies, is the immediate focus of aesthetic engagement.

The point concerning Duchamp is, I think, true of Designated Art in general. Because work of this kind involves the recognition of Found elements, it follows, accordingly, that it will be the sensibly embodied idea and its imaginative ramifications, rather than the visual character of the object alone, which tends to form the main channel of aesthetic response.

Such works can, of course, fail as art—as in those cases where we have only a visually indifferent, sufficiently paraphrasable idea. However, they can also have great imaginative success. Indeed, in my examples extending from Duchamp to Dam and Abramovic, I have tried to show how Designated Art gives the aesthetics of phenomenological depth a distinctively existential inflection.

As most of the traditional idioms have now exhausted their potential for large-scale innovation, future art practice is likely to be driven by conceptual approaches which combine traditional idioms with Found material and the use of new technology. I shall address some of the issues here in Chapter 9.

8   The Phenomenology of Photography

Introduction

Picturing and sculpture, of course, have evolved over many thousands of years, and their origins cannot be assigned with any certainty. Photography, in contrast, was *invented* by specific individuals in the early nineteenth century.

Despite its recentness, however, photography's particular dimensions of phenomenological depth have only been theorized in a partial way. The dominant approaches are reductionist, and one of them—that of Pierre Bourdieu—shows just why photography is so problematic in theoretical terms. He remarks that

> The position of photography within the hierarchy of legitimacies, halfway between 'vulgar' practices, apparently abandoned to the anarchy of tastes and noble cultural practices, subject to strict rules, explains . . . the ambiguity of the practices which it provokes, particularly amongst the members of the privileged classes. The efforts of some devotees to establish photography as a fully legitimate art practice almost always appears foolish and desperate because it can do practically nothing to counteract the social key to photography, which is never recalled so strongly as when one seeks to contradict it.[1]

Bourdieu's point here is that photography is more than common visual communication, but is, nevertheless, *so* useful in terms of its mundane social documentary functions that these functions always subvert attempts to present it as high art. Issues of technique and form can never quite overcome the spectre of documentary significance.

However, this is not the insuperable problem which Bourdieu takes it to be. The key is to find an explanation of what makes photography art, which is based on factors involving both technical and formal achievements, *and* photography's documentary functions.

As one might expect, this amounts to a sustained analysis of photography's *phenomenological depth*. Most interestingly, this task of analysis can draw on a very unexpected source—Roland Barthes.

His emphases on the 'death of the author' and 'intertextuality' have tended to shift attention from questions of form to ways in which patterns of signification are historically acquired and distributed in art, and also to the shifting social codes which are implied in such signification.

One major consequence of this is the view that meaning in art cannot be fixed without 'closure', i.e. an arbitrary delimiting of its potentially endless generative scope. (It is to suggest this scope that Barthes prefers the playful neologism 'signifiance' rather than the term 'significance' in relation to artistic meaning.)

A further consequence of the approach is that the subject is, to all intents and purposes, understood mainly as an effect of the signs through which desire is articulated. This renders the subject highly amenable to psychoanalytic interpretations.

The problematics of such interpretations have already been dealt with at length earlier on in this book. For present purposes, I shall focus instead on an extraordinary transformation. In *Camera Lucida* (the last book published by Barthes in his lifetime) we are told that

> It is the fashion, nowadays, among photography's commentators (sociologists and semiologists) to seize upon a semantic relativity: no 'reality' (great scorn for the 'realists' who do not see that the photograph is always coded), nothing but artifice.[2]

Against these reductionist approaches Barthes asserts that

> realists do not take the photograph for a 'copy' of reality, but for an emanation of past reality: a magic, not an art. To ask whether a photograph is analogical or coded is not a good means of analysis. The important thing is that the photograph possesses an evidential force, and that its testimony bears not on the object but on time. From a phenomenological viewpoint, in the photograph, the power of authentication exceeds the power of representation.[3]

What Barthes recognizes here (and develops throughout his book) is that photography has unique characteristics as a medium, and that these give it distinctive effects. It has—in the terms of the present work—phenomenological depth.

In this chapter, then, I start from Barthes' approach and take it much further. Part One offers an exposition of the main claims in *Camera Lucida*. In

Part Two, these are addressed in more critical terms so as to develop his intuitive insights concerning phenomenological depth and its key existential implications. This approach is then taken further through critically engaging with some ideas from Susan Sontag in Part Three.

Part One

Barthes identifies the core of photography's meaning in terms as follows:

I call 'photographic referent' not the optionally real thing to which an image or sign refers but the necessarily real thing which has been placed before the lens, without which there would be no photograph.[4]

Both the photograph's 'That-has-been' character and its distance from the original referent are founded on the mechanical and chemical basis of photography as a technical process.

From a real body, which was there proceed radiations which ultimately touch me, who am here; the duration of the transmission is insignificant; the photograph of the missing being, as Sontag says, will touch me like the delayed rays of a star. A sort of umbilical cord links the body of the photographed thing to my gaze: light, though impalpable, is here a carnal medium, a skin I share with anyone who has been photographed.[5]

On these terms, then, the referent of the photographic image *must* have existed at some time or other by virtue of what photography is, in ontological terms. Autographic media such as painting and sculpture offer only direct traces of those gestures by the artist, *by means of which* the referent is represented. In such cases, whether or not the subject ever existed in reality is not an issue which can be resolved with certainty purely on the basis of the image's mode of representation.

The photograph, in contrast, is *causally rigid* in terms of its relation to the referent (though Barthes himself does not put it like this). What we see is, by virtue of the mechanical and chemical processes involved, a direct causal trace of the referent's visible being. And even if the photo is a fake, it is composed of elements that involve the physical traces of some visual item or states of affairs that have actually existed.

On the basis of this distinctive causal rigidity, photography can be characterized in terms of three fundamental aspects—the viewpoint of agent, subject, or spectator.

These factors overlap, especially in relation to what Barthes calls the 'pose'. He interprets this as follows:

> Looking at a photograph, I inevitably include in my scrutiny the thought of that instant, however brief, in which a real thing happened to be motionless before the eye. I project the present photograph's immobility upon the past shot, and it this arrest which constitutes the pose.[6]

This is analyzed in still more detail as follows (first from the viewpoint of the agent of the photograph):

> by attesting that the object has been real, the photograph surreptitiously induces the belief that it is alive, because of that delusion which makes us attribute to Reality an absolutely superior, somehow eternal value; but by shifting this reality to the past ('this has been'), the photograph suggests that it is already dead. Hence it would be better to say that photography's inimitable feature (its *noeme*) is that someone has seen the referent (even if it is a matter of objects) in *flesh and blood*, or again *in person*.[7]

On these terms, the taking of a photograph is testimony to fact that what is photographed was, thereby, witnessed by someone. The complex ramifications of this entwine with what happens when one is the subject of a photograph. As Barthes puts it:

> In front of the lens, I am at the same time: the one I think I am, the one the photographer thinks I am, and the one he makes use of to exhibit his art.[8]

More complex still,

> the Photograph (the one I *intend*) represents that very subtle moment when, to tell the truth, I am neither subject nor object but a subject who feels he is becoming an object: I then experience a micro-version of death (of parenthesis).[9]

The existential complexity of engaging with the photograph becomes even greater when it comes to our role as spectators. Here Barthes emphasizes the photographic image's status as an emphatic particular[10]—a phenomenon which for him, personally, is exemplified most profoundly by a photograph of his own mother as a child.

For Barthes, this image expresses her essential identity *'the impossible science of the unique being'.*[11] This is not just a case of identification. Rather,

> it accomplishes the unheard-of identification of reality ('that has been') with truth ('there-she-is!'; it bears the effigy to that crazy point where affect (love,

compassion, grief, enthusiasm, desire) is a guarantee of being. It then approaches, to all intents, madness.[12]

There are also other spectatorial factors which contribute to this 'madness'. These include a distinction between 'studium' and 'punctum', and the notion of an 'air'. The studium is the dimension of photography which pertains to its narrative/cultural significance; the 'punctum' is an incidental feature—a telling detail or aspect which instigates a wealth of ideas or feelings, and which makes us want to be present in the photographed scene. The 'air' is a specific lucidity of pose which successfully affirms the worth or value of its referent, as well as its identity. (The photograph of Barthes' mother is—for him at least—an example of this.)[13]

One other spectatorial aspect of the photograph is of profound significance. For Barthes, what the photograph says of its referent is, in effect, 'that is dead and that is going to die'.[14] This paradoxical conjunction suggests a connection between photography and resurrection—not in the sense of the photograph bringing back the dead, but rather in its radical affirmation that it represents something which actually existed.

A key factor here is what Barthes calls 'concomitance'—things existing together or in connection with one another. This encompasses both items in the photograph, and their relation to the viewer. The photo

> makes me lift my head, allows me to compute life, death, the inexorable extinction of the generations . . . I am the reference of every photograph, and this is what generates my astonishment in addressing myself to the fundamental question: why is it that I am alive *here and now*?[15]

Given all these considerations, it is hardly surprising that Barthes should conclude that through photography's embodiment and articulation of 'intractable reality' it attains its own kind of 'ecstasy'.[16] This is not just the *signifiance* of textual meaning noted in the Introduction to this chapter; it is an affective response based on what is distinctive to photography—i.e. its phenomenological depth.

Part Two

Having identified and connected the key points in Barthes' position overall, it is now time to engage with them more critically. A first problem to note is that whilst he emphasizes the phenomenological aspect of his approach, some important contextual phenomena of an existential kind are built into it.

In this respect, we will recall Barthes affirmations of the 'punctum'—or telling incidental detail, and the 'air'—a compositional or stylistic factor which unselfconsciously discloses the worth or value of something. We will also recall his important clarifications of the introspective richness of how we relate to the camera in terms of the one who takes the picture, the one who is thus pictured, and the one who looks at the photograph. Each of these aspects involves complex *intimations of mortality*.

Now the punctum and air are not features which are in any way intrinsic to photography (though Barthes seems to think that they are). The famous little mirror in van Eyck's *Betrothal of the Arnolfini*, for example, is a telling example of the former, whilst the tender gesture of the elder in Rembrandt's *Jewish Wedding* is a perfect example of 'air'. It may be that the occurrence of such factors in photography gives them an experiential impact that is different from their occurrence in other media, but they are not features intrinsic to photography itself.

Barthes' linkage of photography to intimations of mortality, in contrast, is grounded on factors which *are* distinctive to photography. But we must make an important qualification here. For whilst these responses are grounded in the ontology of photography, whether or not they are manifest is a function of the relation between particular photographs, and particular individuals, in particular historical circumstances. They are privileged interpretative perspectives based on photography's causal rigidity, but not features which are themselves intrinsic to the description of what photography is (i.e. to what Barthes calls its *noeme*).

Daguerrotypes and the very earliest photographs, for example, involve long time-exposures, and a limited range of immobile subjects. This means that whilst the ontological structure of photography is in place, it is not historically and technologically developed enough to bring out all the distinctive intimations of mortality noted by Barthes.

Indeed, whilst Barthes takes the photograph to be an intrinsic testimony to someone having witnessed the referent, this does not have to be the case. There are circumstances where photographs are taken without someone looking through the lens, or without having seen the referent as presented to the lens. This means that the link between photographic agency and spectatorship cannot be intrinsic to photography *per se*.

Now it might be thought that Barthes' position here is actually a very commendable one. What really counts is not the ontology of the photograph *per se*, but rather the special responses which it enables under different contextual conditions.

However, whilst these responses are important there remain some key factors still to be clarified in terms of photography's basic ontology. In fact, it is this material which gives photography its most significant phenomenological depth.

To see why, we can start from Barthes' claim that photography is violent—in the sense of filling the spectator's sight with an image-content whose existence is not subject to the will. As he puts it,

> until this day no representation could assure me of the past of a thing except by intermediaries, but with the Photograph, my certainty is immediate: no one in the world can undeceive me. The Photograph then becomes a bizarre medium, a new form of hallucination: false on the level of perception, true on the level of time . . .[17]

On these terms, then, whilst reality's perceptual mobility is distorted by photography's static images, such images express temporal truth. They testify that there was at least one moment in time, necessarily, when their referent(s) existed.

It is interesting that Barthes also links this truth to the 'unique' and 'contingent' character of such images but without clarifying this linkage's broader philosophical ramifications. I shall now do this.

First, we must inquire about the sense in which a photographic image is unique. One can, of course, have many copies of a print or digital original, but these are taken from a negative or from a specific configuration of electrical signals (as in digital photography). In such cases the prints are tokens of a type, and it is the type which is unique.[18]

Of course one can take photographs of the same immobile object at different periods of time, but in every such case, the original negative or configuration of signals is literally unique—even if one cannot tell the prints taken from different originals, apart from one another. No matter how perceptually indiscernible they may be, the type or original presents the referent as it appeared at a unique moment in, or for a unique period of, time.

This has some remarkable consequences. Every appearance of a visible item is contingent, in the sense that it can be seen from a number of other possible perceptual viewpoints. However, each of the item's actual appearances, i.e. ones which are realized through the item being perceived or through its appearance being mechanically recorded at a specific position in time and, where relevant, space, is a part of that object's full identity, henceforth, ontologically speaking. It forms a unique component in the causal history of the item. If it had not been encountered or recorded in just that place and time, its causal history would have been slightly different, and from this slight difference, other differences would have developed exponentially.

Hence, whilst each actual spatio-temporal position of an item comes into being and passes away with seeming contingency, it forms a *necessary* component in the identity of that item. The causal rigidity of the photograph's relation to its referent not only shows that the referent once existed, it also reveals one of the particular visual aspects which is a necessary factor in that referent's identity.

Ironically, through being photographed, the aspect comes to exist independently of the object as a causal trace. But because of the causal rigidity of its relation to the referent, we know that this trace presents an inescapable aspect of that referent's identity. The photograph not only testifies to the necessity of its referent having existed, but also to features which were, or are, *essential* to that existence. Its expression of the concrete particular is even richer than Barthes imagines.

Let us now think through his insight that the photograph presents its referent as something which is dead and is going to die. Again, this characterization needs qualification. It is literally true of photographs of people or other living things who have died since the photograph was taken.

However, many photographs are of people or living things which are still alive, and many other such images, of course, are of inanimate items—in which case it seems absurd to say that they are dead and they are going to die.

We should, therefore, rephrase Barthes' description so that it is ontologically exact. It would now hold that the photograph shows 'what has gone and is going into the past'. If something is in a photograph, then even if it still actually exists, the image shows one of its past appearances in the form of a present one.

The notion of 'form' needs remarking on here. Obviously the photograph is not a duplicate of its referent, but because of the existence and identity factors analyzed above, it is ontologically bound to it. Whilst the photograph survives, so does the form of some of its referent's visual aspects—and it is the visual dimension which describes what is most fundamental to something's existence and identity, namely its mode of occupying space.

But the visual aspects of the referent in the photograph are from time past.

It presents something which is known to have gone but which is always accessible through the immediately present trace of its visible aspects. Barthes observes rightly that

> What the photograph reproduces to infinity has occurred only once: the photograph mechanically repeats what could never be repeated existentially.[19]

His own emphasis is on the temporal dimension. My analysis, however, emphasizes the trace of visual form, precisely because of the ontological fundamentality of the spatial dimension outlined above. It is, indeed, the creative tension between temporal loss and spatial presence which makes of photography much more than the imprint of something which has existed at least once.

The significance of this may range deeper still in metaphysical terms. Nietzsche proposed that every event recurs eternally. His reasons for this belief are quite specific and complex.[20] But it is possible to give it a broader justification.

For if reality exists independently of the human perception of it, this means that the ultimate nature of the event cannot be given a sufficient characterization from the finite human viewpoint. In terms of reality *per se*—wherein there is no single absolute position in relation to which things can be described as past, present, or future—any event is, as it were eternally embedded in the whole. It does not go away—except from the finite viewpoint.

Such eternal embeddedness within the whole cannot be perceived, of course, in literal terms by a finite subject. There is a spatial whole combined from heterogeneous elements which—from the human perspective—*appears* as an event. In the context of the whole, it does not have that event-character. However, it can at least be understood through an image—the idea of eternal recurrence. We make sense of the eternal embeddedness of events through the *idea* of them recurring without end.

And this offers a startling connection with the photograph. The photographic image is itself a crude partial sensible presentation of the idea of the eternal recurrence of spatial events. In this way, it offers an intuitive sensible *image of an image* of a truth about reality as it exists in its ultimate form.

Hence, if this metaphysical reading is correct, it follows that not only does photography offer a crude preservation of the passing event, but, in so doing, it also points to a broader fabric of the real wherein that event is eternally inscribed. The photographic image, therefore, is a psychologically profound exemplar of our complex mode of belonging to reality.

Part Three

There are several other key aspects of photography's phenomenological depth which remain to be dealt with. One of them constellates around a factor that is rather submerged in Barthes' approach but which surfaces very markedly in Susan Sontag's ideas. Like Barthes, she notes that

> All photographs are *memento mori*. To take a photo is to participate in another person's (or thing's) mortality, vulnerability, mutability. Precisely by slicing out this moment and freezing it, all photographs testify to time's relentless melt.[21]

However, Sontag develops these points in a direction very different from Barthes. For her, through photography,

> Reality as such is redefined—as an item for exhibition, as a record for scrutiny, as a target for surveillance. The photographic exploration and duplication of the world fragments continuities and feeds the pieces into an interminable dossier, thereby providing possibilities of control that could not even be dreamed of under the earlier system of recording information: writing.[22]

The details of this in Sontag's theory are most interesting. We are told that

> To photograph is to appropriate the thing photographed. It means putting oneself into a certain relation to the world that feels like knowledge—and, therefore like power.[23]

Indeed,

> To photograph people is to violate them, by seeing them as they never see themselves, by having knowledge of them they can never have; it turns people into objects that can be symbolically possessed.[24]

Sontag holds further that photography offers a kind of 'surrogate possession' of cherished persons or things, which gives the photo something of the character of unique objects. It also sets up a consumer relation to events which is alienating, insofar as rather than experiencing events *per se* we, as it were, 'certify' them through the photograph, and make ending-up-in-a-photograph the reason for searching out the event in the first place. This, and photography's multiple and duplicating possibilities, fulfil a promise which is 'inherent' from the very beginning, namely photography's capacity 'to democratize all experiences by turning them into images.'[25]

Now if these details of Sontag's approach were correct, photography would be a mode of representation which is inherently ideological in the sense of being inauthentic or 'false consciousness'. But this is incorrect. Indeed, Sontag is making some rather more serious errors of the kind which I identified previously in relation to Barthes, namely the conflation of intrinsic with contextual factors.

Consider the claim, for example, that photography involves a kind of aggression insofar as it shows the subject from a position which the subject does not see himself or herself from. There could be some truth in this. Feminist critiques of pornographic representation have put a case for this in terms of photography's use in gender-determined social contexts.

However, in other circumstances it can be argued to have the opposite significance. To see oneself from a position which is unavailable in one's immediate perception of oneself can be an exhilarating and liberating experience.[26] And whilst the photograph in its most basic form offers only a single 'atomized' perspective on the real, its very singularity can illuminate and act as a focal point for unconventional understanding as well as for mundane visual documentation. Its ontological detachment can, in other words, in some contexts energize its interpretative potential.[27]

Sontag is certainly correct to note how photography can usurp the function of genuine experience (e.g. in holiday snapshots) but again viewing reality in terms of its photogenic character need not always have this alienated character. It may lead one to attend closely to the visual details and complexities of persons and places, in a way that one would not otherwise do. This might serve an educative function in terms of how such a person negotiates the aesthetic and poetic dimensions of the visual.

The awkwardness of Sontag's approach is focused in a major contradiction. Having emphasized photography's intrinsically aggressive character, she then backpedals on the claim. We are told, for example, that photography is 'essentially an act of non-intervention.'[28] Indeed,

> Between photographer and subject, there has to be distance. The camera doesn't rape, or even possess, though it may presume, intrude, trespass, distort, exploit, and, at the farthest reach of metaphor, assassinate . . .[29]

Clearly, the point is here that, in many circumstances, the photo can be taken irrespective of whether the subject of the image chooses it or not and will only focus on a limited range of visual aspects. But whilst this can be existentially negative in the way it is done or used, this is not absolute. Some element of passivity on the photographer's part will also be involved. He or she has by no means total control of the situation.

Sontag's problems here are extremely instructive in terms of their origin. Her analysis constellates, in effect, around the implications of *snapshot* photography. She emphasizes factors which are mainly functions and effects of the instantly captured image realized in specific kinds of socio-historical context.[30]

However, the wealth of factors which Sontag identifies, and the very fact that she sees them as intrinsic to photography, points towards an interesting and decisive issue. It is that of whether there is something about the snapshot *itself* which is of intrinsic significance for the ontology of photography.

Now historically speaking, the technology of the snapshot is secondary to that of time-exposure, and it arose in a specific cultural context. However, in ontological terms, there is a case for regarding it as prior—as something which is intrinsic to the medium *in its most complete form*.

This is because (whilst there is still a role for time exposure) *the immediate shot makes time—and thence the recording of action—into an active feature of the photographic image*, rather than a factor which has to be overcome in order to even take a picture.

The image taken by the immediate click of the shutter, in other words, is what photography must tend towards if the full range of its semantic possibilities is to be realized.

This offers a broad parallel with the achievement of fully developed linear perspective in pictorial representation. Through linear perspective it becomes possible to represent visual reality as a *systematically* connected continuum, of which the particular picture functions as a spatio-temporal cross-section.[31] This brings with it an enormous expansion of the picture's informational uses and aesthetic possibilities.

Analogously, the snapshot allows photography to encompass the realm of action, thus enabling the single photograph to offer a spatio-temporal cross-section of systematically continuous reality.

Again, this brings a massive boost in terms of photography's informational and aesthetic possibilities. Indeed, (though Sontag clearly does not realize it) the atomized character of the photograph is primarily a *physical* characteristic of its status as a single print or whatever, and is much compensated for by that systematic continuum of reality beyond its physical edges, which it posits in virtual terms.

Conclusion

By analyzing Barthes and Sontag's ideas then, I have identified photography's causal rigidity and particularity, and the significance of the snapshot, as the basis of photography's phenomenological depth. The former factors establish an intrinsic connection between the photograph and the existence and essence of its referent, from which many distinctive effects flow. The snapshot is a refinement of photography's basic ontology which allows it to make time into an active factor in photographic meaning rather than an obstacle which must be overcome in order to take a photograph.

One issue, however, remains. It does not feature much—if at all—in Barthes' and Sontag's approaches, but, curiously enough, is one of the most perceptually central features of the photograph, despite not being remarked upon under normal circumstances.

I am referring to the scalar variation of size which the photograph characteristically performs in relation to its referent. Photographs are very rarely life-size, and when they are, it is generally through being turned into a poster rather than being an actual photograph.

The question arises, then, as to whether this photographic diminution of scale is a mere contingency of the medium, or something more meaningful. In terms of a particular photograph being larger or smaller than its referent, this is entirely contingent upon personal and historical contexts. However, the sheer capacity to vary the size of the referent *per se* is something intrinsic to the ontology of the medium itself.

It is not, of course, unique to photography, insofar as similar transformations of scale are also intrinsic to any pictorial art. However, in photography, it takes on a distinctive and extraordinary power precisely because the variation of spatial scale constellates around a causally rigid trace of the referent's visual appearance. This, of course, is a constraint, but at the same time it means that in varying the scale of the image one is acting on a causal trace of the real, in a way that one is not so doing in drawing or painting the referent.

There is some analogy here with photography's character as an image of recurrence (outlined at the end of Part Two of this chapter). There the photo enables its referent to recur in symbolic terms both spatially and temporally. This gives a kind of transcendence of finitude which is, nevertheless, based on factors—bound up with existence and identity—which are basic to finitude.

In the case of scalar variation, one has a kind of symbolic power over the referent's appearance which transcends what is physically possible in relation to it. But what one varies here is visual appearance, i.e. the fundamental expression of that which is the basis of any existence, namely space-occupancy.

The ontology of photography, then, is intrinsically connected to factors which are basic to our embodied inherence in the world. Our intuitive fascination with this is the basis of photography's phenomenological depth. The fact that photography has such intrinsic meaning is precisely what enables its informational function to be *reconfigured* as an object of aesthetic, and thence artistic significance, in its own right.

9 Ontology and Aesthetics of Digital Art

Introduction

Many would claim that the traditional idioms of visual art have lost their capacity for large-scale innovation. Arthur Danto,[1] for example, has argued that the exhaustion of innovation is symptomatic of art having completed a historical process of self-investigation (aimed at clarifying its own essence).

I have indicated some of the problems with Danto's approach elsewhere.[2] There is no 'grand narrative' of art's self-discovery at issue. The exhaustion of large-scale artistic innovation is due, rather, to the *structural* conventions and properties which are constitutive of pictorial representation simply being incapable of further significant development *at the structural level itself.*

There are limits to new ways in which the representation of three-dimensional material can be achieved within the traditional idioms alone. The emergence of abstract art opened up new possibilities here, but these too appear to have now been exhaustively developed in structural terms.[3]

In talking of structural factors, I mean specifically two basic conventions, and a group of visual properties. The first convention is the *semantic* capacity to project likenesses of three-dimensional items; the second is the syntactic capacity to represent these as spatially connected states of affairs—where, for example, relations in front and behind can be distinguished from above and below. (Mathematical perspective and its variants are the most systematic forms of this.)[4]

The structurally relevant visual properties include transitions from light to dark, and the relation between contour, mass, and detail in the delineation of form. In painting, of course, these factors must also be related to colour.

Now if we try to explain why a specific artist is so important, or how a new movement or stylistic tendency serves to extend the scope of visual art, then reference to the role of structural features is inescapable. Artists and tendencies refine or innovate by reworking the relation between key structural features so as to open up new possibilities for other artists.

The problem is, however, that the physical nature of media such as drawing and painting places constraints on how far the structural features can be taken in new directions. To give an important example (which I will return to in Part One of this chapter), when creating a picture, an artist operates, *necessarily*, along an axis defined by two logical extremes. The picture can be created either by marking out the *contours* of a three-dimensional object *or* by assembling and blending marks so as to represent its *mass*, or, of course, by combining elements of both.[5] How the artist relates to this axis is a matter of choice, but that he or she *must* relate to it is determined by what a picture is—as a function of line or mass, or combinations thereof.

Because this axis is so inescapable, it is hardly surprising that it has sustained a great deal of artistic innovation. An artist who achieves things of substance in relation to this—or other structural properties and conventions—at the same time opens up possibilities of relevance to other artists also.

Ingres' drawings, for example, are executed with an economy and precision of contour which is almost astonishing. They are exemplars of what might be got from a contour-orientation. At the other extreme we find someone such as Frank Auerbach whose paintings show the dramatic visual potential of creating form from mass by using impastos piled up to such a degree that an element of relief-modelling appears.[6] Now artists may come along whose control of contour is even finer than Ingres, or whose creation of mass is even more painterly than Auerbach. But the point is that they will only be working around extremes which have already defined the broad scope of the contour-mass structural axis.

With more analysis, similar considerations could be shown to hold also in relation to the other structural conventions and properties. Since their basic scope has already been established through the work of many individuals and movements, they cannot be developed significantly further so as to sustain radical new movements or 'isms'.

Of course, it is still possible for artists to achieve *individual* creative styles. It is also possible for them to use the established idioms in new and interesting ways—often by combining them, or linking them to critical ideas about the nature and function of art. But these are creative in terms of how established media are *used*, rather than in terms of developments which expand the very structure of picturing, sculpture, or abstraction, *qua* modes of representation.

Obviously, the points which I am making require much more substantial argument in order to be compelling. However, if we can accept them as a viable working hypothesis concerning the limits of traditional art, then it becomes possible to contextualize the potential of new—electronically based—media in very interesting ways.

The basic strategy here is to argue that some aspects of these media actually extend the structural scope of visual representation *per se*. This can involve, on the one hand, significant development of some of the traditional idioms' key visual properties and related effects (roughly paralleling, for example, the way in which the insistent development of chiaroscuro radically changed pictorial art, from the early seventeenth century onwards).

On the other hand, it can involve distinctive ontological factors which involve semantic, syntactic, and broader aesthetic features which build on—and then exceed—what traditional representation and abstraction can offer. This would be structural innovation of the most radical kind.

Innovations in either of these directions can change existing alignments in the relation between object and subject of experience. Literally the world is shown in new ways, which open up new cognitive possibilities in our response to it. This is the realm of *phenomenological depth*.

Now, of course, many new media works combine visual, written, and audio material in ways which obliterate traditional boundaries between art forms. However, many other such works maintain a primarily visual emphasis. These will be the focus of my analysis. I will concentrate specifically on key points of interface and difference between the traditional idioms and those *visually orientated images and configurations which are computer generated or which depend upon computer technology for their full visual realization.*

It is common practice nowadays to use the term *digital art* in relation to such computer-dependent visual idioms.[7] I will follow this usage. Text-based works will only figure in the analysis insofar as they emphasize the text *qua* visual.

Part One addresses some specific hybrids of traditional and digital art, and the way in which the latter radicalizes some of the structural visual properties noted earlier. In Part Two, I identify some ontological features which are distinctive to digital idioms, and which extend the structural scope of visual representation and abstraction. Part Three explores two further important aspects of this extension—namely interactive and evolutionary programs and hardware.

In Part Four, I consider, in detail, the implications of the foregoing for how art might be seen as transformed and taken in new directions, in terms of both the structural scope of visual representation, and the concept of art itself. In the Conclusion, I reflect on the new kind of 'aura' which accrues to digital art, and the possibility of new 'isms'.

Part One

Digital art centres on electronically based technology utilizing mathematical algorithms for the acquisition, storage, processing, and presentation of information. The information in question is often realized in a visual format (rather than through text or numbers alone) and can consist of generated material (based on mathematical formulae or 'painted' using bodily held instruments and dedicated hardware), or of information derived from a scanned source (including already existing images which have been converted to a format which is readable via the appropriate hardware).

In their *discrete* mode (as I shall call it), such images are presented on individual computer screens or larger scale Liquid Crystal Display (LCD) formats directed by computer technology. There are also what I shall call *distributed* modes of digitally generated images or visual environments based on the use of computer-directed optical effects such as Light-Emitting Diode (LED) lights, which are not confined to a single screen, or which are created through linking many such screens and other optical devices. Both discrete and distributed digital imagery have played a decisive role in the emergence of computer-based art since the 1960's.

As a starting point, I shall address some possibilities presented by hybrid combinations of digital art and traditional idioms, looking at the significant ways in which they modify one another.

Two illuminating examples here are Chris Finley's *Goo Goo Pow Wow 2* and Joseph Nechvatal's *birth Of the viractual*, both from 2001. The former work begins with a digital template constrained in terms of shape, form, and colour, by the imaging program through which it is realized. The compositional elements are combined and varied digitally, and then executed as a painting by the artist himself—working within the formal constraints inherent in the original imaging program.

Nechvatal's work involves compositional elements modified by a virus-like program. The files of this interaction are then sent via the net to a remote location to be painted by a computer-driven robotic machine.

These examples show two basic possibilities—works created by digital programs which issue in artefacts that are hand-made or involve some autographic aspect; or works issuing in traditional art-type artefacts but which are entirely digital in their creation and execution. The digital procedures in both cases are aesthetically validated by the fact that they invest the final image with a distinctive character.

In this respect, two characteristics are of special importance. First the capacity to define forms with hyper-clarity and sharpness; and second, the opposite capacity to blend forms in masses with unparalleled smoothness, nuance, and at levels of the utmost visual complexity.

It should be emphasized that these are not simply opposites. Rather they are the extreme developments of that contour-mass axis which I described in my Introduction. To reiterate: on the one hand, one can create a picture by marking an outline; or, on the other hand, one can create it by linking and blending marks to define spatial masses.

Most pictures of course involve elements of both, and there are endless ways of combining them or articulating them individually. However, the digital or digitally informed drawing, painting, or print, can deploy either or (in some complex works) both of these definitive factors with a precision and complexity that is alien to normal, exclusively gesture-based, image-making.

Some artists, of course, can execute hyper-clear outlines or the most extraordinary intricate nuances and transitions of form by hand, but digital imagery achieves these to a much higher and sustained degree. Indeed, they are the medium's commonplace characteristics, and are found in many works which are digitally realized on-screen without being 'translated' subsequently into an autographic idiom.

It should be emphasized that this clarity and complexity of three-dimensional definition in the most 'realistic' digital imagery is so intense that some artists[8] are occasionally described as producing a form of sculpture—even though the image is still projected on a two-dimensional screen.

Of course, it is not sculpture really, but this very usage, in itself, indicates just how intense digital illusionistic effects can be, and that what is involved here is not just a mode of appearance, but one which is startling and unsettling in a positive way. It invokes a new aspect of phenomenological depth.

The intervention of digital factors is also of the greatest significance for physically three-dimensional work. In this respect, one might consider the importance of *distributed* digital visual configurations (in the sense described earlier) for installation/assemblage art.

Such art involves things brought together by an artist so as to define and give content to a specific viewed space, or space for viewing and acting upon. The space in question can be installed or assembled within an existing one (such as a room) or it can actively modify its location by physical intervention upon it, or by controlling the conditions of visual access to it.

Installation and assemblage art was once very much avant-garde. However, it has become such a familiar idiom since the late 1950's as to be more or less mainstream in contemporary art practice. The significance of distributed digital imaging (and computers in general) for enhancing the visionary scope of installation/assemblage has continuously revitalized the idiom.

An excellent example of this is Erwin Redl's work. His *Matrice* series (ongoing since 2000) uses strings, and as it were, curtains of small LED lights which have been programmed to change colour, gradually. The series has a dominant twofold structure. In some cases, they seem to open up (or amplify) the *interior* physical space of the room in a way that is suggestive of layers of inner atomic structure; in other cases, they virtually extend the walls *outwards* through the suggestion of similar structures.

Now one of the reasons why installation/assemblage art has become mainstream is because it complements a broader characteristic of postmodern culture—namely a suspicion of fixed categories and the idea of things simply being present to perception, or to knowledge, as such. (The widespread interest in deconstructive strategies in various forms of literary thought and cultural analysis is one of the most direct expressions of this.)

Installation/assemblage art allows something of this phenomenological depth to be enjoyed as a sensory spectacle through a kind of optical (or in some cases, tactile, also) deconstruction of the artworks' traditionally unitary visual presence into a function of intersecting elements and layers of meaning.

Digital imagery and control technology is a key factor in such visual strategies. Quantitatively speaking, it enables more visual dimensions to be deployed in the occupied or mediated space; qualitatively speaking, the complexity and nuances of these visual structures are, themselves, only possible through the use of computer-based technology. Redl's work is a splendid example of this.

The function of digital imagery in the work I have considered so far is mainly one of positive intervention upon established artistic idioms. This intervention extends the scope of these idioms, by allowing their fundamental structures to be radicalized in ways which exceed what is available to digitally unassisted artistic practice.

Fig. 12. Erwin Redl, *Matrix II*, 2000, green LED lights, single LED wire strand, hanging mechanism, weights. Collection Museum of Contemporary Art San Diego. Museum purchase with funds from the International Collectors and the Annenberg Foundation. Photographer: Pablo Mason ©Erwin Redl 2000.

However, as well as this interventional role, digital art has more autonomous aesthetic functions. These are based on characteristics which are logically unique to discrete digital imagery. It is to consideration of these I now turn.

Part Two

The first distinctive factor is of a perceptual kind. Any pictorial representation involves the projection of a virtual third dimension from a virtual two-dimensional base. I say 'virtual' here in relation to the latter, because no plane surface is, *qua* physical object, flat in absolute terms. Such things as pictures and drawings have a flat appearance, but under close examination their physically three-dimensional nature (no matter how attenuated) will emerge.

Now the digital image's LCD and other display screens appear rather more insistently two-dimensional than autographic picturing. They are *physically flatter* than such conventional media. However, ironically enough, this flatness actually facilitates their capacity to project three-dimensional content in an especially insistent way. This is because physical flatness has no overtones of autographic presence in a way that even the most well-finished paintings do.

This insistent evocation of intense three-dimensional illusion is enhanced by the (previously discussed) precision and nuanced complexity with which digital imagery can be generated. Such generation involves human intervention and artifice, but because the image is so dependent on hardware and software for its vivid realization this suspends our sense of its origins in such artifice.

It might be thought that since the image is *so* dependent on technological support, this means that that we must be always and inescapably aware of its artefactual origins. However, as in the case of film or TV screens, the supporting technology becomes so familiar as to be unnoticed.

A further contrast with autographic representation arises on ontological grounds. The digital image can be realized at as many different times and places as there are devices to activate it. This *non-local* possibility of realization is an expression of the digital image's ontological character as a *token* of a *type*. In this, it contrasts with the emphatically individual nature of autographic pictures such as drawings and paintings, whose existence at any one time is tied to a single physical location.

Of course, there is a sense in which some autographically created images, namely prints, can be regarded as tokens of a type whose structure is embodied in the original plate. However, the plate *qua* unique physical object is of a different ontological order from the tokens, even though it bears the type-structure which defines those tokens. Indeed, insofar as the tokens are produced by direct causal contact with the plate, it will gradually wear down, the more impressions are taken from it.

In contrast to this, the tokens of a digital type do not degrade.[9] This is because the type they instantiate is of the same ontological order as they are—it is a function of mathematical relations and algorithms. The type-program is created before the tokens are, but in no other respect is it distinct from them; neither is there any difference between the individual tokens (except externally—when the hardware which realizes them is in some way faulty, or there is a problem with the software program). We have a case of absolute *type-token visual identity*.

Again, there are broad parallels to this in the way that some sculptures are made in multiple editions according to the artist's specifications, rather than by hand. But here, in ontological terms, the individual works of any such series must, *qua* three-dimensional physical objects, differ from one another in some specific details—no matter how miniscule. In contrast to the digital work, in other words, the type-token identity in sculptural multiples is not absolute between the tokens themselves.

The algorithmic basis of digital art issues in a further ontological feature which is distinctive to digital imagery, namely the most complete idioms of *morphing*. This allows one form to be changed into another without any perceptible gaps or abrupt changes.

Composite images are of course familiar in the form of 'identikit' images used by law-enforcement agencies, and transparent images layered over one another. But the morphed digital still-image generates its composite in a single, *continuous* electrical/mathematical process.

Through this, the end-product is freed of any visual sense of having been constituted from disparate original elements. Whereas non-digital composites are, as it were, visual mixtures, the morphed digital image programs any scanned material into a whole which is more than the sum of any original scanned material which it may incorporate. This *holistic visual structure* is not a matter of skill in terms of the image's realization, rather it is something *intrinsic* to the digital mode of generation itself.[10]

The distinctiveness of holistic digital morphing is even more pronounced in temporally realized idioms, i.e. ones based on visual narratives whose presentation itself involves the passage of time (over and above that which is involved in perceptually scanning the image *qua* spatial object).

Now it might appear that such imagery should be regarded as an aspect of film or video. Matters are, however, more complicated, and the morphing effect is especially instructive in this respect. Effects of this sort have been attainable in film through cumbersome techniques based on cross-fading. However, digital imagery not only involves a more efficient realization of morphing than film and video does, but has also logically unique aspects.

Temporal realization in film and video is achieved through the successive presentation of individual photographic frames at an appropriate speed. The individual frames have a causal relation to some original visual state of affairs—even though they may make this unrecognizable or incorporate special effects through editing or intervening upon the normal filmic process.

The temporal realization of digital imagery, in contrast, does not need a direct causal relation to that which it is an image of, in order to be created. Such a relation is involved minimally when a pre-existing image is digitized, or where a scanning process is involved. But even here, a massive flexibility enters in, which film and video do not have. Once an image is digitized and incorporated in a program, its nature is to be manipulable, and temporally realizable in ways that differ from the sampled or scanned original.

Of course, film and video can be adapted—but this is achieved through physically editing the original reels or tapes, or by adding new material to them. In digital morphing, however, the originals are transformed in terms of their appearance by their very function within a single program.

Temporally realized morphing, then, is qualitatively distinct from that animation of original discrete units which is the basis of film, video, and, indeed, cartoons. It is much less constrained by the 'real'. (This has important aesthetic implications which I will address later.)

There are two other related factors which set digital art apart from traditional visual idioms. They are of great complexity, and will be the subject of the entire next section.

Part Three

The first factor is the *interactive* dimension. The vast majority of visual artworks allow for alternative viewpoints in how they are perceived, and this will involve active positioning in relation to them. But the audience is not called upon to engage with the work in a way that alters its existing physical and virtual structure by virtue of such repositioning.

In some avant-garde tendencies such as Dadaism, Surrealism, and Conceptual art, objects or scenarios have been created which do solicit such engagement, but this is very much the exception rather than the rule.

With much digital art, matters are the other way round. In the case of digital imagery, significant modifications to the original program can be performed, in principle, wherever and whenever it is realized using the apparatus through which it is realized. The viewer of such digital imagery is, in principle, an active participant in the generation of the work, rather than a passive observer.

This is possible because the digital image's software program, by its nature, allows for further refinement and development. Such a program may become obsolete by virtue of new developments in hardware, but notionally, at least, it is always open to permanent transformation at user-level in a way that film and video are not.

There are five main vectors of interactivity.

i) local and non-local interface—the former where one is in physical proximity to the computer, the latter when one accesses it remotely

ii) where the boundaries of interaction are rigidly set by the artist, i.e. the user's choice is restricted to such things as pressing 'Enter', opening or shrinking windows, or choosing between links. It involves no significant creative feedback from the computer

iii) interfacing based on computer responses to an audience, occurring whether or not the audience is aware that an interaction is actually taking place (e.g. when the computer generates imagery in response to movements by the audience, or to other environmental variables)

iv) by voluntary interface where the user *navigates* a program, i.e. exercises choices which are reciprocated through the computer opening up new creative possibilities of interface in response to them

v) user-transcendent interface—where the user instigates and guides a program which is able to then develop at various levels of autonomy in formulating and projecting visual configurations

Now whilst some of these relationships, can, in principle, be involved in certain machine-based avant-garde art practices (using VCRs, televisions, telephones, and the like) they are not basic to such practices. However, they are integral to major kinds of digital art, and the last two factors—navigation and user-transcendent autonomy—are unique to it. This is because continuously *evolving* or relatively autonomous functions are possible only through digital technology.

The most developed form of navigational interaction, to date, is Virtual Reality's immersion scenarios. Some VR programs involve visual engagement through user-headware, but in projects such as Char Davies' *Osmose* of 1995 the immersion is more total through the user wearing a motion-tracking vest that also monitors breathing and balance.

Osmose offers perceptual virtual vistas of unfamiliar quasi-natural forms and more abstract optical effects. These reconfigure in correlation with the agent's movements and gestures. The sights and sounds thus presented can be projected onto a larger viewing screen for the non-immersive spectatorial audience.

Fig. 13. Char Davies, *Vertical Tree, Osmose* (1995). Digital still image captured during immersive performance of the virtual environment Osmose. ©Char Davies.

In user-transcendent programs, a different level of complexity emerges. The highest stage of this is *autonomous evolutionary imaging* whose structures are spectacularly distinctive to the digital realm. An important example here is Thomas Ray's *Tierra* of 1998.

Of this, Christiane Paul remarks as follows:

> *Tierra*, essentially a network-wide 'biodiversity reserve' for digital 'organisms', is based on the premise that evolution by natural selection should be able to operate effectively in genetic languages based on the machine codes of complex software: the *Tierra* source code creates a virtual computer and a Darwinian operating system, so that machine codes can evolve by mutating, recombining, and ultimately producing functional code. The self-replicating machine code programs were able to 'live' in the memory of a computer or even a computer network.[11]

Evolutionary imaging is not tied to biological models necessarily in its program designs. All that is required is the use of algorithms for generating and developing autonomous digital objects and characters capable of continuous development (even in the absence of further interventions from the programmer or user). This has enormous developmental scope in many different directions.

Having identified some of the features which are distinctive to digital imaging, the term has come to consider their aesthetic and artistic implications.

Part Four

It will be recalled that earlier on I noted how digital works had reopened the possibilities presented by the foundational contour-mass axis of pictorial art. Indeed, we also saw how the illusionistic aspect of such representation is massively accentuated through the fact that the digital screen has no autographic surface markings to distract from the projection of its content.

The automated mechanisms whereby digital programs are designed and realized gives them a kind of formal completeness in terms of the basics of projecting three-dimensional forms in two-dimensional media. Their precision and complexity radicalize the contour-mass axis and offer a kind of purer, more absolute illusion of three-dimensional items and states of affairs.

One might describe this as an aesthetic of illusional *purity*. In terms of phenomenological depth, it allows us to engage with the world in an unsettling combination of half-magic, and half, as it were, absolutely hygienic or cleansed visual appearance. The capacities for trans-ostensive projection which enable perception and self-consciousness are here augmented in the most radical terms.

Another aspect of more traditional art is radicalized in a related way by digital work. In Chapter 2 I discussed, at length, the *modal plasticity* of picturing, i.e. the fact that it is not tied to the representation of things which actually exist or which have the possibility to exist, but can even present nomological *im*possibilities—situations which could never physically be, or which involve combinations of properties in an object or event which would not be possible for it to have in 'real life'.

Digital imaging not only extends this to the temporal realm, but through its capacity for holistic visual morphing, does so in a way that is psychologically and perceptually more insistent than the modal plasticity of static images.

As we have already seen, even photographic or related material which is scanned in the preparation of the program becomes representationally malleable—a vehicle for projections which are developed in scenarios different from those presented in the original scanned material. Its exact causal link to any scanned original is exceeded. In this sense, digital morphing might be said to have a *transcausal* rather than causal relation to reality.

Indeed, through its manipulation of abstract or peripheral glimpses of real things (as in Char Davies' *Osmose* VR program) it can create the optical and auditory impression of *totally* alternative physical and perceptual environments.

All in all, then, the enhanced modal plasticity of digital imaging makes it a more total vehicle for fantasy than static picturing or film and video. It has the power to virtually reconfigure the real in transcausal terms, and to do this in a sustained and ever-transforming way.

Through this, an aesthetic of the *quasi-magical* is generated. We have the visually unlikely or impossible presented in the most insistently 'realistic' visual terms. In terms of phenomenological depth, there is a permanent dialectical/aesthetic loop wherein the real and its opposite find an unexpected co-existence.

Now whilst I have emphasized the continuities between digital art and traditional idioms in the foregoing arguments, it is important to emphasize now how digital work extends visual representation in distinctive new directions. These, indeed, involve potentially far-reaching transformations of the nature of visual art itself.

In this respect, it will be recalled that earlier on I gave some emphasis to the way in which digital art involves a type-token relation based on absolute visual identity between the type and its tokens. This has some important implications.

First, it means that the dimension of creativity in digital art is mainly in the dimension of the *design* of programs. This may suggest that the aesthetic dimension assumes a mainly secondary importance. However, the situation is otherwise. Design problems range far beyond questions of mathematical or technological competence alone. The creator must gear his or her creation to the structure and conditions of a specific type of visual realization.

Structural factors concern how the imagery will look, and relate to basic questions of spatial composition and (where relevant) visual narrative construction. They also involve the endeavour to go beyond established imaging programs and outcomes by refining them in new directions, or by more fundamental innovations.

Some digital programs present a special creative challenge in terms of their dynamic potential for further development. Earlier on I stressed the importance of the interactive dimension of digital art. In its navigational forms, this means that the viewer/user of a program can explore and extend its scope on the basis of choice and (in the case of games) an element of skill.

When navigation admits of this evolutionary possibility, there are grounds for saying that the concept of visual art itself is on the threshold of a radical diversification. The traditional artwork involves an individual artist or creative ensemble who make an individual work. Revisions of it or additions to it are not normally accepted unless they are performed by the original creators, or, more exceptionally, by someone else who has been granted permission by them. Even then, such additions or revisions are very unusual.

Now some orally transmitted works—such as Homer's stories—have been finalized in a form which must have involved changes to the narrative in the course of transmission from generation to generation and place to place. The 'final' form might thus be seen as an arbitrary intervention on an artistic idiom which exists through flexible interactions with a core set of narratives and characters.

Of course, it is difficult to determine what level of change can be allowed before we find ourselves with a different oral work than the one started out from. Indeed, the criterion of a 'beginning' for such a transmitted work raises issues of some philosophical complexity in its own right.

The navigable digital work avoids these problems. It combines the stability of an artwork which is definitively embodied in physical terms, with the openness to evolutionary change of the orally transmitted idiom. In many cases, whilst the viewer/user makes a necessary contribution to the way in which the work is realized on a particular occasion, there will be no question of this, in itself, making it into a different work of art.

There are, however, two contexts in which this does become a possibility. In relation to one of them, the oral tradition is again instructive. Such traditions engender great figures who are noted for their skills of verbal delivery. Their virtuoso role, indeed, is also akin to that of great musical performers.

Now it might be that if the right kinds of digital technology develop, visual idioms may emerge where the virtuoso interpreter takes on something of the same significance as the creator of the work. On these terms digital visual art might move in the direction of musical performance with the work being increasingly presented as a vehicle for such interpretation rather than an individual visual artwork *per se*. There would be a gradual realignment in our paradigm of what visual art is.

This possibility is on the horizon. As digital technology becomes cheaper and simpler, and initiation into its use comes in childhood, then game-formats and the like might become as central to visual education as drawing and painting has traditionally been. From such game-formats much more sophisticated evolutionary possibilities might emerge—possibilities which may demand digital interpreters of virtuoso standard.

In this respect, for example, VR systems have great promise. At present they are very much orientated towards the immersant eliciting responses from the program. But it is easy to conceive of programs where it is not the elicited VR environment which is important so much as the use to which the immersant puts it. (In this respect, for example, consider how a program attuned to nuances of movement might be realized by an immersant trained to professional ballet standards.)

The second context wherein navigable digital works might challenge existing notions of visual art is in terms of collective authorship and the possibility of open-ended works. Much complex software or hardware already requires teams of specialists to design and produce it, rather than the usual creative individual of autographic visual art-making. However, even such autographic idioms can involve teamwork on occasion (especially in relation to large-scale projects), so if we are to identify the more distinctive possibilities opened up by digital works in terms of collective creatorship it is to the work itself that we must look.

In this respect, the evolutionary navigational programs discussed earlier should be recalled. If a digital work is capable of constant development, this opens up the possibility that this development can be structured through interfaces with many different individuals at many different times and places. Even if these contributions are carried out within basic parameters established by the original creative individual or team, it may be that the work grows far beyond them, taking on a new identity on the basis of how it is realized by new generations of users.

Of course, such a work might amount to no more than a composite entity where the individual contributions to the whole can be recognized clearly. But the possibility also exists for the evolving whole to completely absorb such contributions. The fact that it takes on a new character at a specific point shows that one identifiable contributor or group has made a major contribution, but the nature of the contribution does not declare itself, independently, within the evolving phenomenal structure of the work.

Here there is a contrast. Collectively created visual works (say, those painted on the walls of a cave over generations) constitute a visual palimpsest, with clearly apparent layers. Even when, say, a team of artists cooperate in painting a single work where the contributions of the individuals are meant to merge perceptually, there is always the possibility of ultra-sensitive forensic instruments which could map these individual contributions.

In the collective visual digital work just described, in contrast, we have a *holistic* phenomenal structure. All individual contributions to its evolution are absorbed seamlessly within the whole. They cannot ever be detected from analysis of the imagery's visual appearance alone. At every new stage of its development it creates a new type which is then instantiated as a token by the other users. But the purpose of the whole enterprise is to prevent the work from congealing into a type whose characteristics are fixed.

The significance of such an open-ended work is that, in it, creatorship involves membership of a community—but one whose cohesion is not that of a shared everyday language, location, and culture. The creators are bonded through an artistic structure that can, in principle, continue indefinitely. Here the work offers, in effect, a limited ideal of community, lifted out, through its non-local character, from some of the vicissitudes which lead real communities to divide and disintegrate over time.

This is not to say that the relationships involved will not develop distinctive tensions of their own. However, the very fact that it is an aesthetic structure which is being created rather than a purely social one means that risks such as this might be addressed creatively and taken account of in each new program-modification strategy.

Now the degree to which the distinctive features and transformations of visual art described in this section are developed is contingent on many factors—not least of which is the availability of the appropriate technology on a large-scale.

It might be thought that some of the factors described are no more than elaborate game-playing. But such playing is taken to a higher order when the rules of the game themselves are a major player in its evolving transformations. This may issue in an art form whose character is much more that of 'being-in the-world' rather than that of visual perception and amusement alone—the more so if the work's evolving aesthetic structure is able to model broader physical, perceptual, social, and psychological processes.

In fact, the various aspects of digital art which I have emphasized most—namely extremes of contour and detailed mass, type-token absolute visual identity, visually holistic morphing, and navigational and evolutionary potential—each engage with phenomenological depth in individually striking ways that I have scarcely even begun to indicate. There is room, accordingly, for detailed further phenomenological analyses which can elaborate these, individually, and as a field.

I shall now indicate, briefly, some of these possibilities and their limit.

Conclusion

Walter Benjamin famously claimed that the mechanical reproduction of images destroyed the 'aura' of original works by making them available in times and places other than that defined by their immediate physical presence.[12]

This theory is demonstrably false. Indeed, its exact opposite is true. Far from negating the aesthetic impact of the original work, mechanical reproduction has amplified it to the highest degree. Through being reproduced so often in books and on the net, etc., the original seems even more extraordinary, *vis-à-vis* its very power to have issued in so many mechanical copies. Its aura is not destroyed, but transformed, rather, into a veritable *halo*.

It becomes imperative to see the sacred original in direct perceptual terms without the intermediary of reproductions. (The massive expansion of visits to art galleries in late modern and postmodern times, and the incredible market appetite for original works, are powerful testimonies to this continuing need for acquaintance with the original.)

Given this, it is worth reflecting on the aura of digital works. Because they can be realized in the non-local terms described earlier, it may seem that they can have no aura, because there is no perceptually privileged 'original'—we have only programs.

However, this—in conjunction with the other important features which I have emphasized—surely invest the digital work with aura of a quite distinctive aesthetic kind. Not being tied to existence in one place and time, and, in many cases, being navigable or having evolutionary potential, is something with intrinsic fascination.

On the one hand the work is disembodied in terms of parallels with traditional art 'objects', but at the same time the fact that it can be realized in times and places determined by the user means that it has an intimacy and special status through being realizable very much in one's own personal space. It is embodied as the user wills . . .

Even if a such a digital work is encountered in a gallery, one knows that it can, in principle, inhabit many such spaces simultaneously. It can converge on where and when the viewer is, whereas in traditional art objects, the viewer must seek out the unique space occupied by the object.

There is a kind of liberation from physical constraints here which gives the digital work its distinctive aura. Indeed, there is something about—to use a crude metaphor—the aesthetic 'feel' of digital art *per se* which has its own special iconological character. Exemplification of, or reference to, the hyper-precision and complex subtleties of the digital image to some degree expresses the visual style of the present age.

In its extreme clarity and complexity, for example, the digital image exemplifies the postmodern age's characteristic hi-tech and informational aspects. This is achieved through forms which combine presentational precision and accessibility with a sense of the depth and extensiveness of the digital medium's informational scope.

I have argued, then, that digital art both perfects some structural visual properties which are basic to pictorial art, and also takes visual representation into new territories on the basis of its distinctive ontologies. I have argued also that these developments may be signs that the concept of the traditional art object will itself be transformed by such factors.

This being said, there is no reason to rule out the development of tendencies and 'isms' of the kind associated with more traditional visual art. Indeed, those autonomous programs such as Thomas Ray's *Tierra* (discussed earlier) already demand something like the term 'evolutionism' to signify that they are aspects of a shared digital strategy which—whatever its different realizations—moves in the ever-accelerating direction of programs which involve a central dimension of self-creation and development.

One might also usefully employ the term 'digitalism' within the more traditional field of painting to signify those works (such as Finley's and Nechtvatal's, and many many others) which are possible only through digital interventions.

The possibilities of 'isms' here are manifold. Large-scale innovation in the visual arts is still possible but is now located in the continuing development and use of digital idioms, *and* their relation to the more traditional modes of visual art.

It is important to emphasize this latter relation. For—despite the extravagant claims sometimes made for digital art—such works will never supersede the older autographic modes. The digital 'aura' of non-local realization has its own magic, but the human subject is embodied, and will always need to find something of its own identity restored through the felicities of touch and individual physical presence. Drawing, painting, and sculpture have always been, in part, concerned with the answering of these needs, and will, no doubt, continue this ministry.

10   The Body of Architecture

Introduction

I turn now to the last major idiom of visual art which has not been addressed in detail earlier—namely, architecture. The phrase 'body of architecture' is used here with two meanings, that of the medium's distinctive physicality and that of the human body's engagement with it.[1] This engagement involves a complex interplay between physical realities and symbolic meanings. To understand the interplay is to understand architecture's phenomenological depth at the profoundest level.

The task is formidably difficult. This is not only because it demands thinking across boundaries (in aesthetics, epistemology, and cultural and architectural history), but, more fundamentally, because architecture is an art form which has no established convention of 'reading' akin to that which enables us to recognize, say, a picture or sculpture as being 'of' such and such a thing.[2] The symbolic dimension of architecture is, accordingly, hard to determine in exact terms. It involves an image-character, but one that is as open and allusive as that of abstract art.

For this reason, at points in the coming discussion I will use 'suggestive of', 'analogous to', 'symbolic of', and cognate phrases to indicate specific aspects of architecture's wealth of symbolic associations. Some of these associations may seem curious. A number of them, indeed, may seem almost childish in their obviousness, whilst others may appear somewhat vague.

These extremes are, however, by no means a symptom of weak analysis. They are indicative, rather, of the extraordinary phenomenological depth of architecture. This art form is one whose distinctive nature impinges on many levels of self-knowledge and world-perception. Its meanings connect basic functionality and the simplest morphological analogies to much deeper epistemological relations between subject and object of experience. To do justice to architecture, one must be prepared to embrace the whole range of relevant associations.

This discussion, accordingly, adopts the following strategy. Part One is a logical analysis of the basic functional criteria which define building, and the grounds which enable building to be interpreted artistically, as *architecture*. Part Two considers the phenomenological link between the body and architecture's expressive character in great detail, and highlights some unfamiliar and complex idealizing aesthetic effects.

The basic theory is then made more specific in Part Three through discussion of key historical examples—specifically, classical temples, triumphal arches, Renaissance and Baroque churches, and a variety of Modern and Postmodern works. In Part Four the theory is taken to its highest stage. The relation of body and architecture is shown to have key relevance for a mode of spatial experience which enables the evolutionary/historical emergence of embodied subjectivity *per se*.

The Conclusion considers, very briefly, some possibilities of the body/architecture relation in terms of future architectural practice.

Part One

Architecture centres on the enclosure and/or declaration of space for functional purposes. Of necessity, this involves the connecting and/or working of three-dimensional material.

The origins of architecture probably lie in the transition from shelter *found* through occupying or adapting pre-given natural formations (such as caves) and from edifices built from the piling up of stones and the like, through to the construction of shelters and other edifices from hewn wood or stone. Buildings constructed from stone (or cognate enduring materials) using physically bonded units are the end-product of this transition.[3]

The distinctive character of architecture in relation to the other visual arts is implicit in all aspects of this transition. Whereas, for example, pictorial art is three-dimensional in *virtual* terms predominantly, architecture involves works which are physically three-dimensional; and whilst sculpture shares this character, the architectural work is three-dimensional in a further way through actively facilitating occupancy of, and movement through the work, as well as perception of its external three-dimensional features. This means that it has an intrinsic connection with functional possibilities in a way that other art forms do not.

Of course, there are some postmodern architects (such as Bernard Tschumi in his *Parc Villette* project) who, in effect, challenge the division between architecture and sculpture. And there are others such as Peter Eisenman who (in a work such as *House VI*) challenge the functional ethos. Specifically, Eisenman claims:

> My work attacks the concept of occupation as given. It's against the traditional notion of how you occupy a house.[4]

However, in addressing the architecture/sculpture divide, or in challenging 'given' notions of occupancy, these strategies will, nevertheless, be dependent, by definition, on the centrality of that which they are challenging (a point I will return to in Part Three).

The deconstructive strategy, therefore, involves playful gestures of re-arrangement, rather than genuine challenges. For whatever genuinely interesting games might be played at its periphery, architecture's central function will always be *inescapable*. The making of other forms of art and our encounters with them are largely a matter of personal choice, but a relation to architecture (in the western world, at least) is thrust upon us through our basic need for shelter.

Of course, it might be argued that building *per se* answers this basic need, and that architecture is a great deal more than this alone. It is building created as, or made into, art. Hence, whilst building is inescapable, architecture is not.

Against this, however, it must be stressed that, once one lives in a community where there is *choice* as to how shelter can be constructed from available materials, then building itself already involves more than basic function alone. *How* the building is constructed becomes a significant consideration in its own right. Once basic physical needs are covered, then an array of correlated psychological needs demand satisfaction also. These involve the articulation of both personal and collective identities.

In this respect, Christian Norberg-Schultz has noted that architecture exists to give humankind an 'existential foothold' as well as answering practical needs. Such a foothold requires 'symbols' 'that is works of art which represent "life-situations".'[5]

Understood in modest terms, this symbolic loading is true of even the humblest habitation's form. Such buildings will express the character of a community in terms of preference for such things as materials, the shape of a structure, or the particular way in which this structure is informed by choice concerning key features such as windows or chimneys.

Another decisive factor will involve how the structure is adapted in relation to the social units who are meant to occupy it—such as single families or more extended groups. Explicitly intended or not, buildings will exemplify more specific priorities or values pertaining to the community which constructs them.

This symbolic dimension means that *all* building—once there is room for choice in how it is constructed—has a basic architectural *character*. The transition to architecture as an explicitly pursued *art form* occurs when this dimension of choice—the style in which building is constructed (and thence its symbolic meaning)—becomes an object of community concern in its own right, and can be pursued in a variety of ways.

Such a concern arises *internally*, or *externally*. The former is the case when a community is in a material position to choose between various building options, each of which can answer a basic functional need equally well. In such cases, the particular way in which a building is constructed (*vis-à-vis* such things as shape, materials, and location) becomes a source of community interest in its own right.

At first, such interests may be tied closely to broader social functions. But once these functions themselves admit of alternative means of equally valid realization *qua* function, then a dimension of aesthetic preferences comes into play. Freedom, in the sense of choice between alternatives, is intrinsic to the establishment of architecture as an art form.

Now when a culture enjoys the material conditions which allows such preferences to be exercised, it can relate them to buildings constructed by other communities—even though those communities may exist under material conditions which do not allow much scope for choice in how buildings are made. This external standpoint allows the alien buildings to be regarded as architecture through interpreting them in relation to a comparative interpretative framework established within the community's own form of life.

On these terms, then, architecture as an art form arises from *building viewed comparatively in a context of choices*. Its enduring, functionally grounded and publicly sited character has broader implications, however, in terms of artistic significance. As Roger Scruton observes,

> the existence and predominance of an architectural vernacular is an inevitable
> consequence of the distance that separates architecture from the other arts,

of the relative absence from the art of building of any true artistic autonomy, of the fact that, for the most part, a builder has to fit his work into some pre-existing arrangement of unchangeable forms, being constrained at every point by influences which forbid him the luxury of a self-consciously artistic aim.[6]

A further decisive aspect of architecture's artistic significance should be noted (one, indeed, which deserves rather more emphasis than it has received in the existing literature.). It is architecture's status as a *non-autographic* visual art.

In the case of traditional idioms of picturing and sculpture, for example, the creative outcome most often centres on the artist's personal physical working of the medium in question.[7] But whilst an architect might, in principle, be involved in some aspect of the actual making of his or her building it is extremely rare, and is in no sense a central presupposition of architectural art. The building is designed by the architect, and it is in the realization of the design rather than his or her involvement in the process of building *per se* which is decisive for the finished artwork.

As I will show, this factor mediates the aesthetic status of architecture in important ways. To see why, we must now address the relation between the body and architecture in great detail.

Part Two

Architecture involves three-dimensional spatial unity. This means that, unlike the arts of temporal realization (whose unity involves their elements being perceived in an exact order of linear succession), the part/whole structures of building can be comprehended in any order which one's perceptual positioning allows.

Such unity, of course, encompasses experience of the building's interior as well. The space which it occupies is not only physically continuous with that of our embodied existence, but is so in *enveloping* terms. One cannot form a full sense of a building's character unless one has perceived its exterior, *and* been inside it.

Here is a first loose, but interesting, connection between building and embodiment. The human condition involves a constant reciprocity between our sense of having a body, and our sense of being 'in', or, better, of *inhabiting* a body. Our personal identity involves both the body's present character and networks of memory and imagination which inform present awareness and make it intelligible.

The fact that the self exists in such an horizon of past and possible experiences means that it can never know itself sufficiently as just this immediately given physical body. It *inhabits* that body in the sense of being able, as it were, to wander introspectively through memory and imagination to places, times, and situations other than those of its present embodiment. Our sense of the present 'outer' body and its 'inner' experiences are reciprocally dependent. One cannot have the one without the other.

This reciprocity of external aspects and inner features also characterizes the architectural work—except that here the 'inner' aspect is literal rather than metaphorical. The rooms of a building, 'like' the other stages of our lives (in networks of memory and imagination) are places we can explore and make discoveries in.

Of course, the analogy here is not at all exact. But the loosely shared 'inner/outer' character is enough to suggest some elementary kinship between the embodied subject and building (and in Part Three we shall see a very interesting variation on this).

The kinship just described may be significant in its own right. However, it is probably subsumed, for the most part, within a network of more direct associational affinities between the body and architecture.

These affinities are based on the dynamic character of experiencing architecture. The experience's cognitive aspects constellate around the body's movement through space, and the positive physical arrest, or direction, of such movement (as determined by the location and layout of the building). And whilst one can perceive and move only in terms that the building allows physically, some works are articulated in a way that stimulates avenues of more focused perception, and imaginative association.

To understand what is at issue here, it is worth considering some key insights from the history of architectural theory. Schopenhauer, for example, claims that architecture exemplifies specific Ideas.

> Such Ideas are gravity, cohesion, rigidity, hardness, those universal qualities of stone, those first, simplest, dullest visibilities of the will, the fundamental bass notes of nature; and along with these, light, which is in many respects their opposite. [More specifically] the conflict between gravity and rigidity is the sole aesthetic material of architecture; its problem is to make this conflict appear with perfect distinctness in many different ways. It solves this problem by depriving these indestructible forces of the shortest path to their satisfaction, and keeping them in suspense through a circuitous path . . .[8]

Schopenhauer's position here is based on a broader metaphysic which holds that the forces and forms of the phenomenal world are Ideas through which the 'World Will' objectifies itself. The material of architecture involves the crudest level of such objectification.

However, the key issue can be developed without reference to this metaphysic. For it is clear that the most general problem faced by the architect is how to a create a specific mode of space occupancy based on the erection of structures from substantial materials. This involves building an edifice whose form not only defies gravity, but does so in a way which both fixes and thematizes its own style of erection. In this, it exemplifies that dimension of choice between alternatives which, in Part One, I argued to be the basis of architectural character.

Now in all this, the building's relation to light is of paramount importance. It is light which illuminates both whole and parts with shifting emphases (through different times of day). This not only draws attention to how the work is present as building, but re-activates the complex and, as it were, arrested dynamics of the building's upward thrust.

It should be emphasized that in talking of 'erection' and upward 'thrust' in this context, a key relation to the body's spatial aspect is suggested. It consists not in some facile analogy with male sexual arousal but more fundamentally in the fact that, when waking, the human body characteristically erects itself through an expenditure of energy—taking it from an immobile recumbent posture to an active upright position. Indeed, the capacity to maintain, and act from, an upright position, is (along with other distinctive aspects of human embodiment) profoundly implicated in the genesis of rationality itself. As Merleau-Ponty observes,

> it is no mere coincidence that the rational being is also the one that holds himself upright or has a thumb which can be brought opposite to the fingers; the same manner of being is evident in both aspects.[9]

A completed building, then, is suggestive of *achieved and active upright posture*. Features such as the mutual arrest of gravity and rigidity noted by Schopenhauer are involved in such association. They are noticed when achieved-uprightness is something striking, and we are made attentive to *how* it is achieved in both perceptual and physical terms in this particular work.

To appreciate in these terms is a special case of appreciating the *style* in which the whole relates to the parts and vice-versa. The criterion of parts and whole here, is of course, not that of visual appearance alone but the way in which this is informed by balance and related factors which are achieved in the 'play-off' between the physical, gravitational, and lighting factors described before.

The general involvement of the body in aesthetic responses to architecture can be stated in even more precise terms. Schmarsow, for example, asserts that

> The intuited form of space which surrounds us wherever we may be and which we always erect around ourselves and consider more necessary than the form of our own body, consists of the residues of sensory experience to which the muscular sensations of our body, the sensitivity of our skin, and the structure of our body all contribute. As soon as we have learned to experience ourselves and ourselves alone at the centre of this space, whose coordinates intersect in us, we have found the precious kernel, the initial capital investment so to speak, on which architectural creation is based . . .[10]

Schmarsow's point here is that the body not only moves through the space of buildings but is the basis of axial coordinates around which this space constellates and receives a distinctive character. The building is not a neutral or passive container but one whose construction actively accommodates the body's sensorimotor orientations. Schmarsow provides more details as follows:

> Next to the vertical line, whose living bearers resolve space by our bodily orientation into above and below, front and back, left and right, the most important direction for the actual spatial construct is the direction of free movement—that is, forward—and that of our vision, which, with the placement and positioning of the eyes, defines the dimension of depth. For the viewing subjects, this dimension is so necessary, for it represents the measure of our free movement in a given space since we are accustomed to looking and moving forward.[11]

Wolfflin takes a similar approach:

> Our own bodily organization is the form through which we apprehend everything physical.[12]

Indeed,

> as human beings with a body that teaches us the nature of gravity, contraction, strength, and so on, we gather the experience that enables us to identify with the condition of other forms.[13]

In relation to architecture, this means that we look for organic unity that can parallel that of the human form, and are also able to recognize and identify with, shared physical characteristics which bond our corporeal being and the world of things. Factors such as regularity, symmetry, proportion, and harmony, for example, are vital elements in the disposition of part to part, and to whole, in all organic structures and, especially, the human body. They are also basic to architecture. Hence Wolfflin's further observation that

> there is no oblique line that we do not see as rising and no irregular triangle that we do not perceive as unbalanced. It hardly need be said that we do not experience architectural creations in merely geometric terms but rather as massive forms . . . Instinctively we animate each object. This is a primeval instinct of man.[14]

One might ask, as a matter of analytic urgency, why this instinct should be *so* primeval, and indeed, why it should be treated as anything more than a curious tendency—akin, perhaps, to seeing faces in clouds. Why should it be found *expressive?* Surely the mere analogy with bodily factors *per se* is not enough to explain architecture's *profundity* of expressive aesthetic power?

To deal with this worry we need to emphasize that what Wolfflin and Schmarsow are describing is, in effect, a correlation of body and world which has (though they do not much remark upon it) distinctive *cognitive benefits.* The building's articulation of form, shape, and mass in enduring materials, on the basis of symmetry, proportion, and the like, offers a kind of rectification or *idealization* of the body's vectors of sensorimotor activity.

Traditional notions of the Ideal in pictorial art emphasize the elimination of particularities, and enhancement of factors such as regularity, symmetry, proportion, and harmony. These enhancement factors are central to architecture, but in a perceptually active rather than a contemplative sense.

In this respect, for example, there are many physical and perceptual situations where we lose our balance, or are overburdened, or are unable to make sense of something given in perception. Architecture, however, offers a realm of artifice where clarity and order is achieved in concrete, enduring terms. Indeed, the giving of form to massive and resistant material such as stone means that what is most basic to human gestural artifice—namely the giving of form to matter—is exemplified in terms which are both profound and spectacular.

The fact that all this involves the suggestion of bodily movement—the carrying out and arrest of activity in ways described by Schmarsow and Wolfflin—allows us to explain what gives architecture its special expressive power. Through architecture, *the spaces we must negotiate are made familiar and coop-*

erative through their analogy with the body and its activities. They are not just aesthetically lucid configurations of whole and parts, but rather ones whose physical structure seems itself to exemplify aspects of the body and its vectors of activity.

Hence, whilst building, literally, provides places where we are at home with the world, in architecture this meaning takes on an added and quite distinctive aesthetic character through architecture's special kind of expressiveness.

This links up with the non-autographic significance of architecture as an art form. In painting or sculpture, the physical effects of the artist's own gestures are necessary conditions of the work *qua* picture or sculpture. Both the how and the what of representation are grounded in the physical effects of the artist's intended gestures—a feature which is the basis of picturing and sculpture's distinctive meanings.

In architecture, however, the work is defined mainly through the creator's design, rather than the effect of his or her gestures. This has its own special significance. As Wolfflin notes:

> Since only the human form . . . can express all that lies in humanity, architecture will be unable to express particular emotions that are manifested through specific faculties . . . Its subject remains the great vital feelings, the moods that presuppose a consistent and stable body condition.[15]

Architecture is not the human body, nor is its physical fabric constructed through the architect's own gestures. This means that whilst its forms have those important correlations with the human body noted earlier, its expressive meaning will lack the gestural specificity which identifies an exact emotion. It will, nevertheless, allow the viewer an identification with more general and very basic 'vital feelings' such as elevation, illumination, mystery, security, belonging, or whatever. The non-autographic nature of architecture allows it, in other words, to operate at a more general and basic expressive level than autographic visual media.

I have linked architecture's special expressive power, then, to the way in which its perceptual idealization is achieved through structures which are suggestive of bodily activity. Other, rather more indirect kinds of idealizing effects can be involved also.

The most important of them is suggested by some further ramifications of architecture's non-autographic status. Since the building is not physically made by the architect, this means that the work of many individuals will be involved and transformed within the unity of the finished whole.

This is an ultimate challenge. For the more a whole is composed from parts with a high degree of individual autonomy, the more it can be claimed that its creation embodies an ideal of artefactual unity. The architect's plan must be good enough to both clarify and direct how the specific parts are to be made and/or disposed, *and* to accommodate the inevitable degree of creative licence which will inform the work of those individuals involved in the edifice's construction.

Hence, the achievement of regularity, symmetry, proportion, and harmony in the organization of such autonomous (and thence, potentially wayward) parts means that, in terms of artistic creation, architecture has claim to embody an ideal of *artefactual unity*.

This claim is substantiated further by a point made in the previous section. It is that, unlike other art forms, architectural unity has to be achieved through adapting to external circumstances and surroundings. This, of course, amplifies the range of potentially wayward factors which the architect's creative powers much negotiate.

Now it should be emphasized that whilst being an ideal of artefactual creation in the senses noted, this does not give architecture some hierarchical authority over other art forms. Each such form has its own distinctive characteristics which are not derivable from the others.

With this qualification in mind, we can now consider some further—rarely remarked upon—effects which are also connected loosely with architecture's idealizing significance. To understand the first of them, we must address briefly a recurrent theme in architectural theory. It concerns the mimetic significance of classicism.

In this respect, for example, the columns and architraves of classical edifices are often taken to refer back to architecture's very origins in the use of tree-trunks as vertical supports for other trunks used horizontally as beams; with the capitals referring back to the filled bags used to position beams upon the vertical trunks. This symbolism of primal origins is sometimes taken further to justify the privileged status of classical forms in architectural tradition.[16]

It is important to emphasize, however, the broader significance of this symbolism. Specifically, there is a case for seeing it as more than a passive mimetic relation. For if an architectural work makes us mindful of primal origins, it surely at the same time exemplifies its own significance as an *achieved transcendence* of such origins—as a moving far beyond them to a higher plane of accomplishment.[17]

This effect need not be confined to classical forms. A case might be put for it in relation to any architectural tendency where some symbolic play-off against more basic idioms of building is manifestly to the fore. It is also connected closely with a third achievement-effect.

An interesting example of it is provided by those postmodern 'deconstructive' works noted in Part One. For here, the sophisticated stylistic games played with traditional forms and functions might be seen, in themselves, as a dynamic manifestation of the extraordinary degree to which architecture can transcend its primal origins. A similar claim might also be made for baroque, rococo, and *art nouveau* works, in terms of their superabundance of ingenious rhythmic and ornamental features.

In these cases the primal factor invoked is not basic building idioms *per se*, but rather that dimension of choice between possibilities which is the basis of building's inherent architectural character. Such tendencies affirm, in the most spectacular terms, an *achieved transcendence of brute necessity*. For whilst a basic functional origin in the provision of shelter is always present to some degree, architecture goes beyond it in terms of how this provision is realized. And when this transcendence involves formal means whose visual dynamics involve a dimension of complexity or excess of detail for its own sake, then architecture's capacity to achieve free choice in the interpretation of function is exemplified with especially powerful effect.

A further achievement-effect of architecture is the simplest, but most dramatic. It arises from a contrast of physical scale. The human body is small in relation to the size of most buildings. Yet these large—and sometimes even vast—edifices owe their existence to human artifice. Their sheer scale in relation to the size of the beings which built them, in other words, can evoke wonder at the extraordinary power of human artifice to transcend physical limitations. Here, the achievement-effect is, itself, the effect of achievement.

Having identified architecture's expressive basis and the less frequently remarked upon secondary idealizing factors, the question arises as to their cognitive status. Are they just associational ideas *per se*, or aesthetically significant ones? In this respect we must emphasize two points.

First, the close links between the architecture and the body which I have explored mean that, when we look at a building or explore its internal features, this does not have to be for purely practical ends. The perceptually idealized 'cognitive benefits' which I described earlier are not practical guidelines for clear perception and movement which the building offers, rather they invite us to appreciate aesthetically the way in which such possibilities have been spatially realized in the particular case. The body-architecture resonances described earlier create an *expressive* orientation which points beyond the work's purely functional significance.

This orientation does not have to be 'contemplative' in some passive way. It can involve extremely active perception (elated even). But the fact that it is centred on a parts/whole relation achieved through the creativity of another human being is something that can be enjoyed for its own sake, and thence, aesthetically.

Similar points apply to the *quasi*-idealizing associations which I described. For whilst one can experience architecture as an ideal of artifactual creation at the level of ideas alone, in the actual presence of an architectural work things can be very different. Here what we engage with is not *just* the idea but the concrete way in which it is realized in this particular case. Generated through attentiveness to the particular, quasi-idealizing associations clarify the character of that work *qua* individual, and thence become a factor in its *aesthetic* appreciation.

I am arguing, then, that the relation of architecture and the body extends far beyond issues of shelter for the embodied subject and Vitruvian questions of proportion. It centres on a correlation of body and world which is existentially unique. Architecture involves space created with the interests of bodily exploration as well as practical function in mind.

This deep *affinity* between the body and architectural space enables the subject to animate the building's forms, expressively, in such a way as to evoke an idealized perceptual and symbolic transcendence which is emergent aesthetically from the work's particular way of enclosing and articulating space. Architecture's phenomenological depth centres on is clarification and enhancement of our cognitive inherence in the world as *embodied* subjects.

Part Three

Having explored the relation between the body and architecture in general terms, I will now deepen the account by reference to some specific historical idioms.

The example of classical formats is an obvious starting point. Earlier, I re-

Fig. 14. *Parthenon*, 5th century B.C., Athens, Greece. Photo taken November 12, 2005 by Barcex. From Wikimedia Commons / under GNU Free Documentation License.

viewed the link between classicism and its evocation of more primitive dimensions of building. However, there are other symbolic connotations with more specific reference to the human body.

A first example is the analogy between the columnar structure of Greek temples and the notion of the human frame in upright posture—grouped in protective rows. The *raison d'être* of such edifices is not only to create impressive building, but also to provide a place for the statue of the God—a God which is itself construed in terms of an idealized human form. The columns protect this form by surrounding it with defensive rows, and also—insofar as they bear the weight of the entablature—by exemplifying strength of posture.

In this particular functional context, the carrying of such a physical burden suggests, indeed, a further symbolic burden of spiritual *responsibility*. The *Parthenon* is a decisive example of this. It has a colonnade of Doric columns encompassing the entire periphery of the structure. The 'protection' afforded to the cult God is extended, indeed, through the addition of six columns in front of the two entrances to the temple's inner rooms.

It is interesting that, whilst having a determinate frontage, the columnar structure does not, in itself, mark out a clear main entrance to the place of the God from the outside. The columns represent, symbolically, the community as a closed social group, shielding and protecting the image of their God.

The Roman triumphal arch offers some rather more secular and dramatic associations between the body and architecture. And again, these focus on a relation to posture. For there are strong symbolic suggestions of the victorious warrior standing bestride the defeated, and/or surveying conquered lands. Indeed, there is a sense also of the Arch *itself* standing in a posture of salute to the martial power whose achievements it celebrates. These effects, of course, are a function of both scale and form.

An excellent example here is the *Arch of Constantine*. It stands 21 metres high, 25.7 metres wide, and 7.4 metres deep. The central feature is an arch with two smaller flanking ones (the central arch being 11.5 metres high and 6.5 metres wide, and the flanking ones measuring 7.4 by 3.4 metres each). Four Doric

Fig. 15. *Arch of Constantine*, 312, Rome, Italy. Photo: Alexander Z., from Wikimedia Commons / under GNU Free Documentation License.

columns emerge in partial-relief in each of the walls dividing the arches, giving intense accentuation to the martial bearing of the edifice as a whole.

The fact that the Doric columns here are in partial-relief rather than free standing has, perhaps a symbolic significance in its own right. Their semi-autonomy is suggestive of a free but disciplined acceptance of command—an acceptance which further emphasizes the martial character of the whole. And whereas the columnar structure of the Greek temple conceals the God which is its *raison d'être* from the external viewer, the Triumphal arch's columns proclaim that edifice's rhetorical message insistently, to anyone who even looks towards it.

It is worth noting that this proclamation depends not only on the immediate character of the Arch's size and shape, but also the fact that one knows it to be something one is meant to pass *beneath*. Such passage involves a kind of physical subjugation to the Arch's striding posture.

The Arch is also striking through the character of its decorative friezes. These are a familiar feature of the Greek temple, but here any mythical content serves to provide an allegorical affirmation of specific imperial military achievements.

These friezes are not merely decorative effects, neither are they simple visual documents of triumph. Rather they are a direct narrative focusing of the Arch's physical and formally assertive posture. In psychophysical terms the Arch is a triumphant unity as well as a unity which thematizes triumph. It is a building which embodies thought through making overt narrative meaning central to both its overall structure and specific surface details.

In Renaissance architecture, the symbolic relation to the body is developed in further directions. Of special interest here is the role of the pilaster. In the Renaissance context, the pilaster is, in effect, a classical column whose free-standing, three-dimensional nature has been transformed into the mere appearance of columnar structure. It is now, in other words, a virtual decorative feature rather than a real physical support.

Again, this has some symbolic overtones. Its incorporation of the column within a broader structure which emphasizes geometric exactness and order is, in one sense, an incorporation of the embodied subject within a cosmos. The human frame is an essential part of this order, but its meaning and ultimate function is only intelligible within a broader rational scheme of things. (Here, indeed, this revision of the body's role might be understood further as, itself, emblematic of broader and parallel assimilations—namely Chris-

Fig. 16. Leon Battista Alberti, *Santa Maria Novella*, completed 1470, façade, Florence, Italy. Photo: Georges Jansoone. GNU Free Documentation License / public domain.

tian doctrine's absorption and transformation of pagan philosophy, and the Renaissance's more culturally urbane appropriation of Romanesque or Gothic idioms.)

A key example in relation to all these points is Alberti's façade to the *Church of Santa Maria Novella*, in Florence (1458–1471). Added to a pre-existent Gothic church, Alberti's façade superimposes a sequence of tall, narrow arches. These serve to assimilate the Gothic structure's vertical emphases. The entrance is framed by columns and bounded on both left and right by evenly distributed fluted pilasters. All the elements are connected by marble panels, so as to achieve an overall rhythmic and geometric unity which embodies a classical eurythmic pattern on the 1:2 ratio of the musical octave.

In baroque architecture, a much more complex relation to the body is set up. Consider, for example, Borromini's *S. Carlo Alle Quattro Fontane,* Rome,

Fig. 17. Francesco Borromini, *San Carlo alle Quattro Fontane*, 1638–1641, façade, Rome, Italy. Photo: Gaspa, From Fickr.com / under Creative Commons License.

1638–1641. The façade consists of undulating S-curves mainly, with a central bay entrance which curves into a convex line and then moves into concave bays on each side.

Longitudinally speaking, the building is set out as an oval, with the altar at one end and the entrance at the opposite (a design well-adapted to the church's restricted spatial location). This oval is slightly compressed at each of its extremities, thus setting up a waving contour. The walls of the building are animated likewise with a sense of motion and mobility that seems to carry the more specific architectural features (such as entablatures and mouldings) along in the 'flow'.

Here we have a transposition of the corporeal. Rather than alluding to the human frame in its erect and static 'columnar' posture mainly, the baroque building also emphasizes the mobility and pliancy of form in motion. This, and the avoidance of harsh angularities, give stone itself the appearance of something more fleshy and supple. There is still a strict geometrical order involved, but its exact disposition is more complex, and often in large part concealed. It is analogous to those 'strange geometrick hinges' (John Webster) upon which the motives of an embodied subject's behaviour turn. Such behaviour is rational, but always in motion, and involving unexpected twists and turns.

This animated corporeal emphasis is common to most baroque and rococo work. However, it is also special testimony to both the particular character of architectural expressiveness and the reciprocal dependence of inner/outer (which applies literally to architecture, and metaphorically to the embodied subject).

In respect of the former, we will recall Schmarsow's point that space intuited through architecture

> consists of the residues of sensory experience to which the muscular sensations of our body, the sensitivity of our skin, and the structure of our body all contribute to.[18]

The idioms of baroque work embody these expressive residues with particular insistency.

In respect of the reciprocity of inner and outer, this is, indeed, a strong feature of baroque architecture. But here the link with the body has a different metaphorical emphasis from that described in Part Two. Consider, for example, Bernini's *St. Andrea Quirinale* in Rome (1658–1671). The dramatic façade recedes in a curved proscenium, and is composed entirely from classical formal devices (such as Corinthian pilasters, egg and dart motifs, and triangles and half-circles inspired by Roman sources).

However, there is no trace of classical eurythmic order here. Rather the formal elements are compressed and given a vertically extended emphasis. The escutcheon of Camillo Pamphili (who commissioned the church) animates them by seeming to loom towards the viewer. In doing so, it not only energizes the whole façade, but does so in a way that carries the idiosyncratic overtones of individual *facial* expression.

The analogy can be taken further. For the steep semi-circular array of steps, the pilasters, and narrow free-standing pillars, all serve to dramatically frame and emphasize the entrance to the building. It thus takes on the same kind of formal primacy that the mouth enjoys in relation to the face as a whole.

These facial associations may seem no more than a trite analogy. But it must be remembered that the face has an enormously privileged role in terms of bodily communication, and the mouth especially so. Hence, if a façade suggests these bodily features, then it is surely invested with a kind of visually inter-

Fig. 18. Gian Lorenzo Bernini, *Sant'Andrea al Quirinale*, 1658–1678, façade, Rome, Italy. ©Gross Brothers Media LLC.

rogative assertiveness that is not a characteristic of more classically oriented edifices.

The association between the mouth and the building's entrance invites, indeed, the further association that in entering the building one moves inside a body and encounters its vital organs. This is both intimate and privileged in psychologically associative terms. For one cannot access a living being's bodily interior in such free, explorative terms. And it may be that experiences of this kind are the ones where that elusive sense of one's own body being a building (with the self inside) finds its main architectural analogue.

A point such as this invites obvious caricature. 'If being inside a building is like being inside a body, then which bit is the heart, which bit is the intestine and bladder, and which bits are the lungs?!', etc.

Again, however, the analogies made here can amount to rather more than childish comparison. It may be, for example, that there is some structural principle in a building's layout which directs all the others in formal terms, and/or which enables the flow of building-users to be directed or distributed in practical ways. Thinking about the senses in which something might count as the 'heart' of the building, could, accordingly, offer useful insights on such issues.

Another intriguing example concerns what the 'lungs' of a particular building might be. Obviously, this could encompass literal issues of ventilation and 'airiness' but it might also lead us to consider whether the distribution of light sources within a building represented a kind of inhalation and exhalation process, and the sense(s) in which some of these sources had a dominant role.

Of course, stylistic idioms other than the baroque can carry bodily connotations of the aforementioned kinds, but the mobility and emphatic entrance-framing devices of baroque and stylistically cognate architecture are especially conducive to it.[19]

I shall now address idioms involving a much less direct relation to the body. These are modernism's characteristic *containment* of the body, and postmodern deconstruction's *subversion* of it.

Modern architecture's relation to the body represents, in general, a moment of supreme economy. Its characteristic adaptation of form to function involves a simplification which emphasizes enclosure as the creation of *site* for different practical activities. Such architecture is, fundamentally, the creation of space for enabling and declaring what the embodied subject does in the buildings in question. It is an emblem of the root significance of architecture's enclosing function.

Fig. 19. Le Corbusier, *Villa Savoye*, ca. 1929, Poissy, France. Photo: Valueyou. GNU Free Documentation License/public domain.

In this, the transformation of the column into the piloti is of special significance. Consider Le Corbusier's *Villa Savoye* at Poissy, France (1928–1929), for example. Here, the slender piloti are, in effect, the column *diminished* into a purely functional support item. They exist only to lift the rectangular box structure of the first story, and to divide up the space beneath. There is little more here than an elegantly constrained and enabled space for living—a site for the embodied subject to exist domestically.

This functional approach to domestic space finds its Modern apotheosis in work by another architect—Mies van der Rohe. His *Lakeshore Drive Apartments*, Chicago, 1951, consist of two identical 26-story towers separated by an interval of 46 feet, with their long axes aligned perpendicular to one another. The skeletal steel frame is manifest in the elevations, by means of steel sheets painted in black, which cover the columns and beams.

Each building's face is addressed uniformly, the component bays subdivided into four window units by means of three steel mullions. Within this frame-

Fig. 20. Mies van der Rohe, *Lake Shore Drive Apartments*, finished 1951, Chicago.
©Photo: Jeremy Atherton, 2006, from Wikimedia Commons / under Creative
Commons License.

Fig. 21.   Daniel Libeskind, *Food Theatre Café (The Serpentine Gallery)*, 2001, London. Courtesy Studio Daniel Libeskind, ©H. Binet.

work are set floor-to-ceiling windows in aluminium frames. At the base of both structures are rows of, as it were, gravitationally challenged pilotis—which scarcely appear with any distinctive identity of their own, in the context of the whole.

Buildings such as this are highly characteristic of Modern architecture's relation to the body. It contains the body through enclosure, but its architectural means are not themselves informed by the body's form (and its correlated modes of mobility) either as morphological features, or even in looser associational terms.[20]

Postmodern architecture involves, characteristically, a different relation to the body. Such architecture, is of course, extremely diverse, but in its most distinctive postmodern form—the 'deconstructive'—it brings about a subversion of the body.

In this respect, consider Daniel Libeskind's *Food Theatre Café* in London (2001). This space is not fully enclosed, but consists, rather, of a loose assemblage constructed from an aluminium frame with metal cladding. The whole has a fragmented angular emphasis, providing varying degrees of enclosure. To experience the edifice internally is to encounter a complex play of shapes which vary radically as the viewer changes position.

The key to this work is the mutually deconstructive play-off achieved between the theatre and the café aspects. These two interacting nominal functions gently negate those customary expectations which are based on them individually considered. One goes to the theatre to see a performance given by others, a performance whose significance is representational rather than as an actual sequence of actions *per se*. But here, the focus is on the building where events occur and on the people who, in a theatre, would normally be the audience.

And, from the other direction, a café is a place where one goes to eat. True, one can do this in spectacular locations where one is invited to 'take in the view' as well as eat. But with Libeskind's edifice, the setting is much more insistent. To eat in this place is, of necessity, to do much more than that. The experience of dining in this particular café extends beyond the satisfaction of mere physiological appetite—and this is true, surely, even if one did, in fact, enter the edifice with no other reason than to eat. Once 'inside' it, one is displaced by the uncanniness of the spatial site where this specific bodily need is to be realized.

In all this, the body has not been eliminated. Rather its activity is rendered awkward or incongruent as one's awareness shifts constantly between the two dislocated functions. This means that the body is subverted, in the sense that its normal vectors of sensorimotor engagement are made problematic. In this respect, we will recall Peter Eisenman's observation quoted in Part One:

> My work attacks the concept of occupation as given. It's against the traditional notion of how you occupy a house.[21]

I suggested that such aspiration is 'play' rather than a real elimination of architecture's functional orientation. We are now in a position to understand a further key meaning of this play. For whilst it subverts the body's customary expectations—in the sense just noted—its more far-reaching effect is to make us more aware of the scope, direction, and limitations of the body's customary expectations.

Function in deconstructive architecture does not disappear; in other words, it just tells us things about our orientation towards building which we could not countenance before. Hence, whilst such architecture will always be para-sitic on the functions which it is challenging, it has, in contemporary parlance, 'added value' in terms of how it creatively thematizes the relationship of build-ing and the body.

Such thematization is not just some fashionable 'idea' which happens to characterize one tendency within postmodern architecture but is, rather, a principle which provokes new and satisfying forms of building. It creates spaces which engage our attention and which surprise and delight and more through a deep fusion of the unsettling and the spectacular.

This reaches its highest and most disturbing point, perhaps, in Libeskind's *Jewish Museum* in Berlin (2001). The external layout of the building has mor-phological affinity with an unravelled Star of David. This—in conjunction with its position in the heart of Berlin, near Hitler's Bunker—gives the build-ing extraordinary power as a marker of inseparable historical, geographical, and cultural location, and, simultaneously, *dislocation* (topics I will return to in Part Four).

Fig. 22. Daniel Libeskind, *Jewish Museum Berlin*, aerial view, opened 2001, Berlin. Courtesy Studio Daniel Libeskind, ©Guenter Schneider.

In physical terms, the edifice takes up some 10,000 square metres of space—a space which is articulated through such devices as sloping floors, lines of windows suggestive of wounds, empty concrete walls (some of them spiralling), and a windowless tower.

The key connecting feature is the 'void'—an empty space that extends over the building's entire length, and which is devoid of any air conditioning, insulation, or even heating. It signifies those who perished, and does justice to the unimaginable horror of this precisely through not trying to illustrate it in any figurative way. The dead are manifest through an unrelenting and oppressive *absence*.

Through all the aforementioned features, the body is present as that which has been disfigured, mutilated, and eliminated in both physical and psychological terms.

Indeed, the unparalleled evil of the Holocaust is here indicted in terms which are both aesthetic and ethical. It may seem a travesty to even think of the aesthetic in such a context, but that would be, in a sense, to give into the simplistic mind-set of the instigators of the Holocaust. The Museum's architectural excellence provokes the observer to negotiate evil in an experientially deep way. It does so not by preaching about the horrors, but by creating a surprising and unsettling space where the individual can, through perceptual and bodily exploration of the building, negotiate its terrible implications *through imagination*.

By this means, the horrors are brought home at a much more personal and introspective level. The individual is allowed to be a free agent who has responsibility for his or her exploratory actions, and who has to interpret what the Museum presents on his or her own terms. Through its architectural achievement, in other words, the Museum celebrates precisely the ultimate human factor of freedom which the Nazis so grossly abused, and so totally denied to their victims. The building's aesthetic achievement embodies, at the same time, an ethical victory.

Part Four

Having analyzed the relation between body and architecture in phenomenological terms, and then through historical examples, the time has now come to view its more general philosophical significance. For it might be argued that architecture plays a further key role in an area of spatial experience which is fundamental for embodied subjectivity *per se*.

To understand this, consider the general relation between architecture and space. If this relation is not to be emptily abstract, it must be understood in terms of those factors which are most implicated in a body's way of occupying and perceiving space. This means, at the very least, a close attentiveness to details of how it is embodied in specific buildings, *vis-à-vis* the nature of the materials used, and the ways in which these are articulated through details and specific techniques.

However, if one wishes to understand architecture's *full* aesthetic significance, one must be mindful, at least, of how the aforementioned factors *at the same time* reach back to more primordial features of humanity's modes of inhabiting and cognizing space.

In this respect, it is worth considering, first, the significance of space-occupancy *per se*. If something exists then it must occupy some portion of space or—as in the case of events—be the outcome of changes which have taken place amongst space-occupying phenomena.[22]

The embodied subject is a function of both space-occupancy and movement through space. In this respect, the following remarks by Gareth Evans are extremely instructive:

> The capacity to think of oneself as located in space, and tracing a continuous path through it, is necessarily involved in the capacity to conceive the phenomena one encounters as independent of one's perception of them—to conceive the world as something one 'comes across'. It follows that the capacity for at least some primitive self-ascriptions—self-ascriptions of position, orientation, and change of position and orientation and hence the conception of oneself as one object amongst others, occupying one place amongst others, are interdependent with thought about the objective world itself.[23]

On these terms, knowledge of an objective world and the unity of self-consciousness are dependent upon one another. The body in its continuous traversal of space is the common factor whereby the subject becomes aware of itself through becoming aware of objects *qua* objects through recognizing them *as* re-encountered and re-encounterable.

Now the importance of space-occupancy in defining existence and in enabling self-consciousness, already indicates a distinctive status for architecture. Any visual artwork is spatial, but architecture is so, generally, in more emphatically three-dimensional terms. Crudely put, its edifices usually occupy more space than other visual art forms, and, since their overt virtual/representational aspect is usually minimal (or, even more often, non-existent) their physical spatiality, accordingly, tends to be much more perceptually and physically accessible, enduring, and, all in all, insistent than is the case with other visual art forms.

However, architecture's spatial distinctiveness extends beyond mere contrasts with other art forms. To see why, we must now consider Evans' account of how objective knowledge and self-consciousness are correlated through re-encounters with spatial items. For it can be argued that architecture is a decisive factor in such re-encounterability.

This is not just because buildings have the insistent physicality described above, and are things which we encounter a lot. Rather their *architectural character* (in the sense already described) has an additional importance which must now be considered.

In this respect, it must be emphasized that the re-encounterability of spatial objects is not just an abstract formal condition of the correlation of objective knowledge and self-consciousness. It is something which has been *achieved* in evolutionary/historical terms. This means that it has its own different emphases and aspects.

To explain. The minimum condition of re-encounterability consists in the fact that whatever the embodied subject's changes of position, the material bodies which it encounters remain to some degree the same—in terms of their physical characteristics or in their position in relation to other material bodies (i.e. location) or both. There must be enduring *markers* which stabilize the horizon of re-encounterability.

Some such markers may amount to no more than the relative constancy of an object's identifying characteristics. On the larger scale, even location can be defined simply by things which happen to stay alongside one another for a period of time. However, whilst these simple markers may be decisive for the correlation of objective knowledge and self-consciousness in the most primitive terms, the correlation is not static. The formation of deeper competences in language and other symbolic and ritual activities, indeed, surely depends not only on things which happen to be re-encounterable, but even more so on things which are *made* to be.

Tools have this character, but *edifices* even more so. In fact, once shelter is achieved through permanent means such as building in stone; and once this activity is developed as a repeatable competence, then a change has taken place. For *location is now created through the edifices which are made there*, rather than through mere adaptation to pre-given landscape features.

In Part Two of this chapter, I placed great emphasis on the way in which architecture has key symbolic resonances with the human body, most notably uprightness of posture and a host of more specific expressive features. This, of itself, means that it provides works which have a very special significance as markers in the horizon of re-encounterability.

This can be taken even further. In Part One I stressed the way in which architecture involves a choice between alternatives and that such choices can be sources of both personal and community concern. Linking all the aforementioned points, a major conclusion can be drawn. *Through architectural creation, objective knowledge's horizon of re-encounterability is invested not only with a stable framework of markers, but ones with special significance as public embodiments of collective artifice and identity.*

Architecture, in other words, enables the horizon's vectors to be structured decisively by human intentionality at both an individual and collective level. The fixed, multiple, and enduring character of architectural markers is a profound enabler of community identity and broader cultural activity based on social interactions. Through them, physical terrains become humanized.

In this respect, the architectural work's enduring spatial character acts not only as a focus for sharing in synchronic historical terms, but also in diachronic ones. A person meets with the cultural present there, but in a way which affirms a continuity with the past—with those who walked through the same rooms and stood in the same places in the building in earlier times. Continuity of identity with the future is also opened up in that the building can house future members of one's own and other communities.

Of course, one can also have such experiences in the physical presence of other visual art idioms, notably sculpture, but architecture evokes cultural continuity through its *enclosure* of the observer as well as though the observer's beholding of it. And in this, it has a symbolic completeness which the other visual idioms lack. For whilst cultural identity is something one can choose to adopt, more often one is born into it; and even if one has adopted it, to exist in it as a form of life is, speaking metaphorically, to be *enclosed* within a system of beliefs.

A further distinctive feature of architecture *qua* enclosure is the way in which its internal layout can be just as distinctive an expression of cultural identity as its external features. The case of Islamic architecture is instructive here. As Jale Erzen observes in relation to Ottoman interiors,

> the perspectival view giving order to space in relation to the viewer's position, and thus making the viewer the center is not applicable to the visual ordering

in Ottoman ... architecture. Here, man has no monopoly over the visible, he is part of it, immersed in it, and the views open up to him as he moves and discovers.[24]

In all these factors of shared cultural identity, the non-autographic spatial nature of architecture also plays a decisive form. For whilst the architect has designed the work, his or her gestures do not physically inform the stone and thence emphasize the building as their own individual creation. In the absence of such emphasis, the viewer's sense of the work as a place of shared community space and time—as a focus of cultural identity—is more to the fore.

Of course, it is all too easy to think of cultural identity as an analytic term alone. It is not. The term signifies real continuities of value and meaning through time, and it is through this that the nature of being human reaches its fuller disclosure. Heidegger was given to describing language as the 'house of being'. Architecture's manifold symbolism is a major aspect of this. Through its physical and social character, it shows what a culture values, and, through ways of making that exceed functional need, it discloses a relationship to Being in the broader sense.

There is an intriguing contemporary example of a particular aspect of this. The German city of Konigsberg was obliterated in the Second World War, then ceded to the Soviet Union and renamed Kaliningrad. In the late 1960's, the ruins of the great castle in the city were finally completely levelled as part of an ongoing attempt to erase remnants of the city's German past.

However, post-Soviet Russians in Kaliningrad have come to re-appraise this past. Rather than think in terms of historic rivalries, considerable restoration of ruined German edifices has been undertaken. One of the most striking potential contributions to this is Alexander Bazhin's proposal for re-building the castle on the basis of its original structure. This cannot be done on the exact same site for practical reasons, but the very idea of such a project—whether or not it is ever actually realized—has remarkable implications.

These are not just an overcoming of old hostilities, but also a positive affirmation of architecture as the basis for cultural identity of more open kind. If built, the castle will mark out a rebirth of location, which, whilst not restoring the past literally, will connect it to the future as, simultaneously, remembrance and a shared quest for the new. Here architectural creation will bring about a cultural sharing not by levelling out differences, but by *affirming* difference, i.e. the 'return' of an old Germanic castle as a revered marker for a (relatively) new Russian city.

This has metaphysical as well as cultural significance. Being in all its fullness involves difference as a necessary factor in determining the character of the finite. In the present age, however, it has become all too easy to think of difference as something which must be overcome in the name of abstract notions of 'consensus'. The Kaliningrad castle project, in contrast, shows how (through the relation between architecture and cultural identity) the importance of difference as the great *characterizer* of Being can be affirmed.

Such a building would allow cultural differences to grow together. It would achieve something which was new and different from the individual characters of its component cultural identities, but with a particular identity which was inseparable from the active differences between those components.

Of course, it might be insisted that this describes nothing more than organic unity *per se*. In such unities, the whole is more than the sum of its parts, but has a character which depends on the differences between them.

However, in the present case, it is important to emphasize that we are dealing with unity based on the architectural realization of a new *explorative* cultural identity. And, what this is achieved from is itself *fraught* with the continuing dangers of deep-seated historical conflict. It offers unity created from, and in contexts where, difference is still a potentially antagonistic and destructive force.

Here, existential risk and challenge makes the achievement of aesthetic unity all the more poignant, and affirms the deep creative potential of difference in the broader scheme of things.

To some degree, the Kaliningrad castle project is a dramatic exemplar also of a more general truth about architecture and context *per se*. We will recall Scruton's point from Part One that the architect is severely constrained through having to adapt his or her plan to the demands of a pre-existing site and surroundings. Of itself, this difficult zone of differences imports an existential challenge which means that the finished Kaliningrad castle—if realized—will have a unity achieved through its broader setting as well as embodied in its physical structure alone.

Good architecture *per se*, in other words, achieves its effects through negotiating difference in terms that other art forms do not have to (under normal circumstances). Through this, it discloses the aesthetic character of its setting as well as marking it out in physical terms.

The key point to gather from all these arguments, then, is that the architectural marker has an optimum role in the correlation of objective knowledge and self-consciousness which is basic to embodied subjectivity. It not only involves re-encounterable spatial edifices which define location, but also ones which bring members of a community together.

Through this, it establishes conditions of social interchange which facilitate linguistic development and cultural identity to the highest degree, and in special ways. It is a key focus for the body's physical artifice, for its encounters and recognized re-encounters with the spatial object and with other people, and, through this, for the articulation of distinctive ways of disclosing Being *per se*. In this way, architecture's phenomenological depth centres on the further expression of factors that are basic to the physical, historical, and cultural conditions of embodied subjectivity, in the *emergent* dimension.

Conclusion

I have explored the relationship between body and architecture in both phenomenological and historical terms. The relation between the two is profound at the most basic level of our aesthetic responses, and is also capable of significant transformation over time.

Given the latter point, it is worth reflecting on, briefly, how the body/architecture relation might be developed in the future. To date it has been located in morphological analogy or association mainly. However, it might be possible for the relation to be pursued in more explicit terms.

It would be ludicrous, of course, to create edifices which were, at the same time, representations of, say, faces or hands, or the human body *in toto* (except for humorous or critical purposes). But it might be possible to create works adapted to fairly overt interpretations of specific limbs, conjunctions thereof, or body-based activities.

A special challenge would be to find ways of adapting such body-reference to specific functions in the buildings concerned, or to the character of the relevant locales. One possibility would be to base such interpretations not on the macro-body, but on its subcutaneous structures. In the age of sophisticated scanning and imaging devices, cell and tissue structures are easily available for architectural as well as medical investigation. These might well offer visual structures inspirational for an overtly *corporealist* architecture, attuned to new avenues of access to the body.

Conclusion
Art History and Art Practice—
Some Future Possibilities

To conclude, I shall develop some of the broader ramifications of the approach taken in this book.

It began by showing the limits of reductionist art history and theory. In turning away from art's aesthetic significance, such history has tended to fixate one-sidedly on the documentary functions of the image. Through marginalizing or excluding other approaches to art history, it represents the overwhelming of art by a western consumerist mentality.

The bulk of my text has not shown the restrictedness of this approach by critique. It has done so by opening up ways of thinking about art which emphasize the phenomenological depth of its creation and reception. Phenomenological depth is not a question of 'significant form'. It goes far beyond it—through showing what *enables* form to become significant.

This centres on the way in which the making of visual art concentrates and clarifies factors which are central to perception, and to self-consciousness's relation to the visible world. These complex factors constitute the intrinsic meaning or significance of the visual arts.

I have also argued at length, that in order for this depth to engage our attention intuitively, the image must be enjoyable in aesthetic terms, i.e. in terms of the relation between its phenomenal structure and the medium's comparative history. When a work achieves this status, the image's intrinsic significance becomes artistic meaning.

There is one major conclusion that can be drawn. It is that the reductionist tendency in art history misses out on what is, in effect, visual art's *raison d'être*. If art history is to avoid such distorted analytic one-sidedness, it must embrace the dimension of phenomenological depth—at least in those cases where it is negotiating (directly or indirectly)—issues concerning visual art's claim to enduring cultural worth.

In addition to this general normative context, phenomenological depth might be useful to art historical studies in two ways. The more ambitious one would be in sustaining comparative stylistic analysis as a key methodological strategy.

Such comparative art history means, in effect, looking at artistic styles in relation to one another across different cultural times and places. Such a method was practiced in a restricted formalist way by Wolfflin, who tended to reduce issues of style to 'categories of beholding'. I hope to have gone beyond this by providing artistic creation-based concepts and strategies which clarify the character of specific artworks or *oeuvres*, in relation to key aspects of the medium of which they are an instance. Through such clarification, comparative art history overcomes formalism.

The second way in which phenomenological depth might inform work in art history is rather more piecemeal, and can be of use even for (otherwise) reductionist approaches. It involves identifying the way in which such depth-factors are brought about by, or can carry, historically specific meanings 'on top', in a way that allows the historically specific and the aesthetic to mutually complement one another.

Such identifications would not rival or compete with explanations of how the work(s) came to be produced and received in historical terms. Rather they would offer a few insights into how criteria of aesthetic formation might be linked to the more historically specific aspects of selected artists and/or works.

That being said, I am, of course, implying that this kind of connection may admit, also, of much more extensive development by scholars with expertise in both art history and philosophy. Such development would allow for a more balanced *modus operandi* in art history that allowed it to be enriched so as to avoid the dangers of social and/or semiotic reductionism.

In what follows, then, I shall consider a few speculative possibilities for linking phenomenological depth to some historically specific developments in the history of art.

First, Malevich's emphasis on Suprematism's relation to the plane. He argues that

> All that we see has arisen from a colour mass turned into plane and volume, and any machine, house, man, table, they are all painterly volume systems.[1]

Indeed,

> Standing on the economic Suprematist surface of the square . . . I leave it to serve as the basis for the economic extension of life's activity.[2]

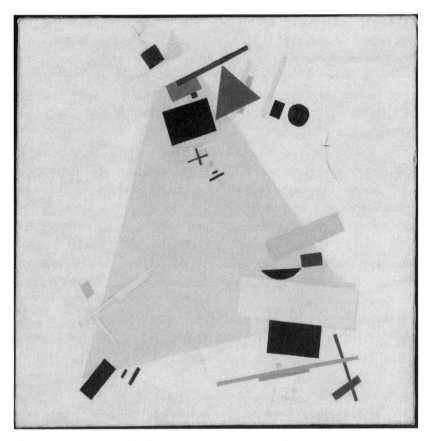

Fig. 23. Kazimir Malevich, *Supremus No. 57*, ca. 1916. Oil on canvas, 80.2 x 80.3 cm. Tate Modern, London. ©Tate, London 2008.

In these remarks from 1919 Malevich is legitimizing abstract art in relation to the demands of the new Soviet state, and also utilizing complex Ouspenskian and Schopenhauerian ideas. However, this emphasis *itself* internalizes features which (in Chapter 6) I showed to be involved in a general theory of meaning for abstract art. There, it will be recalled, I emphasized *optical illusion* as the basis of this. In abstract art this is conventionalized in terms of associations which draw on that *contextual space* of things not noticed (or not noticeable) which subtends all visible things.

This includes visual configurations which arise from the destruction, deconstruction, reduction, reconstruction, or variation of familiar items, relations or states of affairs; and also structural aspects of spatial appearance—addressed individually or in combination. (These aspects include colour, shape, mass, texture, density, volume, and changes of position.)

Now in his Suprematism, Malevich relates to this in an interesting way. The painting *Supremus No. 57*, for example, involves a triangle which is tilted obliquely to the plane. This creates an optical tension which is amplified by a collection of various small geometric forms which constellate around each angle of the triangle.

Through this, the appearance of stasis and action is generated from the optical relation between *real* two-dimensional entities, rather than forms which allude to three-dimensional realities. Structures of spatial appearance are here expressed through a mode of optical illusion which (by virtue of being wholly constituted from real two-dimensional components) is more continuous with the level of our material existence, than are forms which invoke the third-dimension. This is because three-dimensional figures in a plane involve an additional level of illusion which is supervenient on the material reality of the two-dimensional base.

That Malevich's work can express fundamentals of spatial appearance and their possible transformations in such minimal terms is visually remarkable in itself. But what makes it even more interesting is the way in which aesthetic achievement and phenomenological depth is here, at the same time, made into a political gesture by its historical context.

For by developing Suprematism in terms of 'real' two-dimensional forms, Malevich is affirming the possibility of abstract art as a material and artisanal practice—something which has continuity with the world of work and production, as well as embodying spiritual meanings.

In this way, then, Malevich embraces the political circumstances of his times in a way that opens up enduring aesthetic possibilities for other artists. Historical context and transhistorical meaning are made complementary through an original mode of making which constellates around the intrinsic meaning of abstract art.

Another useful example of this harmonizing of reductionism and the transhistorical is found in Barbara Hepworth's sculpture. She was one of the first sculptors to use the hole as a systematic feature of sculptural form. In doing so, she transforms the context of biomorphic imagery in the 1930's.

In her *Seated Figure* of 1932–1933 (Tate Gallery), for example, the holes which define the separation of arms and torso suggest analogies between the human and other natural forms such as (in this case) a tree trunk. But whilst this kind

Fig. 24. Barbara Hepworth, *Seated Figure*, 1932–1933. Tate St Ives, ©Tate, London 2008, ©Bowness, Hepworth Estate.

of isomorphism clearly looks towards the context of Surrealist notions of association, in Hepworth's work, it begins to be significant in a deeper way.

In this respect, we will recall that in Chapter 5, I indicated something of sculpture's distinctive phenomenological depth, on the basis of its magical appearance—in turning the most radically inanimate material into the appearance of living form. Hepworth's use of the hole is a radical contribution to this. As well as suggesting relations between recognizable three-dimensional animate beings, she develops it in a way which *exceeds* that specificity, to some degree. The stone, metal, or wood of the sculpture seems to be material *animated in its own right*. In this way, the work's recognizable biomorphic content seems to be caught *returning* to the level of life's primal emergence from inanimate matter.

Again, in other words, a historically specific innovation in an established context of ideas is able to adapt these in the creation of something which is transhistorically enduring. Indeed, Hepworth's strategy opens up possibilities in addition to that which I have just indicated.

For example, the significance of the hole may radically affect how a sculpture expresses place. It might also be thought through as an interesting interpretation of another feature of Heidegger's approach to art, namely, the emergence of world from earth.

The last example I will consider is that of Jackson Pollock. His move to East Hampton in 1945 brought with it a switch of stylistic orientation away from Picasso and surrealist-inspired imagery to that 'all over' style which Greenberg made so much of. (It is significant that a similar switch of orientation around this time also characterizes Newman, Rothko, and Still's development of the colour-field as a basic compositional format.)

Obviously, this transformation is bound up with personal experiential factors, and it is reasonable to assume some connection between these and artistic sensitivity to the horrors of the Second World War. In the aftermath of Auschwitz and Hiroshima, artists might well feel a need to reconfigure pictorial space in strikingly new terms.

In Pollock's case, the particular form which this reconfiguration takes is very instructive. His drip painting technique—consolidated from 1947 onwards—allows for flatter looking images. However, his images have a discreetly *animated* character which suggests that Pollock was not so concerned with affirming the virtual flatness of the picture plane as formalist critics have supposed.

More specifically, it is striking that in many of his dripped paintings, a small zone or at the edge (often extending around the entire rectangular border area) tends to be left relatively free of forms. This means that a distinct figure/ground relation is set up within the painting. It has the optical effect of activating the pictorial field with suggestions of arrested rhythms or slow processes of biological or other forms of natural change which are unavailable to visual perception under normal circumstances. The drip paintings give distinctive expression, in other words, to a key aspect of contextual space.

This connects to an interesting iconographical factor. One of the first major dripped paintings by Pollock is entitled *Full Fathom Five* (1947).[3] The title alludes to lines from Shakespeare's *The Tempest* (which were featured in an issue of the New York artists' journal *Tiger's Eye*, around the time of Pollock's painting). The relevant lines are

> Full fathom five thy father lies;
> Of his bones are coral made;
> Those are pearls that were his eyes;
> Nothing of him that does fade,
> But doth suffer a sea-change
> Into something rich and strange.

The striking feature of these lines is their poetics of natural transformation and mutability. This factor is also evoked by the optical rhythms of Pollock's painting with its incorporated elements of studio detritus—such as tickets and cigarette butts, which are laid into the work.

It is though symptoms of transience from the macro world are brought in to harmony with the deep-seated natural processes which are the basis of transience. And whilst many of Pollock's subsequent dripped paintings are untitled, others—such as *Sea Change* (a title which also draws directly from the previously quoted lines), *Enchanted Forest*, *Cathedral*, *Autumn Rhythms*, and *Lavender Mist*—are strikingly named in a way which emphasizes their allusive significance.

My point is, then, that the general historical and more specific circumstances of Pollock's drip painting technique focus the allusive power of optical illusion—its phenomenological depth—rather than formal concerns alone. His historical context allows him to give a radical new inflection to contextual space.

One can, of course, find his innovations significant without necessary reference to the immediate historical context in which they were created. But if we do bring in that context, our understanding of the particular work and the scope of contextual space are mutually deepened. The contextual approach and the significance of abstraction's intrinsic meaning here complement one another.

Fig. 25. Jackson Pollock (1912–1956): *Full Fathom Five*, 1947. New York, Museum of Modern Art (MoMA). Oil on canvas with nails, tacks, buttons, key, coins, cigarettes, matches etc., 50 7/8 x 30 1/8' (129.2 x 76.5 cm). Gift of Peggy Guggenheim. 186. 1952. ©2008. Digital image, The Museum of Modern Art, New York / Scala, Florence ©The Pollock-Krasner Foundation ARS, NY and DACS, London 2008.

Again, then, I am arguing that phenomenological depth is not only decisive in terms of the visual arts' intrinsic aesthetic fascination, but allows contextualism not to lapse into reductionism.

In fact, the significance of phenomenological depth for art history ranges broader still. Suppose, for example, that one artist has a preference for a certain range of colours, or subjects, or has the habit of elongating forms somewhat. These may simply be idiosyncrasies of style. They may also play a significant role in giving that artist's work an attractive individual character. Whether or not they have this character can only be determined by comparative stylistic historical analysis (in both diachronic and synchronic modes).

Now it might be that the features whereby an artist establishes his or her individuality turn out to be rather more than that. They might reconfigure factors which are basic to the medium in a new and interesting way. This means that phenomenological depth is implicated in issues pertaining to the possibility of canonic status. For if we link this to how an artist transforms the medium to create new possibilities (rather than judging what he or she does in terms of race, class, and gender positions alone) then we have a case for talking of genuine canonic values.

It may be that the future of art history will be dominated by a consolidation of the present reductionist orthodoxy. However, I hope to have shown how the aesthetics of visual art's intrinsic meaning offers a more diverse future. It could encompass a new comparative approach to art history as the history of styles, as well as a revitalized and more open reductionism.

I turn finally to a few thoughts concerning the nature of art practice itself.

In Chapter 9, I suggested that—in an important sense—the visual arts have reached their creative limits in structural terms. This means that the physical structures of visual art media and the basic semantic and semantic conventions which govern them cannot be extended further. There can still be original work, but not at the level of large-scale innovation which has driven the great 'isms' of western art.

Now, it might be argued that a claim of this sort is wholly unwarranted. It is logically possible that some new Masaccio or Picasso-type genius might emerge and revolutionize the whole artistic enterprise once more.

Such a response, however, misses the point. The problem is not a lack of potentially hyper-creative humans, but rather limits defined by the physical, visual, and referential conventions of visual art media. Even if the geniuses are out there, there is nothing which would allow them adequate expression in terms of far-reaching, structural innovation which would allow art to be done in entirely new ways.

However, I also argued that the development of digital art itself offers some new ways of developing old media as well as fascinating opportunities for significant structural development in its own right.

If this form of visual art continues to be developed, it could involve some radical changes in how art and the artist are conceived. Indeed, it might even be that far-reaching digital innovation takes place alongside the emergence of new technologies which enable artistic innovation or refinement on a scale that parallels or even exceeds the achievement of mathematical perspective.

But even if this occurs, it will not be the whole story. The very abundance of digital imagery—especially of an immersive kind—will always call the viewer back to the being of visual artworks which are two- or three-dimensional physical individuals, rather than visual tokens of electronic types.

Drawings, paintings, and sculptures, for example, are thingly in a way that digital scenarios are not. And for a finite embodied subject, there is a need for examination of and stabilization of the self at that level of re-encounterable particular material items (and stable interactions between them) which enable the correlated development of self and language.

Pictorial and sculptural art work at this same level. Their meaning emerges through being seen, rather than through being electronically activated and then seen (under mechanically determined conditions). Whilstsoever human beings are embodied, the physically individual idioms of visual art will have a continuing ontological priority. This is likely to ensure their survival in the face of any greater innovatory potential opened up by digital art.

However, it might seem that this survival does not amount to much in the final analysis. Individual styles will still be possible, but if these no longer carry the possibility of large-scale innovation, of what use are they really?

We are thus brought to a *foundational* and extremely complex question concerning the nature of art. It is clear that the concept is of mainly western origin. But the reason why the notion of art becomes necessary is because some works manifest their cognitive or narrative content in original ways. This enables an aesthetic empathy with the creator through which we discover new possibilities of experience and opportunities for learning about ourselves.

The making and appreciation of such individualized empathic artefacts as a form of life is the basis of art in the west. And it is an approach which has colonized much of the rest of the world.

We reach the decisive problem. The loss of structural innovation means that the individualistic aspect of visual art has lost its collective expression. It might appear that this is all to the good, insofar as 'isms' offered traditionally a kind of brand identity through which artists could compete against one another in the market.

However, the idea that 'isms' only act as brand identities is, I think, crudely reductive. They have had a much more complex and positive significance in terms of canonic value. That being said, the fact that they are no longer structurally based means that an opportunity may have arisen to establish the constitutive connection between art and individuality on a new basis. There may be room to explore shared values and differences between artist and viewer on more personal and interactive terms.

An interesting case in point here, is the work of Mojca Oblak. Her work is now organized around recognition of the structural limitations of the traditional idioms, and the way in which this can allow the very enterprise of visual art to be reconfigured in terms of more intimate forms of aesthetic and existential discovery.

In 2006, she organized an object- and performance-based event entitled *The Visitation* at the Equirna Gallery in Ljubljana. The immediate stimulus for this was a conjunction of contingent events—her acquisition of a watercolour study of Pontormo's *Visitation* by the Victorian artist G. F. Watts, and her recent study of the philosopher F. H. Bradley's notion of 'active attention'.

In itself, this chance inspiration is of interest. The great body of already created art tends to lie dormant in galleries, the object of gallery visitations, curatorial and historical study, and, occasionally, a source of imagery refined and worked with by contemporary artists in one-off projects. Such work receives attention, but perhaps lacks serious sustained and recurrent *active attention*.

However, Oblak's strategy was to make attentiveness to the theme of the *Visitation* itself into the basis for a series of complex interactions ranging far beyond artistic variations on the Pontormo/Watts image. The gallery event would itself constellate around the idea of 'Visitation'.

To this end, Oblak borrowed some of her pre-existing works from their present owners, and had some flat glass panes in the shape of retorts specially manufactured. The retorts were placed over some new material—incorporating both collage and autographic drawing, with a range of decorative objects placed on top. The retorts would thus be a vehicle of both presentation and transformation (in keeping with the alchemical associations of the retort).

Fig. 26. Mojca Oblak, *The Visitation*, 2006, installation/performance/exhibition, Equirna Gallery, Ljubljana. Courtesy of the artist.

The retorts were, themselves, placed on tables with long flowing fabric beneath, suggesting the possibility of a continuing flow of ideas and exchanges.

One of the pre-existing works included was her *Pythagoras Square* which was hung on a wall in proximity to some brilliantly original women's clothing designed by Jasminka Mitrić as a specific response to factors suggested by the *Square*.

Another aspect of the event was its use in a parallel performance in New York of a piece of music by the artist's sister Jerica Oblak, based on elements from the event, with accompanying interpretations by dancers.

The most decisive factor in the event was the presence of the artist herself during the entire opening hours of the two-week gallery display. During this time she would give lectures about the event, but, much more importantly, talk directly about the works to visitors—not instructing them on the meaning of the individual works, but rather gathering responses concerning both their individual elements and the event itself from the visitors.

These responses opened up the possibility for cooperation between the artist and visitors in future projects—where the burden of meaning would fall on the existential dynamics between the artist and new partners.

This strategy is one of—in Oblak's parlance—*hermetical proximity*. It is something private and hermetically sealed into the specific artist-partner(s) relation, but through this, the two parties come to share an intimate existential proximity with one another. Indeed, the personal relationships involved can be taken to higher and higher levels on the basis of the specific interactive energy which is generated.

Now strategies of audience participation and response are a frequent feature of much conceptual art practice, and, indeed, much earlier avant-garde tendencies. But in the present case there are significant differences.

For here, the premise of the strategy is that art has exhausted its possibilities of structural innovation and must find a new systematic direction. This amounts to *newnesss achieved not through what the artist makes or designs per se, but rather through how these things are used in the context of forming and changing the artist's relation to individual persons (or groups of people) who engage with the work*. In this, there is no hierarchy of media. All idioms can be used, including art of the past.

On the basis of this, original new work is achieved through the creation and confluence of localized channels of creative exploration. As a practice this does not constitute a new 'ism'. Indeed, the whole point is that it shifts the entire trajectory of artistic creativity from the macro level of styles, movements, and great names to a *micro* level of individual personal and collective relationships.

Of course, in the age of global consumerism, such personal emphasis and the giving up of big art 'brand' possibilities may seem hopelessly futile. But perhaps micro art may actually be the best critique of such consumerism. It can deploy the informational means of global technology as well as traditional idioms to achieve a restoration of individual identities at the level where that identity really counts—namely, concrete personal and group relationships. In the terms of the present work, this is its phenomenological depth.

Given such points, it is best to conclude that art in its non-digital idioms has not come to an end. It has, rather arrived at a stage where it can change its creative basis from what can be achieved through specific media development, to what can be achieved through bringing media together in the illumination of specific life-world situations.

In a sense this involves a kind of reconfigured reductionism absorbed explicitly into art practice. But whilst the meanings thus created might be described analytically in terms of the relation between the work and its conditions of production and reception, they would not be *sufficiently* describable in such terms.

There would be an aesthetic bonding between the specific phenomenal character of the work and the specific character of the intended audience. Such bonding would embody an analytically irrecoverable *uniqueness*.

This is not 'posthistorical'. It is art relocated to the microhistorical level of individual artists and those immediate existential relationships created by their work. Maybe this is what art has *always* been tending towards . . .

Notes and Index

Notes

Introduction

1. A recent sustained and impressive attempt to revive the idea of art having a distinctive meaning is Arthur Pontynen's *For the Love of Beauty: Art History and the Moral Foundations of Aesthetic Judgement* (Transaction Publishers: Somerset NJ, 2006). Pontynen's emphasis on beauty, however, is one which separates his position from mine.

2. The great exception to this is Richard Wollheim, most notably in his *Painting as an Art* (Thames and Hudson: London, 1987). However, Wollheim's approach is orientated very much towards the conditions and aesthetics of *spectatorship*. This is even true of the chapter 'What the Artist Does', which gravitates around the notion of 'twofoldness', i.e. our capacity to see painting either as a formal configuration or as an image of such and such a subject-matter. Wollheim does not, unfortunately, do much justice to the way in which the artist's style *interprets* its subject-matter, making it exist in a cognitively and aesthetically enriched way. This enrichment, in contrast, will be a major focus of the present work.

3. See, for example, his book *The Fate of Place: A Philosophical History* (University of California Press: Berkeley and Los Angeles, 2000), where Casey sets forth a phenomenology of place with many aesthetic ramifications, especially in relation to sculpture and architecture. In *Earth-Mapping: Artists Reshaping Landscape* (University of Minnesota Press: Minneapolis, 2007), this approach is extended to a specific idiom of visual art. There have been other recent phenomenological approaches to the visual arts that take a non-exegetical approach. Foremost amongst these is Nigel Wentworth's *The Phenomenology of Painting* (Cambridge University Press: Cambridge, 2004). In this interesting book, Wentworth tends to focus on the relation between the act and materials of painting, and the spectatorial viewpoint. This, unfortunately, misses out on the formative aesthetic character of painting as exemplified in the ontology of the medium. Indeed, Wentworth is driven into rather psychologistic criteria of artistic worth. He suggests, for example, that 'What it is for a painting to work can . . . be understood in terms of the process of trying

to make work. This process requires that the painter does not try to bring about a pre-conceived idea, but rather that he approaches the work with openness, is with the canvas as it is before him, responds to the way he feels it does not work and does what he feels he has to do to make it do so, such as juggling the elements within it until he feels that nothing more needs to be done' (pp. 147–148). Unfortunately these psychological criteria of merit are of limited philosophical substance insofar as even mediocre artists often take their work to be more than it is, precisely because its creation has involved the kind of sincerely felt give-and-take described by Wentworth. What one intends and feels, however, and one's sense of a job well-done, are no guarantee of genuine artistic achievement.

4. It should be emphasized again that this will be a *critical* appropriation. For sophisticated examples of a merging of exposition and critical development (albeit with different philosophical emphases from my own), see Jay M. Bernstein's *The Fate of Art: Aesthetic Alienation from Kant to Derrida and Adorno* (Penn State University Press: University Park, 1991); and Alan Singer's provocative *Aesthetic Reason: Artworks and the Deliberative Ethos* (Penn State University Press: University Park, 2003). The great merit of both these thinkers is that their creative exegesis allows the aesthetic to be thought through non-reductively, in ways that illuminate its broader societal significance.

5. Edward S. Casey provides the best recent phenomenological account of imagination in his *Imagining: A Phenomenological Study* (Indiana University Press: Bloomington, 2000). His approach is orientated towards imagination as experienced by the subject. In chapter 4 of my *Philosophy After Postmodernism* (Routledge: London, 2003), I take a rather different approach which emphasizes the transcendental significance of imagination (in a broadly Kantian sense) as a necessary condition of objective and self knowledge.

Chapter 1

1. Examples of this are in the introductions to W. J. T. Mitchell's *Iconology: Image, Text, Ideology* (University of Chicago Press: Chicago and London, 1987); and Nelson Goodman's *Languages of Art* (Hackett and Co.: Indianapolis, 1976).

2. The convergence in question here now reaches back a fairly long way. See, for example, Dominic M. Lopes *Understanding Pictures* (Clarendon Press: Oxford, 1996), Robert Hopkins' *Picture, Image, and Experience: A Philosophical Inquiry* (Cambridge University Press: Cambridge, 1998); Andrew Harrison, *Philosophy and the Arts: Seeing and Believing* (Thoemmes: Bristol, 1997); Flint Schier's *Deeper Into Pictures* (Cambridge University Press: Cambridge, 1986); and David Novitz's *Pictures and their Use in Communication: A Philosophical Essay* (Martinus Nijhoff: The Hague, 1976). All of these works deal effectively with objections (mainly inspired by Goodman's *Languages of Art*) that resemblance is *not* a necessary condition of

visual representation. Mitchell's *Iconology: Image, Text, Ideology* offers an interesting alternative approach which emphasizes the conceptual and historical diversity of representational forms.

3. This tradition is excellently surveyed and assessed in Michael Podro's *The Critical Historians of Art* (Yale University Press: New Haven and London, 1982). See also a useful collection of primary texts in *Empathy, Form and Space: Problems in German Aesthetics, 1873–1893*, ed. H. Mallgrave and E. Ikonomou (Getty Research Institute: San Diego, 1993). It should be emphasized that Podro's book opens up great opportunities for a critical engagement with far-reaching conceptual issues raised by the German tradition. Unfortunately, the opportunity has not been taken up as widely as one might have hoped. What has happened, rather, is that art history has acquired something of a fad for examining how its own 'conditions of discourse' have been 'historically constructed'. The reductionist approach, in other words, has colonized the German tradition, rather than learned from it. In this respect it is useful to consider Christopher Wood's Introduction to his translation of Erwin Panofsky's *Perspective As Symbolic Form* (Zone Books: New York, 1992). None of the major theoretical implications which Panofsky's arguments raises are addressed significantly except as factors in intellectual controversies during the first part of the twentieth century. The relevance of Panofsky for understanding fundamental structures of pictorial representation *is* addressed in chapter 3 of my book *The Transhistorical Image: Philosophizing Art and its History* (Cambridge University Press: Cambridge, 2002); and in James Elkins' *The Poetics of Perspective* (Cornell University Press: Ithaca and London, 1985).

4. This is especially the case with Clive Bell and Clement Greenberg.

5. See, for example, Michael Podro, *Depiction* (Yale University Press: New Haven and London, 1998); David Summers, *Real Spaces: Art History and the Rise of Western Modernism* (Phaidon: London, 2003), and (amongst many other works by him) James Elkins' *What Painting Is* (Routledge: London, 2000), and Yves-Alain Bois, *Painting as Model* (MIT Press: Cambridge, Mass., and London, 1993). A great deal of good work has also been done by Lopes, Hopkins, Podro, Wollheim, and Gombrich (amongst others) on cognitive issues which relate to the intrinsic significance of the image. Unfortunately, the cognitive issues in question tend to constellate around problems of perception and spectatorship. See, for example, Dominic Lopes, *Understanding Pictures*; Robert Hopkins, *Picture, Image, and Experience*; Richard Wollheim, *Painting as an Art* (Thames and Hudson: London, 1990), and Ernst Gombrich, *Art and Illusion* (Phaidon: London, 1978). Of these, Lopes' book is the most relevant and has quite extraordinary scope and insight *vis-à-vis* his understanding of the diversity of different forms of picturing, and their historical being. Wollheim is extremely good on the nature of spectatorship and expression, but not on the process of making, and what it exemplifies. Gombrich is effective in

describing the artist's use of conventionalized formulae as a means of interpreting shared visual problems, but links this to a historical narrative of progressing naturalism which has found few supporters. (For an effective critique of this narrative, see James Elkins' *On Pictures and the Words that Fail Them* (Cambridge University Press: Cambridge, 1998.)

6. Griselda Pollock, *Vision and Difference: Femininity, Feminism and the History of Art* (Routledge: London, 1988), 7.

7. Norman Bryson, *Vision and Painting: The Logic of the Gaze* (Yale University Press: New Haven and London, 1986), 61.

8. Bryson, *Vision and Painting*, 68.

9. Ibid., 68.

10. Ibid., 68.

11. Ibid., 55–56.

12. 'Defining Art, Defending the Canon, Contesting Culture', *British Journal of Aesthetics* 44, no. 4 (October 2004): 361–377. This reference, 366–367.

13. For a more extended discussion see chapter 2 of my *Philosophy After Postmodernism: Civilized Values and the Scope of Knowledge* (Routledge: London, 2003).

14. Griselda Pollock, *Vision and Difference*, 14. For a striking example of meaning which accrues to the making of visual images in other cultures, see Susan M. Vogel's *Baule: African Art/Western Eyes* (Yale University Press, New Haven and London, 1997).

15. Jonathan Crary, *Techniques of the Observer: On Vision and Modernity in the Nineteenth-Century* (MIT Press: Cambridge, Mass., and London, 1992), 6. A gentle (but extremely decisive) critical disclosure of a number of other contradictory features in Crary's arguments can be found in W. J. T. Mitchell's *Picture Theory* (University of Chicago Press: Chicago and London, 1994), 19–24.

16. For a more detailed refutation see the arguments throughout *Philosophy After Postmodernism* (Routledge: London, 2003).

17. In a work entitled *Defining Art, Creating the Canon: Artistic Value in an Era of Doubt* (Clarendon Press: Oxford, 2007).

Chapter 2

1. This shortcoming covers both main tendencies in contemporary picture theory. The more influential one is the perceptualist approach which—allowing for contrasting emphases and inflections—links pictorial recognition to factors which also determine ordinary visual perception, and assigns a significant role to visual resemblances between the picture and the pictured. The most important exponents of this are Richard Wollheim, Flint Schier, and more recently Robert Hopkins in his *Picture, Image, and Experience* (Cambridge University Press: Cambridge, 1998). The

other major approach is a conventionalist one that emphasizes the significance of modes of picturing as symbol-systems, and which holds that relations between the members of such systems are decisive for pictorial meaning. Its major exponents are Nelson Goodman, W. J. T. Mitchell, and most recently, John Kulvicki in his *On Images: Their Structure and Content* (Clarendon Press: Oxford, 2006). A key thinker who integrates both approaches to some degree is Dominic Lopes. His *Understanding Pictures* (Clarendon Press: Oxford, 1996) is a powerful account of the features which must be taken to be held in common by all modes of pictorial representation. I am in substantial agreement with much of Lopes' argument as far as it goes (with some notable exceptions) but my emphasis on picturing as a formative mode of artifice is something that he does not much negotiate.

2. The major exception is Richard Wollheim's *Painting as an Art* (Thames and Hudson: London and New York, 1990). Unfortunately, Wollheim's approach is heavily observer-based, and negotiates none of the major factors which I address, except in secondary terms. Dominic Lopes' *Sight and Sensibility* (Clarendon Press: Oxford, 2006) addresses criteria of value in the visual arts, but it does not address the key intrinsic links between the nature of pictorial space and the basis of artistic creativity *per se*.

3. One approach which does explore pictorial space in the context of drawing is Patrick Maynard's *Drawing Distinctions: The Varieties of Graphic Expression* (Cornell University Press: Ithaca and London, 2005). However, as the book's title suggests, Maynard's strategy is explorative, rather than one geared towards an integrated theory of drawing and pictorial space. For a magisterial critical discussion of empirical variety in the historical and cultural expression of pictorial space, see David Summers, *Real Spaces: Art History and the Rise of Western Modernism* (Phaidon: London, 2003).

4. A classic account of the issues involved here can be found in Erwin Panofsky's *Meaning and the Visual Arts* (Harmondsworth: Penguin, 1993), 53–67.

5. For interesting and detailed discussions of the main issues involved here, see especially Hopkins, *Picture, Image, and Experience*, 24–93, and Lopes, *Understanding Pictures*, 15–51.

6. In theory, one might paint a picture on one's own body using blood from a wound. However, this far-fetched case would not be analogous to the sufficiency of speech for linguistic communication. For here the blood is being used in a way which is not that of its normal bodily function. It is *used as* a pigment, and in this use becomes, literally, *external* to the body's organs.

7. For an effective observer-based account of the major issues involved, see Lopes' theory of 'aspect recognition' in *Understanding Pictures*, 112–131.

8. In pictures with a strongly individual aspect, the artist will frequently use models or real-life places, but with their actual identities or locations in these re-

spects forming no part of the work's explicit pictorial content. But to understand picturing as a form of meaning is to understand that the work can contain such concealed actual identities, even if we do not know how this applies in the particular case. Unless one's interest is art historical in the main, such mystery enhances our sense of the work's modal ambiguity in positive terms.

9. The only theorists to give due attention to this are German art historians, notably Alois Riegl and Wilhelm Worringer. See, for example, the recurrent importance of the plane throughout Riegl's *Historical Grammar of the Visual Arts*, trans. Jaqueline E. Jung (Zone Books: New York, 2006), and Worringer's *Abstraction and Empathy*, trans. M. Bullock (Ivan R. Dee Publishers: Chicago, 1997).

10. See *Understanding Pictures*, 24.

11. The problematic cases which I now consider are the same ones raised by Lopes throughout *Understanding Pictures*. However, he does not develop their significance in relation to planar structure.

12. The integrating of recognizably three-dimensional subject-matter with the two-dimensionality of the picture plane, and the use of a grid (in the sense just described, are the two features, indeed, which allow Cubism to be identified as a visual style or tendency *per se*.

13. Rosalind Krauss, for example, offers an influential (if philosophically rather superficial) analysis of it in her *Originality of the Avant-Garde and Other Modern Myths* (MIT Press: Cambridge Mass., 1986).

14. In previous works I have discussed this under the label 'aggregate' or 'corporeal perspective'—terms derived from Panofsky.

15. A concentrated philosophical account of mathematical perspective can be found in Hopkins, *Picture, Image, and Experience*, 152–158. A more wide-ranging discussion is in Maynard, *Drawing Distinctions*, 12–52. Both of these approach perspective very much from the recognitional viewpoint.

16. Jacques Derrida, *The Truth in Painting* (University of Chicago Press: Chicago, 1987), 61.

17. Georg Simmel, 'The Picture Frame: An Aesthetic Study', in *Theory, Culture and Society* 11 (1994), 11–17. This reference, 11.

18. Wolfflin's main exposition of this can be found in *The Principles of Art History*, trans. M. Hottinger (Dover Publications: New York, 1950), 124–148.

19. Simmel offers some interesting (if speculative) claims concerning the appropriateness of different kinds of frame to pictorial content. See Simmel, 'The Picture Frame', 13–16. An excellent discussion of the history of the framing function which touches also on some conceptual issues is Barbara Savedoff's 'Frames', in the *Journal of Aesthetics and Art Criticism* 57, no. 3 (1999), 345–356.

Chapter 3

1. There is an interesting complementary approach to the one taken in this chapter, which addresses the role which art *per se* plays in the development of self-consciousness. In a number of important works Ellen Dissanayake has explored what is at issue here in anthropological and evolutionary ethological contexts. See, for example, her *Homo Aestheticus: Where Art Comes From, and Why* (University of Washington Press: Seattle, 1995).

2. This theme is explored in more detail in chapter 5 of my *Philosophy After Postmodernism: Civilized Values and the Scope of Knowledge* (Routledge: London and New York, 2003).

3. See, for example, Henri Bergson, *Matter and Memory*, trans. N. M. Paul and W. S. Palmer (George Allen and Unwin: London 1970), 81–104. Bergson's theory of art is of great interest in its own right, in ways which I cannot explore here. For a useful discussion of it, see Ruth Lorand's paper 'Bergson's Concept of Art' in the *British Journal of Aesthetics* 39, no. 4 (1999), 400–415. Lorand also discusses Bergson in a stimulating broader context in her book *Aesthetic Order: A Philosophy of Beauty and Art* (Routledge: London, 2000).

4. For a parallel notion to this, see Richard Wollheim's concept of 'experiential memory' discussed in his *The Thread of Life* (Cambridge University Press: Cambridge 1980), 104–121.

5. See Kant's discussion in *The Critique of Judgement*, trans. Werner Pluhar (Hackett Publishing Company: Indianapolis, 1987), 182–183.

6. For detailed and probing analyses of the logic of pictorial representation, see Dominic Lopes, *Understanding Pictures* (Clarendon Press: Oxford, 2004); Robert Hopkins, *Picture, Image and Experience* (Cambridge University Press: Cambridge, 1998); and Flint Schier, *Deeper into Pictures* (Cambridge University Press: Cambridge, 1986). An alternative 'Theory' orientated approach can be found in W. J. T. Mitchell's *Iconology: Image, Text, Ideology* (University of Chicago Press: Chicago and London, 1987).

7. See Nelson Goodman, *Languages of Art* (Hackett Publishing Company: Indianapolis 1976), 52.

8. This point and the general themes in this paragraph are explored at greater length in Crowther, *Philosophy After Postmodernism*, chapter 4.

9. The approach to perception taken in this chapter is, in essence, a development of that found in Merleau-Ponty. The theory of picturing and imagination which I have proposed hopefully rectifies some imbalances in Merleau-Ponty's position. For the gist of that position see his *Phenomenology of Perception*, trans. C. Smith (Routledge Kegan-Paul: London, 1974). For more on Merleau-Ponty's treatment of pictorial art, see the key essay 'Eye and Mind', included in his *The Primacy*

of Perception, trans. James M. Edie (Northwestern University Press: Evanston, Ill., 1964). Some important themes from this text are critically analyzed and further developed in the next chapter of the present work.

Chapter 4

1. The differences between painting and literature in terms of temporality are explored in more detail by Gottfried Lessing in *Laocoon: An Essay on the Limits of Painting and Poetry*. A good recent translation of this text can be found in J. M. Bernstein's important edited collection, *German Classic and Romantic Aesthetics* (Cambridge University Press: 2002), 25–130.

2. Analyzing the differences between visual images and forms of linguistic meaning is a central theme in W. J. T. Mitchell's work. He argues, for example, that '(1) there is no *essential* difference between poetry and painting, no difference, that is, that is given for all times by the inherent natures of the media, the objects they represent, or the laws of the human mind;(2) there are always a number of differences in effect in a culture which allow it to sort out the distinctive qualities of its ensemble of signs and symbols. These differences . . . are riddled with all the antithetical values the culture wants to embrace or repudiate' (*Iconology: Image, Text, and Ideology* (University of Chicago Press: Chicago and London, 1987), 49). The problem with this is that the 'differences' which enable a culture to 'sort out' its signs and symbols, and, indeed, the ability to sort anything at all, logically presuppose criteria concerning the correct and incorrect usage of signs and symbols. Such criteria demand recognitional stability in terms of both natural and cultural environment—a stability which is a function of the body's correlation with the world. It is precisely these factors which are the focus of Merleau-Ponty's phenomenology. By exploring his position, it is possible to establish the distinctiveness of painting on grounds which go beyond mere cultural convention. Indeed, as this chapter progresses we will see that there are some features which are distinctive to painting at the level of the medium itself (i.e. in precisely the domain where Mitchell claims there are no essential differences between painting and literary forms).

3. Other central texts include 'Indirect Language and the voices of silence', included in *Signs*, trans. Richard McCleary (Northwestern University Press: Evanston, Ill., 1964); and 'Cezanne's Doubt' in *Sense and Non-Sense*, trans. Hubert and Patricia Dreyfus (Northwestern University Press: Evanston, Ill., 1964). 'Eye and Mind' and these texts are brought together in the *Merleau-Ponty Aesthetics Reader: Philosophy and Painting*, ed. Galen A. Johnson, trans. Michael B. Smith (Northwestern University Press: Evanston, Ill., 1993). This volume has a number of introductory or critical essays. Notable amongst them is chapter 11 of Linda Singer's 'Merleau-Ponty on the Concept of Style', addressing an avenue of connection between perception and art, which I am unable to do justice to in the present discussion.

4. Included in Maurice Merleau-Ponty, *The Primacy of Perception,* ed. James M. Edie (Northwestern University Press: Evanston, Ill. 1964). This reference, 160.

5. Ibid., 161.

6. Ibid., 163.

7. Ibid., 162.

8. Ibid., 162–163. This is the concept of 'reversibility' which is so fundamental to Merleau-Ponty's thought in general. It holds that the division between 'inner' and outer' *vis-à-vis* our relation to the world, is an exaggeration. Both subject and world permeate one another—they are of the same 'stuff'. For a further discussion of this in relation to painting, see chapter 2 of Gary Brent Madison's *The Phenomenology of Merleau-Ponty* (University of Ohio Press: Athens Ohio, 1981). For a very different but equally fascinating treatment of the complexities of vision and representation, see chapter 3 of James Elkins' *The Object Stares Back: On the Nature of Seeing* (Simon and Schuster: New York, 1996).

9. Ibid., 164. This quotation is one of the most direct characterizations of the imagination which Merleau-Ponty offers. Unlike Sartre, his approach to the subject is relatively cryptic and scanty and is scattered throughout his oeuvre. An ambitious attempt to gather up and extend Merleau-Ponty's insights can be found in James B. Reeves, *Imagining Bodies: Merleau-Ponty's Philosophy of Imagination* (Duquesne University Press: Pittsburgh, 2004).

10. Ibid., 166.

11. Maurice Merleau-Ponty, *The Prose of the World*, trans. John O'Neill (Heinemann: London, 1974), 83.

12. Of course, it is almost impossible to be absolutely motionless, but we can be described as relatively so when our cognition involves only eye or head movements and other minor gestures which enable the orientation. The stationary frontal viewpoint which I will emphasize is of this character.

13. Norman Bryson, *Vision and Painting: The Logic of the Gaze* (Yale University Press: New Haven and London, 1986), 89.

14. Free-standing sculpture is the primal form of this medium—in ontological, and, very likely, evolutionary terms also. This is because the easiest way to create a three-dimensional image is to modify a pre-existent three-dimensional entity, which is small enough to be completely manipulable. More advanced sculptural idioms, such as relief carving, or the bust format, are derivative from sculpture thought through in relation to pictorial representation.

15. Relief sculpture, of course, occupies the middle ground between sculpture and pictorial representation. Here the symbolic function of the physical edges is mainly dependent on the individual character of the work in question.

16. I am grateful to students in my Philosophies of Art and Literature course at Jacobs University, Spring Semester 2007, for their helpful discussion of some of

the ideas presented in Parts One and Two of this chapter. Especial thanks to Miruna Cuzman, Christin Hoene, Nikola Ivanov, Julia Klotz, Gabriela Olariu, and Saskia Schirmann.

Chapter 5

1. A useful orientation for material covered in this chapter is William Tucker's *The Language of Sculpture* (Thames and Hudson: London, 1985). An even better—if much harder to find—work, is L. R. Rogers' *Sculpture: The Appreciation of the Arts*, vol. 2 (Oxford University Press: London, 1969). Alex Potts' book *The Sculptural Imagination: Figurative, Modernist, Minimalist* (Yale University Press: New Haven and London, 2000) is far and away the best discussion of the interplay between cognitive and historical demands in the interpretation of sculpture. His discussion of the relation between Merleau-Ponty and minimalism is especially interesting (see pp. 207–234).

2. The point here is that one can recognize what *kind* of three-dimensional thing—in the most general terms—a sculpture represents, simply by looking at it. However, the recognition of more specific individuals or sub-classes of a kind the work might represent requires contextual knowledge concerning the circumstances of its production or the intended audience. In the case of abstract works, the burden of recognition falls on close description of the salient physical and formal properties, i.e. on what material is doing to form (or vice-versa). It follows that, in these cases, the recognition of more specific individual or sub-class reference is even more dependent on knowledge concerning the circumstances of a work's production, or of its intended audience.

3. It should be emphasized that this list of sculptural categories is offered on an empirical rather than strictly conceptual basis. That being said, it might be possible—with more argument—to show that they are conceptually linked to the very notion of 'sculpture' *per se*.

4. The status of Duchamp's 'ready-mades' as 'sculpture, is, of course, highly controversial. An interesting range of approaches to this and related issues can be found in Joseph Mascheck's *Marcel Duchamp in Perspective* (Da Capo Press: New York, 2002). See also chapter 7 of the present work.

5. This offers a very interesting and complex link between transcendence and Kant's theory of fine art. According to Kant, the central property of fine art in relational terms is originality, and in ontological terms its status as an 'aesthetic idea'. In terms of the former, the fine artwork must transcend patterns of sameness and repetition in its medium, and, through these, must give an imaginative expansion to its conceptual content. We have, in other words, a twofold transcendence at the level of history and imagination. See Kant, *The Critique of Judgement*, trans. W. Pluhar (Hackett and Co.: Indianapolis, 1987), 183–185.

6. An admirably restrained use of transcendence as a bridge between tradi-

tional religion and atheism can be found in Jerome A. Stone's *Minimalist Vision of Transcendence: A Naturalist Philosophy of Religion* (SUNY Press: New York, 1992). For the purposes of the present chapter, a more relevant usage of transcendence is found in Gerard Genette's *The Work of Art: Immanence and Transcendence*, trans. G. M. Goshgorian (Cornell University Press: Ithaca and London, 1997). This is not an easy book. As I read him, Genette's doctrine of immanence pertains largely to the ontological structures of art, and, especially, the distinction (following Goodman) between autographic and allographic media. His notion of transcendence (in relation to painting and sculpture) is threefold. First, it encompasses the fact that over periods of time, such works undergo gradual physical change. Second, it is used in those cases where a work has lost a part or parts over time, and where the viewer has, accordingly, to go beyond what is given in order to form a conception of the work as a whole. And third, transcendence is also found in the way the same work can be imaginatively realized in radically different ways by different viewers. My own use of transcendence touches on each of Genette's factors. However, its main emphasis is on transcendence in the sense of a logical movement towards something wherein the sculptural work attempts, through its creative artifice, to comprehend or express various three-dimensional visual aspects of that something. In this sense, my usage is both more specific yet, in another respect, somewhat broader than Genette's.

7. It should be emphasized that the notion of 'disinterestedness' described here is a specifically artistic one—and not that 'apart from any concept' variety described by Kant in the *Critique of Judgement*, 45–46. In particular, the criterion of disinterestedness is here understood as *logical*—rather than the psychological sense of some 'contemplative' attitude. The concept of aesthetic experience with which this logical sense connects has some affinity with Noel Carroll's 'deflationary' account of such experience. His account emphasizes 'design appreciation and/or quality detection' as criteria of aesthetic experience. Now, whilst Carroll explores disinterestedness mainly in relation to the problematics of the link between formalism and beauty, I am arguing for a distinctively artistic version of it. Indeed, it may be that such a variety would have to be invoked if Carroll wished to distinguish between design appreciation and quality detection in say, their technical and professional senses as opposed to their aesthetic modes. For Carroll's discussion of these and related issues, see the sections on 'Beauty and the Genealogy of Art Theory' and 'Four Concepts of Aesthetic Experience' in his book *Beyond Aesthetics: Philosophical Essays* (Cambridge University Press: Cambridge, 2001).

8. For a discussion of these and more general spiritual issues raised by the *Pietà*, see Robert Hupka's *Michelangelo Pietà* (Ignatius Press: Ft. Collins Colo., 1999).

9. The classic study on this topic is Gisela Richter's *Kouroi: Archaic Greek Youths* (Phaidon: London, 1970).

10. The development, key achievements, and complex political controversies surrounding Finlay's oeuvre are surveyed and analyzed in Yves Abrioux's *Ian Hamilton Finlay: A Visual Primer* (Reaktion Books: Edinburgh, 1994).

11. Turrell's work at Roden Crater is insightfully discussed in Craig E. Adcock's *James Turrell: The Art of Light and Space* (University of California Press: Berkeley, 1990).

12. The best sustained discussion of this specific work that I know of is John Golding's *Boccioni: Unique Forms of Continuity in Space* (Tate Gallery Publications: London, 1986).

13. A useful primer on Bernini is Charles Avery's *Bernini: Genius of the Baroque* (Thames and Hudson: London, 1997). An arguably more intellectually wide-ranging account is Rudolf Wittkower's *Bernini: The Sculptor of the Roman Baroque* (Phaidon: London, 1997).

14. For a more detailed discussion see Stephen Polcari's 'Barnett Newman's "Broken Obelisk"' in the *Art Journal* (Dec. 22, 1994); online version accessible via LookSmart.

Chapter 6

1. The secondary literature, almost without exception, addresses how individual abstract artists or tendencies relate to the historical and cultural contexts in which their work was produced and received. There have been few attempts to determine a general theory of abstraction—though many of the artists' own manifestoes have talked as if they were offering general theories (mainly concerning abstraction's 'spiritual' significance). This is especially true of Kandinsky and Mondrian, who offer a number of interpretations of the meaning of abstract forms that turn out, ultimately, to be dependent on contextual factors in order for this supposedly universal meaning to emerge. I have negotiated these theories in some detail in my book *The Language of Twentieth-Century Art: A Conceptual History* (Yale University Press: New Haven and London, 1997). These same artists are discussed, critically, in the course of Mark Cheetham's *The Rhetoric of Purity: Essentialist Theory and the Advent of Abstract Painting* (Cambridge University Press, Cambridge, 1991). However, the burden of analysis in this—and other works by him—falls on the historical and theoretical contexts implicated in abstract art's *historical* emergence. There is no clear attempt to establish a transhistorical dimension of meaning for such work. A rare (and good) *general* discussion of abstract works is Briony Fer's *On Abstract Art* (Yale University Press: New Haven and London, 1997). However, her treatment is of selected aspects, and does not amount to a general theory of meaning, as such. And this is true, in general, of all recent art-historical studies of abstraction.

2. T. J. Clark, *Farewell to an Idea: Episodes from a History of Modernism* (Yale University Press: New Haven and London, 1997), 311.

3. Michael Fried, *Art and Objecthood: Essays and Reviews* (University of Chicago Press: Chicago and London, 1998), 32.

4. In what follows, I develop an approach to perception which is broadly consistent with that of Merleau-Ponty.

5. Merleau-Ponty, *The Primacy of Perception*, 166.

Chapter 7

1. The classic statement of this is Danto's *The Transfiguration of the Commonplace: A Philosophy of Art* (Harvard University Press: 1981). In his *Kant After Duchamp* (MIT Press: Cambridge Mass. and London, 1997), Thierry de Duve rightly emphasizes that Duchamp's work should be validated on the basis of aesthetic criteria rather than purely theoretical considerations. Unfortunately, he attempts to do this through an interpretation of Kant's aesthetics which demands changing the reading of terms that are fundamental to Kant's meaning, e.g. using the term 'art' where Kant uses the term 'aesthetic'. The upshot is an analytic model that, in effect, makes aesthetic criteria apply to any feature that informs the creation of Duchamp's work, including the things he refrained from doing. In consequence, the notions of art and the aesthetic are emptied of any substantive meaning.

2. It is worth emphasizing that this critical point is capable of being developed in much greater depth, and in different directions. However, since the intention of the present work is mainly constructive I refer the reader to the critical discussion of Insitutional theories found in chapters 1 and 2 of my book *Defining Art, Creating the Canon: Artistic Value in an Era of Doubt* (Oxford University Press: Oxford, 2007), 15–64.

3. In what follows, I use a considerably modified and extended version of the approach first set out in the Conclusion to my book *The Transhistorical Image: Philosophizing Art and Its History* (Cambridge University Press: Cambridge, 2002); see especially, 180–184.

4. Whitney Chadwick, *Women, Art, and Society* (Thames and Hudson: London and New York, 1996), 382.

5. For a much more detailed and extended discussion of Kosuth and, indeed, conceptualism in general, see chapter 8 ('Aesthetic Ideas versus Conceptual Art') of my book *The Language of Twentieth-Century Art: A Conceptual History* (Yale University Press: New Haven and London, 1997).

Chapter 8

1. Pierre Bourdieu et al., *Photography: A Middle-brow Art*, trans. Shaun Whiteside (Polity Press: Cambridge, 1990), 97. Bourdieu's approach interprets photography primarily in terms of the class viewpoints embedded in the social patterns of its practice. Other reductionists attempt to assign a socially critical and/or psy-

choanalytic function to it, through the relation between the photographic image and its cultural and textual settings. Examples of this include John Roberts' *The Art of Interruption: Realism, Photography and the Everyday* (Manchester University Press: Manchester, 1998), and Victor Burgin's *In Different Spaces: Place and Memory in Visual Culture* (University of California Press: Berkeley and Los Angeles, 1996). In neither of these authors is photographic meaning interpreted in terms much beyond the documentary significance of the image *per se*, or (in Burgin's case) its supposed psychoanalytic relevance. Photography's distinctiveness as a medium is, at best, marginalized. This becomes strikingly obvious in the collection of writings and dialogues entitled *Photographic Theory*, ed. James Elkins (Routledge: New York and London, 2007). This is an important and informative volume, but one that is caught between the social functions of photography and elements of technical detail, in a way that misses the central features of photography as an art form imbued with a highly distinctive phenomenological depth The only recent approach which really does justice to photography as a medium and its specific aesthetic status is Jonathan Friday's excellent *Aesthetics and Photography* (Ashgate: Aldershot, 2002). His approach rightly foregrounds the distinctive referential structure of the medium. In contrast to him, I develop the metaphysical implications of this, rather than direct aesthetic issues.

2. Roland Barthes, *Camera Lucida: Reflections on Photography*, trans. Richard Howard (Jonathan Cape: London, 1982), 88.

3. Ibid., 88–89. The idea that 'authentification exceeds the power of representation' comes as a terrible shock to devotees of Barthes earlier reductionist treatments of photography and its relevance to '*signifiance*'. Foremost amongst these devotees is Victor Burgin. In an embarrassed and evasive discussion of *Camera Lucida*, he attempts to deflect attention away from the phenomenology by claiming that this approach only works if we forget the rest of Barthes, i.e. the reductionist semiotics. Burgin concentrates his analysis on the punctum/stadium distinction which, ironically enough (as I shall show further on), is actually not distinctive to photography. Burgin seems unable to countenance the idea that Barthes genuinely changes position, so as to hold that the ontology of photography demands an entirely different treatment from literary texts. See Victor Burgin, *The End of Art Theory: Criticism and Postmodernity* (Macmillan: London, 1986), 71–92.

4. Barthes, *Camera Lucida*, 76.

5. Ibid., 80–81. This passage introduces what I shall label, in the subsequent, 'causal rigidity'. This centres on the final photographic image's causal dependence on a specific visual relation with its subject-matter. Everything of interest in photography as a medium flows from this. Barthes does great justice to it, but many other commentators do not. In Elkins' *Photographic Theory*, for example, insofar as the topic is discussed, it tends to gravitate around the Peircean notion of an *indexi-*

cal sign. This has little analytic power, as it is a notion with applications far beyond photography. And the particular ways in which it is explored in the dialogues in Elkins' book converge on a one-sided equivalent of causal rigidity that emphasizes the physical character of the photographic process rather than its image-outcome. This philosophical weakness (and others) is given a witty critique by Patrick Maynard's contribution to the same volume—see Elkins, *Photographic Theory*, 320–333.

6. Barthes, *Camera Lucida*, 79.

7. Ibid., 79.

8. Ibid., 13.

9. Ibid., 15.

10. Barthes' corresponding idea (ibid., 34) that a photograph is restricted in terms of its general symbolism is overstated. Any picture of a place is literally a metonym of that place. And some images have content which is so stereotyped as to be unmistakably symbolic of a quite specific general attitude, e.g. the standard pornographic image's presentation of women as objects of sexual consumption.

11. Ibid., 71.

12. Ibid., 109.

13. Barthes actually conflates two slightly different meanings of punctum; on the one hand there are those effects which are integral to photography's *noeme* ('this dead and this is going to die') and little telling incidental contingencies within specific photographs which dominate our attention, and make us feel that we want to be there. This latter sense of punctum, however, is something which photography shares, in principle, with every other art form. (I will show a couple of examples of this from painting, a little further on.)

14. Barthes, *Camera Lucida*, 91.

15. Ibid., 84.

16. Ibid., 119.

17. Ibid., 115.

18. This point is an important corrective to Walter Benjamin's claim that after early pioneer work (such as Atget's), photography loses its aura in favour of 'exhibition value' (as remarked in his *Illuminations*, trans. Harry Zohn (Fontana: London, 1970), 228). Because the phenomenon of uniqueness is intrinsic to the photographic work's status as an individual type, there is no compelling reason why this uniqueness cannot play a continuing auratic role. Indeed, as my discussion develops this point will be further emphasized, indirectly.

19. Barthes, *Camera Lucida*, 4.

20. Nietzsche's major presentation of the idea is in *Thus Spoke Zarathustra: A Book for All and None*, trans. W. Kaufmann (The Modern Library: New York, 1995), 157–159. Although Nietzsche purists disavow *The Will to Power* as an authentic work, he offers there a more sustained metaphysical justification of the idea. In broad

terms, it is based on an argument which claims that whilst time is eternal, space and its contents are not. From this, it must follow that spatially based events recur eternally. See *The Will to Power*, trans. W. Kaufmann and R. J. Hollindale (Vintage Books: New York, 1967), 544–550. (It should be emphasized that my interpretation of the significance of eternal recurrence is independent of this account.)

21. Susan Sontag, *On Photography* (Anchor Books: New York, 1990), 15.

22. Ibid., 156. Sontag's work was known to Barthes before *Camera Lucida* was written. The relation between Sontag and Barthes' theories is discussed in D. D. Guttenplan's 'Snap Judgements' (a review of Geoff Dyer's *The Ongoing Moment* (Little Brown, 2004)) in the *Times Literary Supplement* (Jan. 6, 2006), 3–4. The review emphasizes Sontag's highly politicized agenda.

23. Sontag, *On Photography*, 4.

24. Ibid., 14.

25. Ibid., 7.

26. In this sense, photography might be interpreted in one respect as a kind of extension of the imagination (insofar as that cognitive capacity allows us to articulate possibilities of how we might appear to other people).

27. In Gadamer's terms, it might be described as bringing about an 'increase of being' for the referent. For a discussion of this possibility in relation to pictures, see H.-G. Gadamer, *Truth and Method*, trans. W. Glen-Doepel (Sheed and Ward: London, 1975), 124.

28. Sontag, *On Photography*, 11.

29. Ibid., 13.

30. This is also true of Barthes in some respects, but through his emphasis on the *noeme*, he stays closer to what is genuinely intrinsic to photography *per se*.

31. I discuss the idea of linear perspective as a cross-section of the spatio-temporal continuum in chapter 3 of my book *The Transhistorical Image: Philosophizing Art and Its History* (Cambridge University Press: 2002). See especially 57–60.

Chapter 9

1. Danto's most sustained presentation of this is in his *After the End of Art: Contemporary Art and the Pale of History* (Princeton University Press: Princeton, New Jersey, 1997). A rather more focused and philosophically stimulating account of Danto's main thesis can be found in the final chapter of his *The State of the Art* (Prentice-Hall: New York, 1987), 202–218. Here Danto considers the possibility of art having exhausted itself through having run out of possibilities, but he neither follows this idea up nor considers it as the basis of an alternative to his main thesis.

2. In 'Postmodernism and the Visual Arts: A Question of Ends', included in a number of anthologies, most recently *Contextualizing Aesthetics: From Plato to Lyotard*, ed. H. Gene Blocker and Jennifer M. Jeffers (Wadsworth Publishing Company:

Belmont, California, 1999), 239–251. For some interesting alternative approaches to Danto, see the special issue of *History and Theory*, 'Danto and His Critics: After the End of Art and Art History', vol. 37, no. 4 (Dec. 1998).

3. I discuss the structural basis of abstract idioms at length in Chapter 6 of the present work. See also chapter 5 of my book *The Transhistorical Image: Philosophizing Art and Its History* (Cambridge University Press: Cambridge, 2002), 143–165.

4. Of course, it is possible to create or use an image in a context where the distribution of the image's virtual spatial connections is meant to be read on the basis of codes or stipulations which accrue to the context. But the decisive sense of syntax in visual representation is the principle of unity which governs the distribution of virtual spatial relations *within* the work's internal resources. The external codes or stipulations just add an extra level of syntactic meaning to the work.

5. An artist's position on the contour-mass axis is determined on a comparative basis. This means that whilst there will always be some artists who are emphatically contour- or emphatically mass-orientated, there will be others whose orientation in these terms is much more dependent on exactly which other artists they are being compared with.

6. It should be noted that Ingres and Auerbach are by no means the first and certainly not the only artists to work at these respective extremes.

7. An excellent introduction to this topic can be found in Christiane Paul's *Digital Art* (Thames and Hudson: London and New York, 2003). Journals such as *Leonardo* feature regularly discussions of a technical nature concerning digital art. In contrast, the philosophical literature is not as developed as one might have hoped. One source of good material is Patrick Maynard's important guest-edited issue of the *Journal of Aesthetics and Art Criticism* addressing 'Special Perspectives on the Arts and Technology', vol. 55, no. 2 (Spring, 1997). Two papers, in particular, are relevant to the present discussion. Timothy Binkley's 'The Vitality of Digital Creation' (106–116) contains some worthwhile (if scattered and undeveloped) insights on the distinctive character of key aspects of digital phenomena. David Z. Saltz's subtle and searching 'The Art of Interaction: Interactivity, Performativity, and Computers' (117–127) takes things much further. Of particular importance is the fact that Saltz notices that computer works relate significantly to the type-token relation. He does not, however, explore this much except on the analogy between a musical work and its performance—an analogy which he himself takes (rightly) to break down in the case of interactive computer works.

8. Robert Lazzarini's *Skulls* of 2000 is an excellent example of this 'sculptural' emphasis.

9. As Lev Manovich points out, there is some degradation when digital images are formatted for transmission. However, if the right technology is used, such degradation is not inherent to digitization in the way that it is to the relation of

prints taken from a plate. For more on digital degredation and cognate topics, see Manovich's brilliant book *The Language of New Media* (MIT Press: Cambridge, Mass., London, 2001), 49–61.

10. The most complete account of the technical dimensions of morphing can be found in Ron Brinkmann's *The Art and Science of Digital Compositing*, The Morgan Kaufmann Series in Computer Graphics (Morgan Kaufmann Press: New York, 1999).

11. See Christiane Paul, *Digital Art*, 143.

12. See Walter Benjamin, *Illuminations*, trans. Harry Zohn (Fontana/Collins: London, 1973), 222–224.

Chapter 10

1. Links between architecture and the human body have, of course, been noted at least as far back as Vitruvius. In *The Ten Books of Architecture*, trans. Morris Hicky Morgan (Dover Publications: New York, 1960), 72–75, he emphasizes the harmony between architectural proportions, and symmetry and proportion amongst bodily parts in relation to the human frame as a whole. As we shall see in due course, factors of this kind are important. However, making sense of the 'body of architecture' in its fullest sense demands attention to much broader issues of the kind considered in the main body of my text.

2. There is, of course, a similar problem superficially, with abstract art. However, in the case of abstract art, there is a presumption of virtuality set up by basic formats, e.g. the work being in a frame. This leads us to look for 'external' factors which the work might be referring to, even if these are elusive to identify. I explain this theory in the greatest detail in Chapter 6 of the present work.

3. For Vitruvius' version of this, see Vitruvius, *The Ten Books of Architecture*, 38–40. He is rightly attentive to the way in which the physical character of a locale can determine the kind of building to be constructed there.

4. Peter Eisenman quoted in the *Deconstruction: Omnibus Volume*, ed. A. Papadakis, C. Cooke, and A. Benjamin (Academy Editions: London, 1989), 142.

5. Christian Norberg-Schultz, *Genius Loci: Towards a Phenomenology of Architecture* (Academy Editions: London, 1979), 5.

6. Roger Scruton, *The Aesthetics of Architecture* (Methuen: London, 1979), 17.

7. There are some exceptions to this, of course, in those cases (such as Rubens) when studio assistants do much of the work. But in such cases, the artist at least does central features of the project, and the finished work is assigned to him or her.

8. Arthur Schopenhauer, *The World as Will and Representation*, vol. 1, trans. E. F. J. Payne (Dover Publications, New York, 1967), 217.

9. Maurice Merleau-Ponty, *Phenomenology of Perception*, trans. C. Smith (Routledge Kegan-Paul: London, 1970), 170.

10. August Schmarsow, 'The Essence of Architectural Creation', included in *Empathy, Form, and Space: Problems in German Aesthetics, 1873–1893*; ed. H. F. Mallgrave and E. Ikonomou (Getty Research Institute: Chicago, 1994), 281–297. This reference, 286–287.

11. Ibid., 289.

12. Heinrich Wolfflin, 'Prolegomena to Psychology of Architecture', included in Mallgrave and Ikonomou, *Empathy, Form, and Space,* 149–190. This reference, 151.

13. Ibid., 151.

14. Ibid., 151–152.

15. Ibid., 152.

16. For an interesting discussion of this, see Edward Winters, *Aesthetics and Architecture* (Continuum: London and New York, 2007), 15–17.

17. Such transcendence is achievable in other visual art forms too. As we have seen already, in Chapter 5, there are important connections between transcendence and sculpture. The sense under present consideration has application there—most notably in relation to many of Michelangelo's works where there is a tendency to leave manifestly unfinished features. The aesthetic effect here centres on form emerging from stone—i.e., that primal level where the intractable materiality of the medium is overcome.

18. Schmarsow in Mallgrave and Ikonomou, *Empathy, Form, and Space,* 286–287.

19. It is worth noting that some Mannerist buildings even have entrances which are made deliberately to look like open mouths, e.g. the monster's head grotto in Bomarzo Park near Viterbu, Italy—commissioned around 1560 by Vicino Orsini.

20. Of course, there are some key Modern exceptions to this, most notably in the work of Gaudi.

21. See 'Peter Eisenman: An *Architectural Design* Interview by Charles Jencks', included in A. Papadakis, C. Cooke, and A. Benjamin, *Deconstruction: Omnibus Volume,* 140–149. This reference, 142.

22. Peter Strawson once posited the idea of a purely auditory world, in chapter 2 of his *Individuals: An Essay in Descriptive Metaphysics* (Methuen: London, 1971). However, this was conducted as a thought experiment primarily.

23. Gareth Evans, *Varieties of Reference* (Clarendon Press, Oxford, 1982), 176.

24. Jale Nejdet Erzen, *Sinan, Ottoman Architect: An Aesthetic Analysis* (Middle Eastern Technical University Faculty of Architecture: Ankara, 2004), 15.

Conclusion

1. Kasimir Malevich, 'Non–Objective Creation and Suprematism', included in his *Essays on Art*, trans. A. B. McMillin, X. Glawacki-Prus, and David Miller (Borgen: Copenhagen, 1968), 121.

2. 'On New Systems in Art' in Malevich, *Essays on Art*, 85.

3. In *Full Fathom Five* and the other dripped paintings from 1947, the edge-space effect which I have just described is local and spasmodic, rather than covering the entire border area. In Pollock's works after 1947, however, it tends to be extremely pronounced.

Index